BEST PERENNIALS
FOR THE ROCKY MOUNTAINS AND HIGH PLAINS

by
Celia Tannehill
James E. Klett, Ph.D.

Department of
Horticulture and Landscape Architecture
Colorado State University

Bulletin 573A

CONTENTS

Introduction   6

W.D. Holley Plant Environmental Research Center (PERC)   7

Rating Method   8

A Guide to the Plant Descriptions   9

Acknowledgments   10

Plant Descriptions of the Best Performing Perennials at PERC   13

Plant Descriptions of Best Performing Ornamental Grasses at PERC   83

Glossary   89

Appendices

   1. Charts of Average Bloom Times of Flowering Plants at PERC   93
     a. Bloom Times for White Flowers   94-96
     b. Bloom Times for Yellow and Orange Flowers   97-99
     c. Bloom Times for Red Flowers   100
     d. Bloom Times for Pink Flowers   101-104
     e. Bloom Times for Blue and Purple Flowers   105-108

   2. Plant Lists   109-113

   3. Featured Plants From First Publication Not Found in This Revision   113

   4. Taxa Not Included In This Publication   115

   5. Taxa Still in Evaluation   117

   6. Colorado State Noxious Weed List   118

Scientific Name Index   119

Common Name Index   123

References   127

INTRODUCTION

This publication is a revision of the 1989 technical bulletin, *Flowering Herbaceous Perennials for the High Plains*, by J.G. Strauch Jr. and James E. Klett, Ph.D. The original publication reflected observations from 1980 through 1988. This edition incorporates the 10 years of data taken from 1989 through 1999 from the W.D. Holley Plant Environmental Research Center (PERC), Colorado State University, Fort Collins, Colorado. The plants featured here must have had at least three years data to be considered for the publication. Many are suitable for xeriscape landscapes (water efficient or water wise gardens), rock gardens, and wildflower gardens as well as the traditional perennial border. Other plants are attractive to bees, butterflies and hummingbirds.

The performance information presented in this publication was collected from the herbaceous perennial research, teaching, and demonstration gardens at PERC by students and faculty in the Department of Horticulture and Landscape Architecture. Plant descriptions indicate the conditions under which a given plant is grown. Many will perform satisfactorily in more stressful situations such as receiving less moisture or in a more exposed site. It is also important to note that some perennials are short-lived by nature. Others have a tendency to self sow. These traits as well as other points of interest are indicated in the species description sections.

By describing the cultural requirements and landscape characteristics of the most reliable herbaceous perennials, we consider this publication a necessary tool for the horticulture industry, landscape architects and designers, park personnel, Colorado State University Cooperative Extension agents, garden club members, homeowners, and horticulturists in the Rocky Mountains and High Plains regions.

W. D. HOLLEY PLANT ENVIRONMENTAL RESEARCH CENTER

The perennial gardens at Colorado State University began in 1980 with four beds and grew to 14 beds by 1999. PERC allows students, researchers, landscape professionals, and homeowners the opportunity to observe horticultural research and demonstration projects grown in a dry climate, intense sunlight, frequent winds, and open winters combined most often with heavy, alkaline clay soils. These conditions present a challenging environment in which to grow the traditional plants found in American landscapes and offered by mainstream nurseries.

Currently PERC contains more than 650 different taxa. Many more taxa planted in the past 20 years failed for various reasons. All perennials in the garden are weeded, deadheaded, and divided as time and labor allow. With the exception of a few in partial shade, all plants are grown in full sun. Often plants receive less than optimal care, but many have performed well regardless. The growth, cultural and landscape characteristics of each taxon is evaluated annually and results are compiled into an extensive database, which reflects the suitability for use in Rocky Mountains and High Plains landscapes.

The soil at the demonstration/test site is a clay loam with a pH of 7.2. The organic matter content was originally 1 percent in 1980, but has increased to 5 percent over 20 years by the addition of compost, sphagnum peat moss and composted manures. Normal precipitation in this area is about 14.5 inches per year. Additional water is added from late April or early May to late October or early November and during dry periods in the winter and early spring.

During the growing season, the garden is watered with overhead sprinklers as needed, usually with about 1 inch on a weekly basis. Slow-release fertilizer, with a 14-14-14 analysis, has been added every year for the past ten years. A winter wood-chip mulch is applied mid to late November and removed from the individual plants (but left in the beds to help conserve moisture) in March or April.

The grounds at PERC are located in the south-west corner of the Colorado State University campus (630 West Lake Street) and are open to the public year round. Other features at PERC include: a woody plant arboretum, annual flower and vegetable trial gardens, small fruit demonstration plots, turf research plots, a hedge collection, and other landscape horticultural research plots. Tours and field days are given for industry personnel and homeowners at various times of the year. For more information, call the department of horticulture and landscape architecture at (970) 491-7018.

RATING METHOD

Performance data has been collected on all the taxa present in the garden at least once a year from the time each species was planted. In some cases, a plant has thrived in the garden since its inception. In other cases, a plant that did not survive over the winter months or for any other reason is relegated to the dead inventory list.

Plant evaluation methods have evolved over the years. The present system, in practice since 1994, uses a standardized form, which requires the evaluator to judge performance in areas of flowering ability and plant aesthetics. Evaluators are asked to choose the best fit under a series of choices regarding plant and flower traits. Plant characteristics evaluated include but are not limited to: landscape uses, estimated plant height and width, color of foliage, fall foliage effect, winter injury, and ornamental fruit qualities. Disease and insect problems are noted as are cultural problems that might make the plant less desirable. Once in bloom, the evaluators note the color and size of the flower. Weekly data is also collected on the percentage of plant covered by flowers so that the length and season can be represented graphically (see appendix 1).

Each year the overall aesthetics of each plant was rated excellent, good, fair, or poor. These ratings were converted to a numbered scale (excellent = 10 points, good = 7 points, fair = 4 points, and poor = 1 point) and scores were averaged. The plants featured in this publication fall within the good to excellent range and have thrived for at least three years in the garden. Perennials that rated slightly below good (score 7) were considered on an individual basis.

It is important to note that the information provided in the plant descriptions reflect the trends shown by the data. For instance, evaluators did not take raw measurements, but were asked to indicate the best choice in size from categories already provided on a standardized form. Original plantings of three or five individuals of one species have often grown into an impressive mass over the years. Thus, heights and widths could not be averaged. The sizes shown in this publication are a gauge for the reader and most often represent a group of plants that can no longer be treated individually. Those species that have been present since the inception of the garden may have been lifted and divided several times.

A Guide to Plant Descriptions

The plant descriptions are listed in alphabetical order by genus then species. A short introduction to the genus is given when represented by two or more species at PERC. Those cultivars rated highly are listed under the species and briefly described. Each plant description has a heading that includes the scientific names according to *The New Royal Horticultural Society Dictionary of Gardening* published in 1999 and originating in the United Kingdom, one or more widely used common names, and the family name. Alternative names are provided in parenthesis. For easy access, symbols representing culture, use and important characteristics are included as follows:

❍ = full sun
◗ = partial shade
● = full shade
✂ = useful as a fresh cut flower
✿ = use flower or fruit in dried arrangements
❧ = useful as a ground cover or foliage plant
❖ = a plant designated for xeriscape gardens by the Denver Water 1998 publication *Xeriscape Plant Guide* and by Jim Knopf's 1991 publication *The Xeriscape Flower Gardener*
= North American native plant
= fragrant flower and/or foliage
= attractive to bees and butterflies
= attractive to hummingbirds
! = caution! all or part of plant may cause dermatitis or be poisonous if ingested, see plant description

PPY = named the Perennial Plant Association plant of the year

PS = introduced and/or recommended by Plant Select®, a program designed to seek out and distribute the very best plants for gardens from the high plains to the intermountain region

(5) = indicates the number of years the plant has survived at PERC

Information on the landscape uses, growth habit, approximate height and spread under conditions at PERC, color of foliage and bloom, months of flowering, and size of bloom are presented in bulleted form. This information reflects the data and the categories evaluated over 20 years at PERC. Heights, widths, and size of bloom are ranges, not absolute values. Definitions of landscape uses and of growth habit are found in the glossary. Unless otherwise specified, the plants highlighted in this publication have been reliably cold hardy along the Front Range of the Colorado Rockies (USDA hardiness Zone 4b to 5.) Fort Collins averages 144 frost free days in the growing season. The average last frost date is May 8th and the average first frost date is September 30th. Fort Collins is located at an elevation of 5007 feet and at a latitude and longitude of 40.30.32N, 105.04.40W.

The main description gives general features of the plant, how it performed at PERC, recommendations, and possible uses. The PERC gardens are located away from roads, sidewalks and buildings and are somewhat cooler than surrounding urban areas. Thus, plants at PERC usually begin to bloom a few to many days later than those in protected areas and last a few days longer. Bloom dates vary with geographic location. The season in Denver usually begins one week or more earlier than it does in Fort Collins, while it is much later in mountain areas. On the other hand, the relative period of bloom for different taxa generally will be consistent among different sites.

Color photographs are used to illustrate the growth habit, flowers and/or fruit. An appendix graphically illustrating bloom periods is included as a guide to select plants according to size, color of flower and time of bloom. Other appendixes list plants by a desirable trait or cultural requirement so that readers may easily find plants to fill a specific niche.

ACKNOWLEDGMENTS

The Colorado State University Department of Horticulture and Landscape Architecture, the Colorado State University Agricultural Experimental Station, and Colorado State University Cooperative Extension has helped produce this publication. The authors are grateful for their support.

Over the past 20 years, the installation and care of the perennial garden has been performed by many undergraduate and graduate students as employees, class members and volunteers. The Larimer County Cooperative Extension of Colorado master gardeners have also enthusiastically volunteered to plant, weed, divide, fertilize, and maintain the garden as part of their community service. An undertaking this large would be impossible without the efforts of many committed plant lovers. Their efforts are much appreciated.

The authors wish to express thanks to horticulturists Andrew Pierce, Steve Newman, Ph.D. and Carl Wilson for reviewing the original manuscript. Gratitude is also extended to Glen Rask Ph.D. for many helpful suggestions. Computer technical assistance was given by Edward Peyronnin, who compiled the data into easy-to-read reports. The photography was done by Bryan W. Baker Ph.D., former Larimer County Colorado master gardener and amateur photographer. Pictures were also used from James Klett's extensive slide library, taken over the years by David Staats, James Klett and J.G. Strauch Jr.

In addition, thanks is extended to Debby Weitzel, publications and promotions specialist with Colorado State University Publications and Printing, for editing and production coordinating, and to Cathay Zipp, graphic designer with Colorado State University Publications and Printing, for design and layout.

The plants and seeds for the herbaceous perennial trial garden were donated by many public and private arboreta and botanic gardens, educational and research institutions, commercial seedmen and nurseries, and individuals throughout the United States. We thank all of those listed below for their generosity.

American Horticultural Society	7931 E. Boulevard Dr., Alexandria, VA. 22308	703-768-5700
American Penstemon Society	c/o Ann Bartlett, Membership Secretary	800-777-7931
	1569 South Holland Ct., Lakewood, CO. 80232	
Arnold Arboretum	125 Arborway, Jamaica Plain, MA. 02130	617-524-1718
Bailey Nurseries, Inc.	1325 Bailey Rd., St. Paul, MN 55119	800-829-8898
Bath Nursery	2000 E. Prospect Rd., Fort Collins, CO. 80524	970-484-3718
Bluebird Nursery, Inc.	519 Bryan St., P.O. Box 460, Clarkson, NE 68629	800-356-9164
Bluestone Perennials, Inc.	7211 Middle Ridge Rd., Madison OH. 44057	800-852-5243
Center Greenhouses, Inc.	1550 E. 73rd Ave., Denver, CO. 80229	303-288-1209
Colorado Garden Show, Inc.	9200 W. Cross Dr., Ste 512	303-932-8100
	Littleton, CO. 80123	
Conard-Pyle Company	572 Rose Hill Rd., West Grove, PA. 19390	800-458-6359
Country Lane Wholesale Nursery	2979 N. Hwy 83, Franktown, CO. 80116	303-688-2442
DeGroot, Inc.	P.O. Box 934, Coloma, MI. 49038	800-253-2876

Denver Botanic Gardens	909 York St., Denver, CO. 80206	720-865-3500
Environmental Seed Producers	P.O. Box 2709, Lompoc, CA. 93438	805-735-8888
Forrest Keeling Nursery	88 Forrest Keeling Lane, Elsberry, MO. 63343	573-898-5571
Fort Collins Nursery	2121 E. Mulberry, Fort Collins, CO. 80524	970-482-1984
Green Acres Nursery, Inc.	4990 McIntyre, Golden, CO. 80401	303-279-8204
Gulley Greenhouse	6029 S. Shield, Fort Collins, CO. 80526	970-223-4769
Gurney Seed & Nursery Company	110 Capital St., Yankton, SD, 57079	605-665-1930
Hines Nursery	12621 Jeffrey Rd., Irvine, CA. 92720	800-444-4499
Klehm Nursery	197 W. Penny Rd., South Barrington, Il. 60010	847-551-3710
Little Valley Wholesale Nursery	13022 E. 136th Ave., Brighton, CO. 80601	303-659-6708
Minnesota Landscape Arboretum	3675 Arboretum Dr., P.O. Box 39 Chanhassen, MN., 55317	952-443-1516
Monrovia Nursery	P.O. Box 1385, Azusa, CA. 91702	818-334-3126
Morris Arboretum	100 Northwestern Ave., Philadelphia, PA. 19118	215-247-5777
Mountain Meadow Nursery	62821 LaSalle Rd., Montrose, CO. 81401	970-240-2810
North Central Regional Plant Introduction Station	Iowa State University, Ames, IA. 50011	515-294-4111
North Dakota State University	Department of Plant Sciences Fargo, N.D. 58105	701-231-8062
Northern Colorado Iris & Daylily Club	c/o George M. Houston Gardens 515 23rd Ave., Greeley, CO. 80634	970-353-4837
O.E. White Research Arboretum	Box 175, Boyce, VA. 22620	703-837-1758
Paulino Gardens, Inc.	6300 N. Broadway, Denver, CO. 80216	303-429-8062
Plants of the Southwest	Aqua Fria Rt. 6, Box 11A Sante Fe, NM. 87501	800-788-7333
Sherman Nursery Company	1300 Grove St., Charles City, IA. 50616	515-228-1124
Springbrook Gardens, Inc.	6776 Heisley Rd., Mentor, OH., 44061	440-255-3059
Synnestvedt Nursery	24550 West Highway 120 Round Lake, Il. 60073	847-546-4700
Timberline Gardens	11700 W. 58th Ave., Arvada, CO. 80002	303-324-4060
University of Wyoming	Plant Science, P.O. Box 3354, Laramie, WY. 82071	307-766-5117
Upper Colorado Environmental Plant Center	5538 R. B. County Rd 4, P.O. Box 448 Meeker, CO. 81641	303-878-5003
U.S. National Arboretum	3501 New York Ave., N.E. Washington, D.C. 20002	202-245-4523
Walters Gardens, Inc.	P.O. Box 137, Zeeland, MI. 49464	616-772-4697
Washington Park Arboretum	University of Washington Box 358010, Seattle, WA. 98195	206-543-8800
Welby Gardens Company, Inc.	2761 E. 74th Ave., Denver, CO. 80229	303-288-3398

THE FOLLOWING INDIVIDUALS HAVE ALSO CONTRIBUTED PLANTS TO THE GARDEN:

Barbara Boardman
Robert Cox
Howard Hill
Carl Jorgenson, Professor Emeritus
Chi Won Lee, Ph.D.
Stan Metsker
John W. Pohly

Acanthus balcanicus

Achillea filipendulina 'Parker's Variety'

BEST PERFORMING PERENNIALS

Acanthus balcanicus   Bear's Breeches
(aka *A. longifolius, A. hungaricus*)   ◖ ◗ ✿ ✂ (4)
Acanthaceae
Landscape use: Specimen, border, cut and dried
flower
Growth habit: Clump
Size of plant (height x width): 1' to 2' x 1' to 2'
Foliage color: Medium green
Time of bloom: Late June to early September, peaking
in July
Color of bloom: Pale pink or white and mauve
Size of bloom: Individual flowers 1" to 2.5";
inflorescence > 5"

This genus, named from the Greek work *akantha*
or "thorn", has several species known for their
unusual foliage and flower. *A. balcanicus* forms a tidy
rosette of glossy green, deeply dissected basal leaves
resembling those of thistles, but without the spines.
The flowers are borne on a long, terminal raceme.
Each white or pale pink flower is capped by a spiny
mauve bract. Gloves are handy when cutting the
inflorescence for use fresh or dried, or let the flowers
remain to add architectural interest to the winter
perennial border.

Bear's breeches prefers well-drained soils and
flowers best in full sun with sufficient moisture. It
survived three warm winter years at PERC without
injury. Protect it from excessive winter moisture. It
has not been invasive.

Achillea   Yarrow
Asteraceae (Compositae)   ◖ ✿ ✂ ❖ 🦋 ✿
Landscape use: Massed, border, background,
wildflower and xeriscape gardens, cut and dried
flower

Growth habit: Upright, spreading
Time of bloom: June-October (frost), peak in July and
August
Size of bloom: Inflorescence 2.5" to 5"

The genus *Achillea* was named for the Greek hero
Achilles, who is said to have used these plants for
healing. There are over 85 species and many cultivars.
Yarrow are useful in shrub and perennial borders, or
more informal settings. They are easy to grow and
tolerate a wide range of soils if given good drainage.
Many species have fern-like leaves that are attractive
even without the brightly colored flowers. Several
species and hybrids trialed at PERC have done well
with few problems.

A. filipendulina   Fernleaf Yarrow
(aka *A. eupatorium*)

The foliage of this yarrow is finely divided, fern-
like and aromatic. The flowers are held in rounded
to flat-topped corymbs and make excellent fresh cut
or dried flowers. Cut before pollen development for
best color retention. Deadheading prolongs flowering.
Fernleaf yarrow spreads rapidly in moist soils, but
is less aggressive when grown in dry, sunny sites.
Divide the main plant every three years.

A. filipendulina 'Parker's Variety'   (16)
Size of plant (H x W): 2' to 4' x 4' to 6'
Foliage color: Light to medium gray-green
Color of bloom: Golden yellow

'Parker's Variety' is coarser in texture than some
yarrows. The five plants grown since 1984 have
spread to create an imposing mass. The golden yellow
flowers, less than 0.5 inches individually, are clustered
in terminal corymbs up to 5 inches wide. Long flower

Achillea x filipendulina 'Coronation Gold'

Achillea 'Moonshine'

Achillea ptarmica 'The Pearl'

stems are excellent for cutting. Due to its size, plants in flower tend to lodge and may require staking. Deadheading is recommended since the spent blooms detract from the overall appearance. Cutting back after bloom stimulates production of fresh foliage.

A. x filipendulina 'Coronation Gold' (20)
Size of plant (H x W): 1' to 3' x 4' to 6' (4 plants)
Foliage color: Light gray-green
Color of bloom: Bright yellow

Achillea filipendulina is one of the parent plants of the garden hybrid Coronation Gold . These plants are smaller in stature than 'Parker's Variety' and require no staking. The fine textured gray-green foliage contrasts nicely with the flat heads of the bright yellow flowers. This hybrid is especially heat tolerant and makes an excellent dried flower. The spent blooms detract from the appearance and should be deadheaded.

A. millefolium   Milfoil, Common Yarrow
Size of plant (H x W): 2' to 4' x 2' to 4'
Foliage color: Medium green
Color of bloom: White or pink

This yarrow has finely-divided leaves, hence the species name millefolium or "thousand leaves". They are alternate, soft and feathery. Culture and care is similar to A. filipendulina. Common yarrow does well in dry sites. Due to its vigorous spreading nature, frequent deadheading and division is advised. The species often is used in wild flower mixes or for naturalizing. It can become a lawn weed. Staking keeps the flower stalks from lodging. Although the species was removed from the PERC garden, several cultivars have performed well.

A. millefolium 'Red Beauty' (5)
A crimson red flowering cultivar which blooms from late June until frost.

A. millefolium 'Rosea' (17)
This cultivar has pink blooms that fade to softer shades, depending on flower maturity. Peak bloom began in July and continued to early August.

A. 'Moonshine' (20)
Size of plant (H x W): 1' to 3' x 2' to 4'
Foliage color: Silver gray
Color of bloom: Pale yellow

The pale yellow blooms and soft silvery foliage make this yarrow especially attractive. In 20 years, five plants have spread to 4 feet in width. The flowers turn brown as they mature and are best deadheaded. Two minor problems are spider mites and chlorosis. This hybrid is a less aggressive spreader than other yarrows. 'Moonshine' blooms from early June until hard frost.

A. ptarmica 'The Pearl'   Sneezewort
Size of plant (H x W): 1' to 2' x 2' to 4' (12)
Foliage color: Dark green
Color of bloom: White
Size of bloom: Individual flowers 0.5" to 1"

A. ptarmica differs from other yarrows by having dark green, linear, toothed leaves. 'The Pearl' has a double white, button-like flower held in branched clusters. It makes an excellent cut flower. Peak bloom is in July and early August. Spent blooms turn brown and detract from the overall appearance. Lodging may also be a problem. The plant is loose in habit and spreads by rhizomes. Although this cultivar is less aggressive than the species, give it plenty of room in the perennial border or use it in a naturalized setting.

Agastache
Lamiaceae (Labiatae)
Landscape use: Border, wildflower and herb garden, massed, cut and dried flower
Growth habit: Erect clump

Agastache barberi

Agastache rupestris

Size of plant (H x W): 2' to 4' x 1' to 3'
Size of bloom: Individual flowers 0.5" to 1",
inflorescence > 5"

This genus contains approximately 30 species of perennials, the majority having stiff, angular stems and fragrant, opposite, toothed foliage. The tubular, two-lipped flowers are characteristic of the mint family. They are arranged in whorls around the flowering stalk. *Agastache* spp. provide a rich nectar source for bees, butterflies and hummingbirds.

A. barberi   Giant Hummingbird Mint
Foliage color: Medium green   (4)
Time of bloom: Late June-October, peaking mid-July to early August
Color of bloom: Pinkish purple

Giant hummingbird mint grows best in a sunny spot in average, well-drained soil. Although it is a member of the mint family, it is not aggressive. It established quickly at PERC, but after three years is less vigorous, due to competition with aggressive neighboring plants. Place *A. barberi* close to a path so its fragrance can be enjoyed. It is drought tolerant. Cut back after frost. It is a native of Arizona and New Mexico.

A. rupestris   Sunset Hyssop
Foliage color: Gray-green   PS-1997(3)
Time of bloom: Late July to October, peak in September
Color of bloom: Pinkish orange

This southwestern native is heat and drought tolerant. It is bushy with gray-green foliage that has a root beer fragrance. The scented flowers are pinkish in bud and open a soft orange. Culture and care is similar to *A. barberi*. Sunset hyssop has been endorsed for use in the Rocky Mountain and plains states by the Plant Select® program since 1997.

Ajuga   Bugleweed
Lamiaceae (Labiatae)   ○ ◐ ● 🐌 🦋
Landscape use: Border, ground cover, erosion control, woodland garden
Growth habit: Creeping, semi-evergreen
Size of plant (H x W): 1" to 6" x indefinite
Foliage color: Dark green
Time of bloom: May-October (frost), peak in late May
Color of bloom: Dark blue to purple
Size of bloom: Inflorescence 2.5" to 5"

Ajuga spp. has the square stem and rhizomatous habit characteristic of the mint family, but without the fragrant foliage. The leaves are opposite, glossy and in mounded rosettes. Flowers are whorled around the stem of leafy spikes. Each flower has a reduced upper lip and a three-lobed lower lip. Bugleweed is an excellent ground cover that can spread rapidly in moist, fertile soils invading lawns if planted too close. Depending on the species, bugleweed spreads by rhizomes or stolons. It is easy to divide in the spring or fall. *Ajuga* spp. prefer part shade to full shade exposures but can be grown in full sun with sufficient moisture and protection from winter winds.

A. pyramidalis **'Metallica Crispa'**
(aka *A. metallica*)   Upright or Pyramid Bugleweed
                                                (12)

The blooms of upright bugleweed are deep blue to purple. As the name implies, the flower stalks of *A. pyramidalis* are pyramidal in shape. Metallica Crispa is a cultivar selected for its crinkled, slightly metallic, dark green and purple leaves.

The purple-leaf varieties color better in the sun, but tend to scorch midsummer. Hard frost browns the leaf tips, yet the foliage retains some color into winter. Although this bugleweed at PERC had few problems, leaf curling aphids disfigured the foliage for part of the growing season.

15

Ajuga reptans 'Bronze Beauty'

Alcea rugosa

A. reptans 'Bronze Beauty'   Common, Carpet, or Blue Bugleweed (20)

A. reptans spreads from above ground stolons. It is capable of effectively covering an area, even in poor, dry soils or when under trees. The plants can spread indefinitely and cover an area quickly in more moist conditions. Consider the aggressive nature of this plant when choosing a site.

The cultivar Bronze Beauty has dark green to purple, oval to oblong leaves. It was more vigorous than Purple Brocade, another purple-leaved variety trialed at PERC. The foliage is semi-evergreen at PERC. Blue to purple flowers appeared in May and June with a minor rebloom later in the summer.

Alcea   Hollyhock
Malvaceae   ○ ✄ 🦋
Landscape use: Specimen, background, border, and cut flower
Growth habit: Mounded clump, erect flowering stems
Foliage color: Medium green
Time of bloom: July-September
Size of bloom: 2.5" to 5"

Hollyhocks are cottage garden favorites. Originally called holy hock or holy mallow, members of this genus were brought to England during the crusades. There are over 60 species of hollyhocks. Depending on the species, bloom height can range from 3 feet to 8 feet. Traditionally, the flowers are cup or funnel shaped and have 5 petals.

Hollyhocks grow best in full sun, moderately fertile and moist soil. Tall forms need a sheltered spot or can be staked in case of wind. Deep watering promotes a root system that will support the height of a mature plant.

A. rosea Chater's Double Hybrids   (6)
(aka *Althaea rosea*)
Size of plant (H x W): 2' to 4' x 1' to 2'
Color of bloom: Assorted

Alcea rosea is not reliably perennial, but most often biennial. Seedlings carry on when the mother plant dies. The leaves are alternate, rough and lobed. They form a basal rosette early in the spring. Later the stems elongate to reach heights of 4 feet or more. The flowers are borne on terminal racemes with the lowest buds opening first. Blooms may be single or double and there are many colors to choose from.

The Chater's Double Hybrids grown at PERC have double blooms in many bright to pale shades. Those at PERC were originally in shades of peach, yellow and red. Over five years in the garden, red and yellow seedlings survived and perpetuated. Seedling plants in 1999 were crowded, shorter, and less vigorous than in years past. White flies, chewing insects, and rust have been a problem.

A. rugosa   (5)
(aka *Althaea rugosa*)
Size of plant (H x W): 4' to 6' x 2' to 4' in bloom
Time of bloom: Mid-July to September
Color of bloom: Pale yellow

A. rugosa is a giant among hollyhocks. Its deeply lobed, medium green leaves are somewhat wrinkled and prominently veined. The flowers are held on long, unbranched stalks reaching to 6 feet and beyond. The pale yellow blooms have the classic cup shape of the old-fashioned hollyhocks. Flowering begins mid July and continues until frost. Care is similar to *A. rosea*.

A. rugosa self-sows freely. Rouge out seedlings from areas that cannot accommodate the mature size. Deadheading encourages a fresh rosette of leaves after bloom.

Alchemilla mollis

Anaphalis margaritacea

Alchemilla mollis Lady's Mantle
(aka *A. vulgaris*) ◐ ◗ ✄ ⚘ (12)
Rosaceae
Landscape use: Ground cover, mass, border, wildflower, herb and woodland garden, cut flower
Growth habit: Mounded, spreading
Size of plant (H x W): 1' to 2' x 2' to 5' massed
Foliage color: Medium green
Time of bloom: June to early August, peaking in June
Color of bloom: Greenish yellow (chartreuse)
Size of bloom: Individual flowers < 0.5", inflorescence 2.5"-5"

Lady's mantle is an old-fashioned plant traditionally used in herbal medicines. Its rosette of toothed, rounded and scalloped leaves look pleated, much like a lady's mantle. In the morning, each cupped leaf holds the dewdrops from the night before. The flowers are more unusual than showy. Each tiny, chartreuse flower is held in a loose cyme above the foliage. The soft color makes an excellent contrast for bold companion plants or in flower arrangements.

A. mollis is easy to grow given moderately fertile soils and regular water. The plants at PERC receive morning sun and light shade in the afternoon. Cutting the foliage back after bloom results in new growth that is tidy and fresh. This practice also controls self-sowing. Moist conditions encourage vigorous growth and lodging. Excessively dry growing conditions encourage spider mite problems.

A. mollis 'Auslese' (4)

This hardy and vigorous cultivar is more compact than the species. Each plant reaches a height and width of one foot and is mounded in habit. Growing at the base of a tree at PERC, it receives filtered sunlight in the afternoon. The size lends itself well to the front of a border, along a path or in a rock garden.

Anaphalis margaritacea Pearly Everlasting
Asteraceae (Compositae) ◐ ✄ ❀ 🦋 ⚘ (19)
Landscape use: Border, wildflower garden, cut and dried flower
Growth habit: Upright, spreading
Size of plant (H x W): 1' to 3' x 3' to 6' massed
Foliage color: Light gray-green
Time of bloom: Mid-July to September, peak in mid-August to September
Color of bloom: White bracts/yellow center
Size of bloom: Individual flowers 0.5" to 1", inflorescence 1" to 2.5"

This North American native has lance-shaped light green leaves that are covered by fine gray hairs. It is erect in growth habit but spreads by rhizomes, especially in moist sites. Drier sites and poorer soils reduce its tendency to sprawl. The flowers are excellent for cutting and drying. The outer bracts are papery and white. The inner florets are yellow. Cut when the yellow centers can first be seen. The flower bracts remain showy until the seeds are ripe. It is best to deadhead before this stage. The seeds are cottony and blow away, much like dandelions.

Pearly everlasting prefers full sun, but can be grown in light shade. Good drainage is important, especially in winter. It does well in our alkaline soils and can tolerate drought. No insect problems were noticed at PERC.

Anemone
Ranunculaceae ◐ ◗ ✄ 🦋 !
Landscape use: Background (tall species), border, mass, ground cover (short species),wildflower and woodland gardens, cut flower
Size of bloom: 1" to 2.5"

This diverse genus contains approximately 100 species of perennials. The majority are native to temperate Asia. Many are woodland inhabitants, thriving in moist, rich, well-drained soils. They may

Anemone sylvestris   *Anemone hupehensis* 'Prince Henry'   *Anemone tomentosa*

be rhizomatous or tuberous, spring blooming or fall blooming. The species grown at PERC have been cold hardy, relatively free of problems, and long-lived. The only difficulty with these anemones has been containing their vigorous growth. Members of this genus are poisonous to humans and livestock if ingested.

A. hupehensis var. *japonica* 'Prince Henry '
Japanese Anemone (14)
Growth habit: Upright, spreading
Size of plant (H x W): 2' to 4' x 4' to 6' massed
Foliage color: Dark green
Time of bloom: Mid-August to October (frost), peak in late September
Color of bloom: Pink

This selection of the popular Japanese anemone is a PERC favorite. It is initially slow to start growth in the spring, but reaches an impressive height of 4 feet in bloom by late summer. The leaves are three-parted, lobed and toothed. The blooms are a semi-double, rosy-pink and full of showy yellow stamens. They are held on long flowering stalks, perfect for cutting. Bees, wasps and blister beetles are common visitors.

'Prince Henry' is planted in full sun next to equally vigorous, spreading plants. Afternoon filtered shade is suitable. Some minor chlorosis has been noted. The main drawback with this anemone has been its late bloom period. Early fall frosts can end the flower show before full bloom.

A. pulsatilla- see *Pulsatilla vulgaris*

A. sylvestris
Snowdrop Anemone
(*A. alba*)   𝒞 ☙ (6)
Growth habit: Mounded, spreading
Size of plant (H x W): 6" to 1' x 4' to 6' massed
Foliage color: Medium green

Time of bloom: Mid-April to October (frost), peak in mid-May
Color of bloom: White

Snowdrop anemone is an excellent ground cover with early-spring bloom. Its white flowers are single, have showy yellow stamens and are fragrant. Although it languishes in the midsummer heat, snowdrop anemone reblooms when the nights turn cool again.

The plant has a fibrous root system and spreads through root suckers. It is easy to lift and divide if it has outgrown its boundaries. It receives morning sun and afternoon filtered shade at PERC. If not deadheaded, the seeds become a minor cottony nuisance. Although not spectacular, plant foliage colors to purple and bronze in the fall.

A. tomentosa
Grapeleaf Anemone
(aka *A. vitifolia*)   (24)
Growth habit: Upright, spreading
Size of plant (H x W): 2' to 4' x 6' to 9' massed
Foliage color: Medium green
Time of bloom: Mid-July to October (frost), peak mid-August to early September
Color of bloom: Pale pink

The leaf shape of this fall-blooming anemone resembles those of grapes. They are deeply veined and woolly underneath, giving the plant a silvery appearance in the wind. Grapeleaf anemone is rhizomatous. It has spread into the pathway at PERC and requires yearly maintenance. However, it's one of the premier late-summer bloomers. The flowers are pale pink with yellow stamens and borne in umbels. Bees find this plant irresistible.

A. tomentosa is late to come up in spring. Its leaves unfurl much like a fern fiddlehead. The fruit is briefly ornamental, but the cottony seeds may be considered a nuisance by some.

Aquilegia

Armeria maritima

Anthemis marschalliana   Marshall Chamomile
(aka *A. biebersteinii, A. rudolphiana*)   ◯ ◗ ⛌ (12)
Asteraceae (Compositae)
Landscape use: Border, rock and wildflower garden
Growth habit: Clump
Size of plant (H x W): 1" to 6" x 6" to 1'
Foliage color: Light gray-green
Time of bloom: Late May to early July, peak from early to late June
Color of bloom: Yellow
Size of bloom: 1" to 2.5"

This member of the sunflower family has cheerful yellow, daisy-like flowers that bloom in early summer. The flowers are solitary and held about a foot high. The foliage is finely divided, aromatic, and covered with silky gray hairs. Cut back after bloom to improve appearance and encourage fresh foliage growth.

A. marschalliana grows best in full sun but tolerates light shade. It requires good drainage, especially in the winter, and is drought tolerant. No insect or disease problems have been noticed.

Aquilegia   Columbine, Granny's Bonnet
Ranunculaceae (Helleboraceae)   ◯ ◗ ✂ 🦋 ⚘
Landscape use: Border, mass, wildflower and woodland garden, cut flower
Growth habit: Mounded clump
Size of plant (H x W): 1' to 2' x 1' to 2'
Foliage color: Light green to blue-green
Time of bloom: May-July
Color, height and size of bloom: Varies with cultivar

Several species and many cultivars of columbine have been grown at PERC with success. Over the years the parent plants have died out and the seedlings are a mixture of colors. Columbines tend to be short-lived. If you desire a particular color combination, you may have to replant new plants every three or four years.

Columbines have three-part, compound leaves. The blue-green color and soft texture provide an excellent contrast to bolder companions. In the cool temperatures of early spring, the foliage has a hint of pinkish-purple. The plants may go dormant in the summer.

The flowers, made up of five spurred petals and five sepals, may be one color or two. They dangle from the long flowering stalk and are excellent for cutting. Bees and hummingbirds enjoy the rich nectar found in the deep spurs. The Song Bird series includes 'Dove', a white-flowered columbine; 'Blue Bird' is a blue and white bicolor; 'Cardinal' is a red and white bicolor, and 'Robin' is a pink and white bicolor. The Music series features large, long-spurred flowers and six different colors. These series have been trialed at PERC with success.

Columbines can grow in full sun, but their flower colors look more vibrant and last longer in part shade. Plant in moist, well-drained, moderately fertile soil. Sawfly larvae, aphids, and chlorosis have affected the appearance of some of the plants at PERC.

Armeria maritima   Sea Thrift, Common
(aka *Statice maritima*)   Thrift, Sea Pink ◯ ⚘ ✂ (12)
Plumbaginaceae
Landscape use: Border, rock garden, ground cover, and cut flower
Growth habit: Mounded, spreading,
Size of plant (H x W): 6" to 8" x 1' to 2'
Foliage color: Dark green, evergreen
Time of bloom: Mid-May to October (frost), peak in mid-June
Color of bloom: Pink
Size of bloom: Inflorescence 0.5" to 1"

This low evergreen plant gradually spreads into spongy, turf-like cushions. The dark green leaves are linear and ribbed. The dense growth habit makes it an effective weed barrier. Winter desiccation and excess

Aster novi-belgii 'Eventide'

Aster novi-belgii 'Finalist'

winter moisture can be a problem in Colorado. Slight crown injury was noted for several years. Sea thrift grows best in a sunny, well-drained spot in the front of the border, along a path or in the rock garden. It is drought tolerant.

The flowers are tiny and clustered in terminal "pompons" on leafless stems. They resemble chives. Although small, the flowers can be cut and used for arrangements. *A. maritima* blooms heavily in June, with minor rebloom often until frost. Deadheading prolongs bloom.

A. m. var. *compacta* (6)

A similar variety spreading only 2 feet wide in five years. More floriferous than the species.

A. m. 'Dusseldorf Pride' (12)

A German cultivar with rosy-pink flowers reaching 6 inches high.

A. m. 'Victor Reiter' (8)

A dwarf, slow growing cultivar. More floriferous than the species.

Aster novi-belgii New York Aster, Michaelmas Daisy
Asteraceae (Compositae) ○ ◗ ✂ ✉ ⚘ (13)
Landscape use: Mass, border, wildflower garden and cut flower
Growth habit: Upright, spreading
Size of plant (H x W): 1' to 3' x 2' to 4'
Foliage color: Dark green
Time of bloom: August-October (frost)
Color of bloom: White, pinks and purples
Size of bloom: 1" to 2.5"

The *Aster* genus contains over 250 species of perennials and subshrubs, many native to North America. They have become the mainstays of the fall garden, blooming at a time when most other perennials are done. They do best in full sun, but tolerate part shade along the Front Range of the Colorado Rocky Mountains. Powdery mildew has been a problem for many of the cultivars grown

at PERC. Breeders have made selections for more resistance.

There are tall and short asters to chose from, as well as many colors. Tall asters are rhizomatous and spread into a broad mass unless divided every three to five years. Shorter varieties require frequent division to maintain their vigor. Lodging of plants in full bloom is a common complaint especially along the windy Front Range. Staking may be helpful. Pinching back growth early in the season encourages shorter, bushier plants.

The New York asters are native to the East coast from Newfoundland to Georgia. The dark green leaves are glossy, alternate and either sessile or clasping on the stem. The flowers are daisy-like with purple, pink, or white ray florets and yellow disk florets. They are held in showy terminal clusters. Many cultivars are available.

Plants at PERC were not overly tall, although sources report heights from 3 to 5 feet for this species. Problems at PERC have included lodging and powdery mildew. Minor chlorosis was corrected with fertilizer.

A. novae-angliae or the New England aster has also been grown at PERC, but the plants have developed severe mildew infections each year. This old planting is shaded by a tree and does not receive the sun and air circulation necessary to maintain its health and vigor. New England asters are native to the Eastern and Central portions of the United States. They are similar in appearance and habit to New York asters but have slightly pubescent, gray-green foliage. Asters that have performed well are listed below.

A. novi-belgii 'Eventide' (13)

This cultivar has dark purple semi-double flowers.

A. novi-belgii 'Finalist' (17)

'Finalist' is a rose-pink flowering cultivar.

A. novi-belgii 'Violet Carpet' (6)

Aster novi-belgii 'White Opal'

Aurinia saxatilis 'Compacta'

A cultivar with violet blooms and compact growth habit.

A. novi-belgii **'White Opal'** (8)

Compact growth habit and profuse white blooms make this cultivar perfect for the front of the border.

A. novi-belgii **'Winston S. Churchill'** (4)

The double, violet-red flowers of this cultivar are especially bright.

A. **'White Fairy'** (20)

This fall blooming, hybrid aster has a compact growth habit and white flowers.

Aurinia saxatilis 'Compacta' Dwarf Basket-of-
(aka *Alyssum saxatile*) Gold, Golden-tuft Alyssum
Brassicaceae (*Cruciferae*) ○ ❖ (12)

Landscape use: Mass, border, rock, wildflower and xeriscape gardens
Growth habit: Mounded
Size of plant (H x W): 6" to 1' x 1' to 2'
Foliage color: Light green to gray-green; semi-evergreen
Time of bloom: Mid-May to mid-June, peak in late May
Color of bloom: Yellow
Size of bloom: Individually < 0.5", inflorescence 0.5" to 1"

Dwarf basket-of-gold is an easy-to-grow, low-maintenance plant that can be counted on for a spectacular spring display if a few simple needs are met. The hairy gray-green leaves are arranged in a mounded basal rosette. The root and stem bases are woody. Flowers are four petalled, yellow and in a compact corymb-like panicle. It prefers full sun and well-drained soil. Excess water and fertilizer (or overly rich soil) encourages rank, soft growth and reduces winter hardiness. A rock garden, raised bed or retaining wall are excellent choices for this plant, which spills over the edges in full bloom. Shearing by a third after bloom keeps it compact and prevents it from self-sowing.

Although flea beetles are fond of this plant, no other disease or insect problems were noted at PERC. Basket-of-gold can be propagated by division, seed or cutting.

Baptisia australis Blue False Indigo,
Papilionaceae (*Leguminosae*) Blue Wild Indigo
 ○ ◗ ✂ ✿ ! (17)

Landscape use: Specimen, border, wildflower garden, cut and dried flower
Growth habit: Erect, clump
Size of plant (H x W): 2' to 4' x 2' to 4'
Foliage color: Light green to blue-green
Time of bloom: Late April to early July, peak in mid-June
Color of bloom: Blue
Size of bloom: Individual flowers 0.5" to 1", inflorescence >5"

This native North American plant was historically used as a dye substitute, hence the common name false indigo. Leaves are trifoliate and blue-green resembling the clover, another member of the pea family. Foliage is attractive throughout the summer. *Baptisia australis* is an erect, slow-growing plant. Plant in full or part sun and well-drained soil. Since it is tap rooted, transplanting is difficult. It can be grown from seed and transplanted when very young. The deep root system enables the mature plant to withstand drought.

The flowers are the typical pea shape and indigo blue to purple. They are borne on a long terminal raceme. Use the inflorescence for fresh flower arrangements. The fruit matures to an ornamental black-inflated pod, attractive in dried arrangements.

False indigo is long-lived and not aggressive. Plants at PERC have shown some minor chlorosis and

Boltonia asteroides 'Snowbank'

Brunnera macrophylla

damage by grasshoppers and other chewing insects. Since the plant is toxic, do not plant where livestock forage.

Bergenia   Elephant's Ear, Pig Squeak
Saxifragaceae   ○ ◗ ● ⁂ (17)
Landscape use: Border, ground cover, mass, woodland garden
Growth habit: Clump, spreading
Size of plant (H x W): 6" to 1' x 2' to 4' massed
Foliage color: Medium to dark green with red tints, evergreen
Time of bloom: April-May
Color of bloom: Pink
Size of bloom: Inflorescence 1" to 2.5"

Although *Bergenia* spp. rarely bloom at PERC, the foliage of these plants has earned it a place in the shady perennial garden. The thick, leathery, simple leaves are evergreen, paddle-shaped, and sometimes wavy or notched. In the spring and again in fall, the leaves turn a reddish purple. By midsummer they are glossy green with red tints or edges.

Bergenia spp. spread slowly through thick rhizomes. They look best when massed by a path, a pond, underneath trees, or the front of the border. Several groupings at PERC are planted in full sun and the leaves scorch by midsummer. Moist, moderately fertile soil in part shade is ideal.

The flower buds and early spring foliage often are frost damaged. When in bloom, the rosy pink flowers are bell-shaped and held in scapes above the foliage. Hybrid *Bergenia* is less variable in leaf size and form as well as flower color than the species, which is often coarser textured. Two hybrids are grown at PERC and are described next.

B. 'Evening Glow'   (9)
The dark green leaves of this hybrid are 6 inches long and red tinted underneath, maroon in winter. The flowers are semi-double, magenta and held on red scapes.

B. 'Sunningdale'   (9)
This hybrid has rounded deep green leaves that turn copper-red in winter. The lilac magenta flowers are held on red scapes.

Boltonia asteroides 'Snowbank'   Boltonia, False
Asteraceae (Compositae)   Chamomile
                                          ○ ◗ ✄ ⚘ (5)
Landscape use: Background, specimen, border, wildflower garden, and cut flower
Growth habit: Upright, spreading
Size of plant (H x W): 2' to 4' x 2' to 4'
Foliage color: Gray-green
Time of bloom: August-October (frost), peak in mid-September to early October
Color of bloom: White with yellow center
Size of bloom: 1" to 2.5"

This under utilized, aster look-alike is a native of the Central United States. Its height and spreading, wiry stems make a bold statement. The leaves are blue-green, lance-shaped and alternate. The plant is self-supporting if grown in full sun. Flower panicles are 4 to 6 inches wide and loaded with daisy-like blooms. This late summer bloomer is covered with flowers until frost. The cultivar Snowbank is not as tall as the species and has white ray florets with a yellow center.

If grown in part shade, boltonia may develop mildew and need staking. It is not fussy about soil, nor is it aggressive. No problems were reported in the five years boltonia was grown at PERC.

Brunnera macrophylla   Siberian-bugloss,
(aka *Anchusa myosotidiflora*)   Perennial Forget-me-not
Boraginaceae   ◗ ● ⚘ (13)
Landscape use: Border, ground cover, mass and woodland garden

22

Callirhoe involucrata

Campanula carpatica 'White Clips'

Growth habit: Mounded
Size of plant (H x W): 1' to 2' x 1' to 2'
Foliage color: Medium green to dark green
Time of bloom: May to mid-July
Color of bloom: Blue
Size of bloom: Individually < 0.5", inflorescence 2.5" to 5"

Siberian bugloss is one of the few plants that has a true blue flower resembling that of the annual forget-me-not in the genus *Myosotis*. It is an easy plant to grow, given partial shade from PERC's intense afternoon sun. Moist soils are recommended, but at PERC this plant has not received any special attention. In fact, moist conditions tend to encourage slugs, one of the few serious pests of this plant.

In the spring, dainty star-shaped blue flowers rise 6 to 12 inches above the rosette of basal leaves in broadly branched panicles. The leaves are softly hairy, heart-shaped and have long petioles. Until finished blooming, the leaves remain small and tightly mounded. As the season progresses, the leaves and stems continue to expand producing a loose mound of attractive foliage. Siberian bugloss is rhizomatous, yet is not aggressive. Divide it when the center dies out or propagate from root cuttings in the winter. It may self-sow.

Callirhoe involucrata   Purple Poppy
Malvaceae   Mallow, Wine Cup
○ ☙ ❖ PS-1999 (14)
Landscape use: Ground cover, rock garden, xeriscape and wildflower garden
Growth habit: Spreading
Size of plant (H x W): 6" to 1' x 6' to 9' (at least 3 plants)
Foliage color: Medium green
Time of bloom: June-October (frost), peak in July to early August

Color of bloom: Magenta
Size of bloom: 1" to 2.5"

This sprawling floriferous plant requires very little moisture once established. It is perfect for sunny slopes, as a ground cover, or trailing over a wall. It is tap rooted and grows poorly in water-logged soils. If given too much water, the center of the plant may "melt out." The cup-shaped, solitary flowers are a bright magenta with a white "eye." They open wide in the sun and close up in cloudy weather.

Wine cup has attractive foliage. Most leaves are palmately divided and circular, although this is variable. The lobes can be deeply cut. The leaves are arranged alternately on long trailing stems. Minor chlorosis was a problem at PERC. Wine cup has been promoted by the Plant Select® program since 1999.

Campanula   Bellflower
Campanulaceae   ○ ☽ ☙
Landscape use: Border, rock and wildflower garden, mass, ground cover (short species), cut flower
Foliage color: Medium green

This variable genus contains more than 250 species of annuals, biennials and perennials. *Campanula* means "little bell", which aptly describes the typical shape of the flower. Bellflowers vary in height and growth habits. Flowers are typically blue or purple in color, but white and pink also are available. They can be grown in sun or part shade; some are tolerant of full shade. They are easy to grow given well-drained soil that is neither too wet nor too dry. Very little maintenance is required to keep bellflowers healthy. Many cultivars are grown at PERC, with the top performers discussed next.

C. carpatica   Carpathian Harebell,
(aka *C. turbinata*)   Tussock Bellflower ☙ (19)
Growth habit: Clump, mounded
Size of plant (H x W): 6" to 1' x 1' to 2'

Campanula glomerata 'Superba'

Campanula persicifolia 'Chettle Charm'

Time of bloom: Late June to mid-September, peaking in mid-July

Color of bloom: Blue-purple

Size of bloom: 1″ to 2.5″

This mounded, low growing plant has shiny ovate to heart-shaped, toothed leaves. The flowers face upwards, are bell-shaped, and are held above the foliage on 6 inch to12 inch stalks. Deadheading encourages continual flower production throughout the season. Carpathian harebell dies out in the center as it ages. Divide every three to four years to promote vigorous growth. After bloom, shear back to encourage new foliage. Plant this species in full sun or part shade on moist, well-drained soil. The cultivars listed below have been grown at PERC.

C. c. **'Blue Clips'** (3)

This compact German cultivar has blue, bell shaped flowers.

C. c. **'Blue Uniform'** (8)

'Blue Uniform' has darker blue flowers and a mounded, spreading growth habit.

C. c. **'White Clips'** (12)

This cultivar is the white flowering counterpart of 'Blue Clips.'

C. cochleariifolia   Fairies' Thimbles
(aka *C. pulsilla*)   ✌ (8)

Growth habit: Creeping

Size of plant (H x W): 1″ to 6″ x 2′ to 4′

Time of bloom: Mid-June to October (frost)

Color of bloom: Light blue

Size of bloom: 0.5″

This ground cover creeps on slender rhizomes, forming a dense weed-choking mat. Its shiny leaves are toothed and oval to heart-shaped. The small, bell-shaped flowers are held on wiry stems and dangle in the breeze. Fairies' thimbles tolerates dry soils and "melts out" if over irrigated.

C. glomerata **'Superba'**   Clustered Bellflower
                                          ✂ (12)

Growth habit: Upright, spreading

Size of plant (H x W): 1′ to 2′ x 1′ to 2′

Time of bloom: Mid-June to early September, peaking in late June to early July

Color of bloom: Violet to purple

Size of bloom: 0.5″ to 1″

As the common name implies, this species has bell-shaped flowers clustered in a terminal raceme. The cultivar Superba has violet-purple flowers whereas the species may have flowers ranging from blue, lavender, and purple to white. The foliage is hairy, toothed, and ovate to lance shaped. Early in the season, the leaves of clustered bellflower are in 6-inch tight rosettes. Later, the flowering stalks elongate reaching 1 to 2 feet high. The clustered bellflower is perfect for cut flowers and massing. Midsummer heat caused some wilting and leaf bronzing at PERC. Clustered bellflower can be invasive in moist, rich soil.

C. persicifolia   Peach-leaved
(aka *C. persiciflora*)   Bellflower, Peach-bells,
                                   Willow-bell ✂ (9)

Growth habit: Upright, spreading

Size of plant (H x W): 6″ to 1′ x 1′ to 2′

Time of bloom: Mid-June to October (frost), peak late June

Color of bloom: Blue or white

Size of bloom: 1″ to 2.5″

The leaves of this species are linear to lanceolate and semi-evergreen. Basal leaves are rosette forming. Flowering stalks reach 2 to 3 feet and wave in the breeze. The flowers are borne in terminal and axillary racemes. Each flower is nodding and cup to bowl-shaped. Bees are frequent visitors. Peach-leaved bellflowers look attractive in wildflower gardens or massed for effect. It is an excellent cut flower.

Campanula rotundifolia

C. p. 'Chettle Charm' (3)
This bellflower has white flowers with a pale violet margin.

C. p. 'Telham Beauty' (3)
A cultivar with light blue flowers.

C. rotundifolia Harebell, Scotch Bluebell
(*C. polymorpha*) ❖ ⚹ (16)
Growth habit: Clump, spreading
Size of plant (H x W): 6" to 1' x 1' to 2'
Time of bloom: Mid-June to October (frost), peaking in late June to early July
Color of bloom: Blue
Size of bloom: 0.5" to 1"
Scotch bluebell can be found from the foothills to the tundra in Colorado and in the Northern Hemisphere. It is capable of tolerating some drought. Basal leaves are rounded to heart-shaped, toothed and light to medium green. The leaves on the flowering stalks are linear. Scotch bluebell forms a clump, but spreads by rhizomes and seed. Flowers are nodding and held on wiry stems. Old plantings tend to lodge and should be divided.

Centaurea Knapweed, Star Thistle
Asteraceae (Compositae) ◯ ⚹ 🦋
Three of the approximate 450 different species of knapweed are grown at PERC with good results. They are easily grown in full sun, almost any soil conditions and provide good cut or dried flowers. Thistle-like in appearance, each flower is composed of many tubular florets surrounded by an involucre of bracts, which range from papery, to fringed or spiny. In some species the outer florets are lobed or fringed. The three species of knapweed described below self-sow if allowed to go to seed. Deadheading encourages compact growth and rebloom and controls self-sowing. Propagate by seed or division in spring or fall.

C. dealbata 'Rosea' Persian Cornflower (12)
Landscape use: Border, mass, wildflower garden, cut flower
Growth habit: Mounded clump
Size of plant (H x W): 1' to 2' x 1' to 2'
Foliage color: Medium green
Time of bloom: Early June to October (frost), peak in late June
Color of bloom: Rose pink
Size of bloom: 1" to 2.5"
Persian cornflower has deeply divided mid-green leaves that are gray-green and hairy underneath. The foliage forms a neat mound initially. As the plant flowers it becomes open and floppy unless supported. The pink flowers are composed of large fringed outer florets and shorter inner florets that form a tuft on top of fringed involucre bracts.
After peak bloom, Persian cornflower can be cut back heavily to promote a flush of secondary foliage that remains compact and tidy and a minor rebloom until frost.

C. macrocephala Globe Centaurea, Yellow
Hardhead, Big-head Knapweed ✿ (16)
Landscape use: Specimen, background, wildflower garden, cut and dried flower
Growth habit: Erect
Size of plant (H x W): 4' to 6' x 2' to 4'
Foliage color: Medium green
Time of bloom: Late June to mid-August
Color of bloom: Yellow
Size of bloom: 2.5" to 5"
This is a tall, stiff, coarse plant resembling a thistle when in bloom. The leaves are large and rough with wavy margins. Its large yellow, globe-shaped flowers sit in a tuft on top of brown involucre bracts. Globe centaurea makes an excellent fresh cut flower. After blooming, the brown papery seedheads are still attractive and can be used in dried arrangements.

Centaurea macrocephala	*Centaurea montana*	*Centranthus ruber*

Full sun is recommended. Because of its large size, globe centaurea is usually grown singly as a specimen plant. The foliage tends to die back a few weeks after blooming and should be cut to the ground unless seeds are desired.

C. montana   Mountain-bluet, Perennial Cornflower (17)
Landscape use: Border, mass, wildflower garden and cut flower
Growth habit: Upright, spreading to mounded
Size of plant (H x W): 1' to 2' x 2' to 4'
Foliage color: Blue green to gray green
Time of bloom: Mid-May to October (frost), peak in late June
Color of bloom: Violet blue
Size of bloom: 1" to 2.5"

Mountain-bluet is a fairly large, bushy plant with broadly lanceolate, silvery green leaves. It produces violet blue flowers whose widely-spaced florets are deeply fringed and lacy looking. Beneath the florets, the bracts of the involucre are fringed with black hairs. At PERC, flowering peaks in June and continues sporadically until frost. Deadheading encourages more flowers and a longer blooming period. Cutting back hard after the first flush of flowers will stimulate new shoots, a compact plant, and a stronger fall bloom.

Mountain-bluets do well in full sun or partial shade and are moderately tolerant of dry soils. The plants are a good source of long-lasting cut flowers early in the season. This plant self-seeds and can be a nuisance. In overly fertile conditions, mountain-bluets become floppy and can spread aggressively. Leaf curling aphids, leaf spot and slugs have been minor problems at PERC. Divide frequently.

Centranthus ruber   Jupiter's Beard, Red Valerian
Valerianaceae   ◗ ▶ ✂ ❖ 🦋 ✔ 👯 (16)
Landscape use: Specimen, background, cut flower, wildflower and xeriscape garden
Growth habit: Clump
Size of plant (H x W): 2' to 4' x 2' to 4'
Foliage color: Blue-green
Time of bloom: Mid-May to October (frost), peak in mid-late June
Color of bloom: Reddish pink, red, or white
Size of bloom: Individually <0.5"; inflorescence 2.5" to 5"

This old-fashioned plant is a good choice for hot, sunny sites and poor (if well-drained), alkaline soil. Jupiter's beard may be short-lived, especially if grown in heavy, moist soil and has a tendency to self-sow. Seedlings vary in flower color from deep reds to pinkish reds or white. If you are fond of a particular color, it is best to propagate with cuttings and deadhead to discourage self-sowing.

C. ruber is a bushy plant with a woody base. The waxy, blue-green leaves are smooth and fleshy. The flowers are small, tubular and in terminal and axillary clusters. Frequent deadheading produces continuous bloom.
C. r. 'Albus'   (16)
A white-flowered cultivar with characteristics similar to the species.

Cerastium tomentosum 'Silver Carpet'   Snow-in-
Caryophyllaceae   summer, Snow-in-harvest
                                      ◗ ▶ 🌱 ❖ (20)
Landscape use: Ground cover, border, erosion control, xeriscape and rock garden
Growth habit: Spreading
Size of plant (H x W): 6" to 8" x indefinite
Foliage color: Silvery gray, semi-evergreen
Time of bloom: Late May-July

Cerastium tomentosum 'Silver Carpet'   *Ceratostigma plumbaginoides*

Color of bloom: White
Size of bloom: 0.5" to 1"

Snow-in-summer is a favorite ground cover for hot, sunny, infertile sites. The semi-evergreen leaves are linear, woolly and opposite. The plant spreads by rhizomes into a dense silvery-gray mat. It is not tolerant of foot traffic. The white flowers are five-petalled and notched. They are held in clusters of three to 15 flowers each with heaviest bloom in mid-June. Silver carpet is a cultivar grown for its silvery white leaf.

If grown in rich soil or moist conditions, *C. tomentosum* may become invasive or die out in the center. It can suffer from spider mites if grown too dry. Division and shearing are two techniques useful in keeping the plant more compact.

Ceratostigma plumbaginoides   Plumbago,
(aka *Plumbago larpentiae*)   Leadwort
Plumbaginaceae   ◯ ◗ ⁂ 🦋 (9)
Landscape use: Ground cover, border, rock garden
Growth habit: Mounded, spreading
Size of plant (H x W): 1' to 2' x 1' to 2'
Foliage color: Medium-dark green
Time of bloom: August-October (frost)
Color of bloom: Deep blue to purple
Size of bloom: 0.5" to 1"

Plumbago has many features to recommend it. It is mounded with shiny medium to dark green leaves that hold up well to heat. Cool weather turns the foliage a spectacular bronzy red. Stems and flower buds are pink tinged. The flowers are borne in terminal and axillary clusters. The tubular base of the flower broadens to five flared lobes and is a deep indigo blue to purple color.

Plumbago flowers best in full sun but tolerates part shade. It requires well-drained soil of moderate fertility. It is somewhat drought tolerant but competes poorly with tree roots. Plumbago emerges late in the spring. It is frost tender and blackens with the first hard freeze. Cut it back to the ground each year after the foliage dies. Winter mulch is recommended along the front range.

Chrysanthemum x morifolium   Garden Mum,
(aka *Dendranthema x grandiflorum*)   Hardy Mum,
Asteraceae (Compositae)   Florists Mum ◯ ◗ ✂ 🦔 !
Landscape use: Specimen, massed, border, and cut flower
Growth habit: Clump
Size of plant (H x W): 1' to 2' x 1' to 2'; some reaching 4 feet tall
Foliage color: Medium green
Time of bloom: Variable depending on cultivar ranging from July-October (frost)
Color of bloom: Variable depending on cultivar
Size of bloom: 1" to 3" depending on cultivar

Many garden mums have been planted at PERC over the years. Their brightly colored blooms and late summer to fall bloom periods have made these plants a favorite. However, none of the original plants have survived. The average life span for garden mums at PERC has been three to four years, before they fail to overwinter.

Garden mums originated in China before 500 B.C. Hybridization has resulted in many flower types including single, double, pompon, and spoon. Foliage is toothed and aromatic. Colors range from yellow, orange, red, bronze, white, and pink. There are no blue shades. Pinching back is an accepted practice and produces compact, stocky plants and many lateral blooms. Pinch back twice in summer before the middle of July.

Mums prosper in full sun, fertile and well-drained soil. They tolerate clay soils and can withstand minor drought. Although not reliably hardy in the north, chances of overwintering increase with good drainage and mulching. Transplanting is possible even when

Chrysanthemum x morifolium 'Mary Stoker'

the plant is in bloom, but given a choice, divide in the spring. Some people may develop dermatitis upon contact with the foliage. The following mums are currently in the PERC garden:

C. x morifolium 'South Pass' (16)
A yellow blooming, double flowered cultivar.
C. 'Mary Stoker' (1)
A yellow blooming, single flowered cultivar.
C. 'Sheffield's Hillside Pink' (2)
A late bloomer with single, pink flowers.

Chrysanthemum serotinum- see *Leucanthemella serotina*

Chrysanthemum x superbum- see *Leucanthemum x superbum*

Chrysopsis villosa- see *Heterotheca villosa*

Clematis   Clematis, Virgin's Bower
Ranunculaceae   ◯ ◗ ✿ !
Landscape use: Specimen, border, and dried flower
Foliage color: Medium green
This popular genus contains over 200 species, many native to China and Japan. The semi-woody climbing *Clematis* spp. enjoys wide usage. Their showy, petal-like sepals and decorative seed heads provide months of interest. The upright herbaceous species, however, are not as well known in this country. Their flowers often are not as large or showy and are borne on the current year's growth. Three unusual and handsome species were grown with success at PERC. Finding these for your own garden may require some effort. Ask your local nursery, check mail-order catalogs, or try the Internet.
All parts of clematis are poisonous if ingested; some people experience skin irritation upon contact with the plant sap.

Clematis heracleifolia   Tube Clematis
(aka *C. davidiana, C. heracleifolia*   ℮ (5)
subsp. *davidiana*)
Growth habit: Upright, spreading
Size of plant (H x W): 1' to 3' x 1' to 2'
Time of bloom: Mid-August to September, peak in early September
Color of bloom: Lavender to blue
Size of bloom: 1" to 2.5"
Tube clematis gets its common name from the unusual lavender to blue tubular flower. They are slightly fragrant, have recurved tips, and are found in whorls in the leaf axils. Bloom is late summer, early fall on current year's growth and can be terminated by early frosts. The foliage is compound, with three leaflets. Tube clematis is upright until the weight of bloom and seed heads force it to lean over. Support it with a companion plant, or stake it. The seeds have a long, hairy, ornamental style.
Plant this plant in full sun and give it regular water. Cut back to the ground in early spring. All clematis grow best with a cool root environment created by applying a mulch.

C. integrifolia   Solitary Clematis
Growth habit: Upright   (24)
Size of plant (H x W): 1' to 3' x 2 to 4'
Time of bloom: Late May to mid-September, peaking in mid-June to mid-July
Color of bloom: Blue to purple
Size of bloom: 1" to 2.5"
This long-lived clematis is shrub-like, but not self-supporting. Its slack stems terminate with a solitary, nodding bell-shaped flower borne on current year's growth. The yellow stamens make a nice contrast to the bluish-purple flower color. Bloom is followed by the ornamental seed heads typical for the genus. *C. integrifolia* does not have a compound leaf. Instead, the leaves are opposite, simple and sessile.

Clematis integrifolia

Clematis recta

Coreopsis verticillata

Visitors find this species particularly beautiful early in the season. By late summer, the plant has fallen outwards from the center. Propping up the plant with companion plants or other supports will improve the appearance. Cut back to the ground in early spring.

C. recta   Bush Clematis, Ground Clematis F (11)
Growth habit: Clump
Size of plant (H x W): 2' to 4' x 2' to 4'
Time of bloom: Mid-June to mid-September, peak in late June to early July
Color of bloom: White
Size of bloom: 0.5" to 1"

   C. recta is sprawling or rambling and needs lots of room in the perennial border. The stems reach 2 ½ to 3 feet high before cascading over. At PERC, it spills out onto the path. This species is literally covered with small, star-shaped, white blooms in terminal panicles. Stamens are creamy-yellow and showy. The flowers are borne on current year's growth and are fragrant. Seed heads look like silvery pinwheels. Care is similar to the clematis previously discussed.

Coreopsis verticillata   Threadleaf Coreopsis,
Asteraceae (Compositae)   Tickseed ○ ✂ ⚓ (20)
Landscape use: Border, mass, cut flower and wildflower gardens
Growth habit: Upright, spreading
Size of plant (H x W): 2' to 4' x 2' to 4'
Foliage color: Medium green
Time of bloom: Late June to late September, peak mid-July to late July
Color of bloom: Yellow
Size of bloom: 1" to 2.5"

   These members of the sunflower family are long-lived and tolerant of poor, dry soils. They are native to the Southeastern United States. Unlike many other rhizomatous plants, threadleaf coreopsis has proven itself well-behaved and not aggressive. Its fine-textured foliage is an excellent contrast for bolder companions. The leaves are opposite, and palmately divided into three narrow parts. The plant has required no staking at PERC.

   Threadleaf coreopsis is covered by golden-yellow, daisy-like flowers midsummer. If spent blooms are removed, a secondary bloom is encouraged. If not deadheaded, the fruit matures to black and produces an interesting contrast to the soft, lacy foliage. *Koris* and *opsis* means "bug-like" in Greek, and refers to the tiny, black seeds.

   These low maintenance plants perform best in sunny, well-drained sites of low to moderate fertility. They are at home in meadow and naturalized settings. The cheerful flowers are excellent for cutting. Threadleaf coreopsis is slow to emerge in the spring. It is drought tolerant.

C. v. 'Moonbeam'   PPY-1992
   This cultivar has survived at PERC since 1994. It is low growing, reaching heights of about 1 foot. It is perfect for the front of the border. The dark green ferny foliage contrasts nicely with the lemon yellow flowers. The plant was moved to a new spot in June of 1999, and by July was blooming again, regardless of the earlier disturbance.

C. rosea
   This species resembles `Moonbeam' but has rosy pink ray florets that surround the yellow disk. It has grown at PERC successfully for two years.

Delosperma nubigenum   Yellow Ice Plant
(*D. congestum*)   ○ ☙ ❖ (13)
Aizoaceae
Landscape use: Ground cover, rock and xeriscape gardens
Growth habit: Creeping
Size of plant (H x W): 1" to 3" x indefinite
Foliage color: Light green, evergreen

Delosperma nubigenum

Dianthus barbatus

Time of bloom: Late May-July
Color of bloom: Yellow
Size of bloom: 0.5" to 1"

The most cold hardy of the ice plants, this plant also is tolerant of poor soils and hot sites. The flowers are yellow, daisy-like, and close up in cloudy weather. Yellow ice plant requires good drainage, especially in winter, but has done well in the clay soil at PERC. This mat-forming plant has thick, succulent leaves that are easily crushed by foot traffic. The purplish-red winter color is excellent. Fungal diseases can set in if given too much water.

There is some taxonomic confusion about the correct species name for this plant.

Dianthus   Garden Pink
Caryophyllaceae   ◐ ◗ ✂ 🦋
Landscape use: Border, mass, ground cover (select species only), cut flower and rock garden

This large genus contains over 300 species and many hybrids. Most are evergreen and low growing. Foliage is linear to lance-shaped and varies from green to gray-green and blue-green. Many make excellent cut flowers and some have a spicy, clove fragrance. The flowers may be one color, flecked, laced, or picotee. *Dianthus* spp. flourishes in well drained, slightly alkaline to neutral soil and full sun exposures. Excess winter moisture is detrimental. The popular cut flower, carnation, was developed in the 16th century. References to *Dianthus* as the gillyflower or July-flower are found in Shakespeare.

This species are easy to grow, adapt to dry or more traditional watering regimes, and require little maintenance.

D. barbatus   Sweet-William ☿ (5)
Growth habit: Clump
Size of plant (H x W): 1' to 2' x 1' to 2'

Foliage color: Medium green
Time of bloom: June-August, peaking in mid-June to early July
Color of bloom: Various shades of pink and white
Size of bloom: Inflorescence 2.5" to 5"

Sweet-William is an old-fashioned cottage garden flower that is most often biennial, sometimes a short-lived perennial. It self seeds readily and extends its presence in your garden through subsequent generations. Seedlings are not necessarily the same color combinations as the parent plants. The flat-topped inflorescence is showy and often a mix of white, pink, red, purple and magenta in contrasting rings. The flower cluster is surrounded by green bracts. Deadheading produces a smaller secondary bloom in September. In Colorado, sweet-William thrives best in part shade but will tolerate full sun if given sufficient moisture. Although not particularly handsome when not in bloom, sweet-William is an excellent cut flower and bright addition to the border.

D. caryophyllus   Clove Pink,
                                       Hardy Carnation ☿ (19)
Growth habit: Clump
Size of plant (H x W): 6" to 1' x 6" to 1 '
Foliage color: Blue-green to blue-gray, semi-evergreen
Time of bloom: Mid-June to late August, peak in late June
Color of bloom: Pink
Size of bloom: 1" to 2.5"

This tufted, woody-based perennial has been cultivated since classical times. It originated from the Mediterranean region. There are many cultivars, some hardy to zone five. The leaves are flat and have conspicuous nodes and sheaths. The flowers, held on stalks reaching 18 inches, are excellent for cutting. There are many colors to choose from. Flowers are fragrant and some cultivars are double. The species at PERC has ruffled flowers in a deep pink.

Dianthus nardiformis

Dianthus plumarius

There are two separate types of carnations–border and florist. Border carnations are bushier and stockier, a habit you can encourage by pinching back. Florist carnations are propagated in greenhouses and are a popular cut flower.

D. gratianopolitanus 'Tiny Rubies'   Cheddar Pink
(aka *D.* 'Tiny Rubies', *D. caesius*)   🌱 ♺ (6)
Growth habit: Creeping
Size of plant (H x W): 1" to 6" x 1" to 6"
Foliage color: Blue-gray, evergreen
Time of bloom: Late May-July, peak in mid-June
Color of bloom: Pink
Size of bloom: <0.5"
This mat forming, cheddar pink is popular for its low growth and tiny double pink, fragrant flowers. It is useful in rock gardens, along a path and at the front of the perennial border. It is long-lived, given good drainage and protection from drying winter winds. It is evergreen and moderately drought tolerant.

D. hybrids   Modern Pinks
Growth habit: Clump, erect flower stalks   ♺ (4)
Size of plant (H x W): 1' to 2' x 6" to 1'
Foliage color: Blue-green
Time of bloom: Late June-October (frost)
Color of bloom: Varies with cultivar
Size of bloom: 1" to 2.5"
There are several hybrids grown at PERC. They are clump-forming with erect, sparsely branched flowering stalks. *D.* 'Cheyenne' shares its parentage with the hardy carnations. It was developed at the U.S.D.A. Horticultural Research Station in Cheyenne, Wyoming. Flowers are a double pink. *D.* 'Prairie Pink' was developed by Dale Lindgren at the University of Nebraska. This carnation look-alike has blue green foliage and large ruffled, pink flowers. It is fragrant. Bloom is from late June until hard frost. *D.* 'Shadow Valley' has medium green foliage, which combines

well with the deep red ruffled flower. *D.* 'Prairie Pink' and *D.* 'Shadow Valley' did not rate as highly as the other *Dianthus* species discussed here. The hybrids were grown in part shade and in heavy competition with other plants. Late season leaf spot detracted from their overall appearance–hence, their lower score. There are more hybrids and cultivars available that you may wish to try.

D. nardiformis   (6)
Growth habit: Spreading, mounded
Size of plant (H x W): 6" to 1' x 1' to 2'
Foliage color: Light green-gray
Time of bloom: Late June-October (frost)
Color of bloom: Pink
Size of bloom: 0.5" to 1"
This species comes from Eastern Bulgaria and Romania. It is fine textured, with slender, branching stems and a soft, greenish-gray color. The basal leaves are stiff, spiny and needle-like. The pink flowers are generally solitary, at the ends of the flower stalks, which reach to 1 foot in height. Flower petals are toothed. *D. nardiformis* appears to have good cold hardiness and be drought tolerant.

D. plumarius   Cottage Pink, Border Pink
(aka *D. blandus, D. winteri*)   ♺ (13)
Growth habit: Spreading, mounded
Size of plant (H x W): 6" to 1' x 1' to 3'
Foliage color: Blue to gray-green, evergreen
Time of bloom: June to mid-August, peak in mid-late June
Color of bloom: White, many variable cultivars
Size of bloom: 0.5" to 1"
The blue-green to gray-green leaves of this drought tolerant species are linear and taper to a point. The plant is loosely tufted and spreads slowly, while keeping a nice mounded shape. Flowers are solitary and fragrant, reminiscent of clove. The petals

31

Dicentra spectabilis

Dictamnus albus 'Purpureus'

are toothed and can be single or double. Some *D. plumarius* cultivars have bicolored flowers with a contrasting central eye.

The plant at PERC has white flowers and blooms heavily in June. The foliage color, texture and the plant habit are attractive as well. The plant is considered evergreen, although in Colorado some dieback was observed. No major insect or disease problems were noted. *D. plumarius* is a good addition to a rock garden, as well as the more traditional perennial border.

Dicentra spectabilis Bleeding Heart
Fumariaceae ◑ ◗ ● ✂ ! (20)
Landscape use: Specimen, border, wildflower and woodland garden, cut flower
Growth habit: Clump
Size of plant (H x W): 2′ to 4′ x 2′ to 4′
Foliage color: Light green
Time of bloom: Late May-July, peak in mid-June
Color of bloom: Pink and white
Size of bloom: 0.5″ to 1″

Bleeding heart is a garden classic that has proven its hardiness by surviving 20 years in the full sun and heavy clay at PERC. Purplish-pink new shoots emerge in March or April then unfold into deeply cut, finely textured leaves. By midsummer at PERC, the foliage is yellow, sun scorched and tattered. *D. spectabilis* often goes summer dormant in our hot, dry climate.

The best feature of this plant is the pendulous, heart-shaped flowers that are held on arching stems. The outer petals are rosy-pink and somewhat inflated. The inner petals are white. Flower color fades as they mature.

Humus rich soil and part to full-shade exposures are most often recommended for this plant. However, if kept moist, the plants perform in full sun. Plan to have other plants fill in the space left by bleeding

heart, once it goes dormant. Chlorosis has been a minor problem at PERC. Late spring frosts have damaged the early flowers and foliage several years. All parts of *Dicentra spectabilis* may cause stomach upset if ingested. Contact with the foliage can cause dermatitis.

D. spectabilis 'Alba' (6)
This cultivar has a pure white flower and is less vigorous than the species.

Dictamnus albus **'Purpureus'** Gasplant,
(aka *D. fraxinella, D. caucasicus*) Fraxinella
Rutaceae ◑ ✂ ✿ ⚕ ✺ ! (20)
Landscape use: Specimen, background, border, cut and dried flower
Growth habit: Clump
Size of plant (H x W): 2′ to 4′ x 2′ to 4′
Foliage color: Medium-dark green
Time of bloom: Mid-May to early July, peak in late May to mid-June
Color of bloom: Pink
Size of bloom: Individual flowers 1″ to 2.5″; inflorescence >1′

This long-lived perennial is one of PERC s premiere plants. Not only does it have beautiful flowers, but the foliage stays attractive until hard frost. *D. albus* is tap rooted. It forms an impressive clump given full sun, and patience. Site it carefully; it is difficult to transplant. The leaves are glossy, alternate, and pinnately compound. References say the foliage gives off a lemony fragrance when it is crushed. You may not want to try this without gloves, however. Some people are allergic to gas plant and can develop a rash upon contact in hot weather.

The flowers of gas plant are five-petalled and star-shaped. The species has white or light pink flowers held on long terminal racemes. The variety grown at PERC has mauve flowers with dark pinkish-purple veins. The 10 stamens are long and curve out from

32

Digitalis grandiflora

Echinacea purpurea

the center of the flower. Bees are common visitors. The flowers mature to capsule fruit that split open disbursing the tiny black seeds. Spent flower stalks are excellent for dry flower arrangements.

The common name is derived from the belief that the volatile oils given off by the foliage in hot weather can be ignited without harming the plant. Gas plant is drought tolerant and slow growing, but improves with age. In full sun with fertile, well-drained soil, this plant provides rewards for years to come.

Digitalis grandiflora   Large Yellow Foxglove
(aka *D. ambigua*)   ◯ ◗ ! (14)
Scrophulariaceae
Landscape use: Mass, border, wildflower, herb and woodland garden
Growth habit: Upright, spreading
Size of plant (H x W): 1′ to 2′ x 1′ to 2′
Foliage color: Medium to dark green, evergreen
Time of bloom: Mid-June to mid-August
Color of bloom: Yellow
Size of bloom: 1″ to 2.5″

D. grandiflora is a perennial foxglove that grows well in full sun or part-shade. The foliage is evergreen. The leaves are finely toothed, prominently veined and become progressively shorter higher up the stem. The pendulous flowers are held on long, terminal racemes, with the bottom most flowers opening first. The petals merge into a slightly inflated tube of pale yellow, with brown, mottled throats. Large yellow foxglove may not be as showy as *D. purpurea* and other species, but it is an excellent companion plant, mixing well with both cool and hot colors. Deadheading rewards you with a smaller rebloom.

Foxgloves perform best in humus rich soil with regular precipitation. Yellow foxglove tolerates the heavy clay, high pH soil at PERC. The plants in part-shade have not been as vigorous as the ones planted in full sun, which have spread slowly without becoming a nuisance. Given optimal conditions, *D. grandiflora* is reliably perennial. Take care with all species when children and livestock have access to the plants. All plant parts can cause stomach upset if ingested.

Echinacea purpurea   Purple Coneflower
(aka *Rudbeckia purpurea,*   ◯ ◗ ✄ ✿ ❖ ⚘ 🦋
Brauneria purpurea)
Asteraceae (Compositae)
Landscape use: Specimen, mass, border, wildflower and xeriscape garden, cut flower
Growth habit: Clump, erect flower stems
Size of plant (H x W): 1′ to 3′ x 1′ to 2′
Foliage color: Dark green
Time of bloom: Mid-June to mid-September
Color of bloom: Purplish-pink
Size of bloom: 2.5″ to 5″

This North American genus in the sunflower family is known for its bright pinkish-purple ray florets and central cone of brown disk florets. It is stiff and coarse in habit. The stems are hairy and the toothed leaves are ovate to lanceolate. Flowers, held singly on long stems, are excellent for cutting. The color and the amount of reflex found in the ray florets differ depending on cultivar. Although deadheading promotes continual bloom, mature fruits are interesting in dried flower arrangements. Plants allowed to go to seed provide winter food for birds and add winter texture to the perennial border.

E. purpurea tolerates some drought, but grows best with moderate watering. Use it in the moderate watering zone of a xeriscape garden. Full sun is ideal; part-shade may be more suitable for lighter-colored cultivars. *E. purpurea* performs well in most soils and is cold hardy.

Echinops ritro

Epilobium angustifolium

E. p. 'Bright Star' (15)

This cultivar has rosy-red ray flowers. Bright Star blooms heaviest from mid-July through mid-August.

E. p. 'White Swan' (3)

This cultivar has drooping white ray florets with an orangish-brown central cone. Peak bloom is from mid July through August.

Echinops ritro Globe Thistle
Asteraceae (Compositae) ◐ ✂ ✿ 🦋 (16)
Landscape use: Specimen, mass, background, wildflower garden, cut and dried flower
Growth habit: Clump, erect flower stems
Size of plant (H x W): 2' to 4' x 2' to 4'
Foliage color: Medium green
Time of bloom: July-October (frost), peaking in late July to mid-August
Color of bloom: Blue
Size of bloom: Inflorescence 1" to 2.5"

The *Echinops* genus derived its name from the Greek word meaning "like a hedgehog" in reference to the spiny-looking round inflorescence. Although not as prickly as thistles, the leaves have spines and are deeply cut. Stems and the underside of leaves are covered with gray hairs providing a nice contrast to the darker green foliage. The erect habit, prickly leaves and stout stems make a bold accent plant.

Globe thistle flowers are perfect for cutting. For dried use, cut the globes just as the tiny tubular flowers are beginning to open. Bees are attracted to the flowers. Globe thistles self-sow if allowed to set fruit. The purple blooms fade to brown and briefly remain attractive before the globe shatters, disbursing hundreds of seeds. If cut back after blooming, the plants form a fresh rosette of leaves and may bloom again. *Echinops* spp. flower best in full sun, but can tolerate part shade. They are adaptable, tolerating poor soils and some drought once established. Chlorosis has been a minor problem. In the last few years, leaf-curling aphids distorted the leaves, but did not affect the vigor or the blooms of the plants.

E. r. 'Taplow Blue' (20)

This cultivar (also called Taplow Purple) is very vigorous, a bit taller than the species, and has a deeper bluish-purple flower. Peak bloom occurs from the middle to the end of July. It is often sold as *E. exaltatus* 'Taplow Blue'.

Epilobium angustifolium Fireweed, Great Willowherb, Rosebay Willowherb
(aka *E. spicatum, Chamaenerion angustifolium, Chamerion angustifolium*) ◐ ✤ 🐦 🦋 ✦ (17)
Onagraceae
Landscape use: Specimen, background, mass, wildflower and xeriscape garden
Growth habit: Upright, spreading
Size of Plant (H x W): 2' to 4' x 4' to 6'
Foliage color: Medium green
Time of bloom: Mid-June to early October (frost), peak in late June to early July
Color of bloom: Purplish pink
Size of bloom: 1" to 2.5"

Fireweed is a native plant known for its colonization of burned-over land through much of North America. Erect stems bear alternately arranged narrow, medium-green leaves. Its inflorescence is a spike-like raceme up to 1 foot long, of asymmetrical purplish pink flowers. The seeds form an unattractive cottony mass easily dispersed for great distances by wind.

In spite of its beautiful flowers, few gardeners want fireweed in the formal perennial garden because of its aggressive nature. It spreads by underground rhizomes and self-seeding. On the other hand, it is a good plant for dry native areas or for wildflower gardens. If used in a xeriscape garden, plant it in the moderate watering zone near other vigorous plants. It is a favorite of bees and makes excellent honey.

Eupatorium maculatum

Eupatorium maculatum · Joe-Pye Weed
Asteraceae (Compositae) ◖ ◗ ✂ ⚊ 🦋 (9)
Landscape use: Specimen, background, border, wildflower garden, cut flower
Growth habit: Erect
Size of plant (H x W): 4' to 6' x 1' to 2'
Foliage color: Medium green
Time of bloom: Mid-August to early October (frost), peak from early to mid-September
Color of bloom: Pinkish-purple
Size of bloom: Inflorescence >5"

This Eastern North American native gained popularity in England and was initially shunned here. Although its native habitat is sunny, moist meadows and stream sides, *E. maculatum* has survived nine years at PERC after a slow start. The plants are more compact and less prone to spread in our heavy clay soil and hot summer temperatures. Given more moisture and richer soil, Joe-Pye weed can become aggressive, reaching heights of 7 feet.

It is a striking plant with erect, pink-spotted stems and whorled, toothed leaves. The pinkish-purple flowers are held in large terminal clusters. Bees and butterflies are attracted to the nectar. Crushed foliage purportedly smells like vanilla. The genus *Eupatorium* is named for the ancient King of Pontus, Mithridates Eupator, who is said to have used these plants medicinally.

Filipendula vulgaris Meadowsweet, Dropwort
(aka *F. hexapetala, Ulmaria filipendula*) ◖ ◗ ✂ 🌿 (5)
Rosaceae
Landscape use: Mass, border, wildflower and herb garden, cut flower
Growth habit: Clump
Size of plant (H x W): 1' to 2' x 1' to 2'
Foliage color: Medium green
Time of bloom: Mid-June to early July, peak in late June

Color of bloom: White
Size of bloom: Inflorescence 2.5" to 5"

This perennial herb has a long history of use medicinally and as a flavoring. The tender young leaves are sometimes eaten in salads. The basal foliage is finely divided and fern-like. Smaller leaves are found on the branching flower stalks that rise to 3 feet above the foliage. The creamy white flowers are fragrant and clustered in terminal panicles. The overall effect is open, airy and finely textured.

F. vulgaris is more tolerant of full sun exposures and drier soils than other meadowsweet species. The plants at PERC are in part-shade and established well in one season. No insect or cultural problems were observed.

Gaillardia Blanket Flower
Asteraceae (Compositae) ◖ ✂ ❖ 🦋 !
Landscape use: Border, mass, wildflower and xeriscape garden, cut flower
Foliage color: Medium green
Time of bloom: Late June-October (frost), peak in mid-late July
Color of bloom: Yellow, orange, and red
Size of bloom: 2.5" to 5"

Gaillardia spp. are known for their tendency to bloom continually. They tend to be short-lived perennials, whose profuse flowering gradually wears them out. Deadheading encourages this bloom, and is important to consider if you wish to keep the seedling population under control.

Blanket flower performs best in poor soils and declines in heavy, wet clay. Give the following species a well-drained site in full sun. They are heat and drought tolerant performing best in the moderate watering zone of the xeriscape garden. Excess fertility and water produces a lanky, weak plant. Some people may develop dermatitis when in contact with the foliage.

Gaillardia x grandiflora 'Goblin'

Guara lindheimeri

G. aristata   ⤳ (5)
Growth habit: Clump, erect flowering stems
Size of plant (H x W): 2′ to 4′ x 2′ to 4′

    G. aristata is native to the Western United States and Canada. It is a sprawling, coarse plant with a tendency to self-sow. Its large, cheerful daisy flowers are the main ornamental attraction. The plants at PERC are fourth generation seedlings. Flowers are a mixture of yellow, red and orange color combinations much like the popular Goblin cultivar described next. The plant itself is better suited to a wildflower or naturalized area. It mixes well with grasses in a meadow. Otherwise, the sprawling habit can be a drawback in a more formal border. Staking unobtrusively will improve the habit.

G. x grandiflora 'Goblin'   (8)
(aka *G. x grandiflora 'Kobold'*)
Growth habit: Mounded
Size of plant (H x W): 1′ x 1′

    This hybrid blanket flower was developed from a cross between *G. aristata* and *G. pulchella*. 'Goblin' is the most widely sold blanket flower in the trade for good reason. It has a compact, tidy habit, remaining a manageable size. Large flowers are held just above the foliage. Ray florets are red with yellow tips and the disk is red. This cultivar is appropriate for the front of the border and mixes well with more traditional perennials. It still requires full sun and fast-draining soil. Winter moisture may induce crown rot. Cut back in late summer to encourage a new set of basal leaves. 'Goblin' overwinters most successfully this way.

Galium odoratum   Sweet Woodruff, Bedstraw
(aka *Asperula odorata*)   ◗ ● ⤳ 𝒞̃ (18)
Rubiaceae
Landscape use: Ground cover, herb and woodland garden

Growth habit: Spreading
Size of Plant (H x W): 6″ x 4′ to 6′
Foliage color: Medium green
Time of bloom: May to mid-July
Color of bloom: White
Size of bloom: <0.5″

    Sweet woodruff is a spreading herb with whorls of bright green leaves. Small, mildly fragrant, white flowers begin blooming in May. An excellent deciduous ground cover for shady areas and moist, humus soils, it often is used in naturalized settings. It spreads indefinitely when well sited, but can easily be lifted and divided. At PERC, it was planted in full sun and in another shady area under a tree. It did not bloom heavily in either location.

    Sweet woodruff has been used since the middle ages for flavoring wine and brandy. Dried, it can be used in potpourri and sachets where its hay-like scent is said to deter moths.

Gaura lindheimeri   Whirling Butterflies,
Onagraceae   Apple Blossom Grass
                         ○ ✂ ⤳ 🦋 (4)
Landscape use: Specimen, border, mass, cut flower and wildflower gardens
Growth habit: Vase-shaped clump
Size of plant (H x W): 2′ to 4′ x 2′ to 4′
Foliage color: Medium green
Time of bloom: Mid-July to October (frost), peak from mid-late September
Color of bloom: White
Size of bloom: 1″

    This native to North America derives its name, *Gaura*, from the Greek word for "superb." It is vase-shaped, growing upwards from the crown and arching outward with narrow flowering stalks. The leaves are alternate, sessile and lanceolate. The flowers are produced on leafless stems that continue to elongate throughout the season. Each four-petalled

Gentiana septemfida

Geranium himalayense (fall color)

flower opens white, fades to pale pink and lasts only one day. Whirling butterflies begins to flower in midsummer and is sparsely covered at first. As the season progresses, many more blooms are produced. The slender flowering stalks, covered with delicate white flowers, bob in the breeze just like a group of whirling butterflies. Bees are common visitors.

G. lindheimeri may be slow to emerge in spring. It is tap rooted and drought tolerant. Well-drained soils, especially in winter, are essential. Soils low in fertility produce a more compact, robust plant. At PERC several seedlings were spotted but its tendency to self-sow appears to be a minor inconvenience if not a bonus!

Gentiana septemfida — Crested Gentian
Gentianaceae ◐ ◗ (13)
Landscape use: Border and rock garden
Growth habit: Clump
Size of plant (H x W): 6″ to 11″ x 6″to 1′
Foliage color: Medium to dark green
Time of bloom: Late June-early September, peak in early July
Color of bloom: Blue
Size of bloom: 1″ to 2.5″

The crested gentian is one of the easiest species in the genus to grow. It is planted under a tree at PERC and receives filtered sunlight. The leaves are opposite and sessile. Chlorosis has been a minor problem. The flowers are trumpet-shaped and borne singly at the end of the stems. Flowers are an intense blue, with white-mottled throats.

The crested gentian is a clump former, whose stems sprawl on the ground. It would look at home in a rock garden or trailing over a wall. It requires well-drained soils and regular precipitation.

Geranium — Cranesbill, Geranium
Geraniaceae ◐ ◗ ✂ 🐛 🦋
Landscape use: Border, ground cover, erosion control, rock and wildflower gardens, cut flower
Growth habit: Spreading, mounded
Foliage color: Medium green
Time of bloom: Late May- October (frost)

This variable genus contains over 300 species of annuals, biennials and perennials. Common traits include rounded, palmately divided leaves, five-petalled flowers, and beaked fruit that looks like a crane's bill. Most are rhizomatous, making excellent ground covers. *Geranium* spp. are found world wide in cool temperate regions. They should not be confused with the bedding annuals often referred to as geraniums from the genus *Pelargonium*.

True geraniums are useful in rock gardens, as ground covers, in the front of a border, or in more informal settings. Some species can tolerate drought. In general, full sun to part-sun exposures and moderately fertile soils are best. Geraniums are adaptable and do well in an alkaline clay loam.. They often stop blooming in the summer heat and pick up again when nights turn cool. Flowers come in shades of blue and purple, although there are pink and white-flowering species. Many geraniums have excellent fall foliage color turning red, bronze, and purple.

Many different species have been grown at PERC, with the best performers listed next.

G. himalayense — Lilac or Himalayan Cranesbill
Size of plant (H x W): 6″ to 1′ x 2′ to 4′ (9)
Color of bloom: Violet-blue
Size of bloom: 0.5″ to 1″

The lilac cranesbill is a mat forming, rhizomatous plant with broad, deeply lobed leaves. The flowers are saucer-shaped and held in pairs above the foliage. Each flower has a white eye and is veined

Geranium platypetalum

Geranium sanguineum

with purple. Fall foliage color is red and purple. *G. himalayense* spreads aggressively at PERC, requiring periodic division to control its size. Peak bloom is from mid June through early July.

G. macrorrhizum 'Bevan's Variety' Bigroot, Bulgarian, or Rock Cranesbill ☙ (11)
Size of plant (H x W): 6" to 1' x 2' to 4'
Color of bloom: Magenta
Size of bloom: 0.5 to 1"

This geranium has sticky, fragrant, evergreen foliage. It has a dense, mounded growth habit that effectively chokes out weeds. The leaves are deeply lobed with three to five notches at the tips. The leaves turn red, purple and orange in the fall. Bigroot geranium is growing underneath a tree at PERC and has suffered somewhat from powdery mildew and chlorosis. 'Bevan's Variety' has a deeper pink flower than the species. Flowers are held in terminal clusters. The flower petals sit on top of sepals, which are inflated into small red balloons. Bloom has not been heavy at PERC.

G. x oxonianum 'A.T. Johnson' (4)
Size of plant (H x W): 6" to 1' x 1' to 2'
Color of bloom: Pink
Size of bloom: 0.5" to 1"

Leaves of this hybrid are toothed and deeply cut into five lobes. The light pink flowers are funnel-shaped and held on cymes above the leaves. Petals are notched. Despite the fact that this plant was crowded between aggressive neighbors, it bloomed continually from June through early October, peaking from mid June through early July. Fall foliage color was fair, with leaves turning orange and red. This geranium should not be confused with the lavender flowered hybrid 'Johnson's Blue.'

G. platypetalum Broad-petaled Geranium (8)
Size of plant (H x W): 1' to 2' x 2' to 4'
Color of bloom: Purple
Size of bloom: 1" to 2.5"

Broad-petaled geranium has the largest leaf of the many geraniums grown at PERC. Each leaf has seven to nine lobes. Fall color is red, orange and yellow. The flowers are a deep purple and flat to saucer-shaped. Bloom occurs from June through August, with the heaviest bloom occurring in the middle of June. This plant is taller and more erect in growth habit than other geraniums.

G. sanguineum Bloodred Geranium, Bloody Cranesbill ❖ (17)
Size of plant (H x W): 1' to 2' x 4' to 6'
Color of bloom: Magenta
Size of bloom: 1" to 2.5"

G. sanguineum is one of the most common cultivated geraniums in the trade. Its unflattering common name refers to the bright magenta flowers. Bloom is continual from late May until frost, with the heaviest bloom occurring in late June and early July. *G. sanguineum* spreads aggressively by rhizomes, producing a dense mat of variably lobed leaves. Fall color has been excellent with red, purple and orange the predominant colors. Fungal leaf spot and chlorosis have been minor problems. Use this geranium in a moderate watering zone in a xeriscape garden.
G. sanguineum var. prostratum (*G. sanguineum* var. *striatum*)

A varietal selection with light pink petals and red veins. It is lower growing than the species.

Geum Geum, Sweet Avens
Rosaceae ◖ ◗

There are approximately 50 species of *Geums*. The pinnately divided, somewhat hairy leaves are

Geum chiloense 'Mrs. Bradshaw'

Goniolimon tataricum

typically arranged in basal rosettes. The flowers, held on branched stalks, have 5 petals and are most often saucer shaped. The genus offers species with single, semi-double, and double flowers in shades of red, orange, white, and yellow. The achene fruit has hairy styles somewhat like clematis and *Pulsatilla vulgaris*, the European pasque flower. Geums will bloom through the summer if kept deadheaded. Well-drained soil is critical to their success. Propagate by seed or division in fall or early spring.

G. chiloense 'Mrs. Bradshaw' ✂ (13)
(aka *Geum quellyon* 'Mrs. Bradshaw' or *G. coccineum* 'Mrs. Bradshaw')
Landscape use: Border, mass, cut flower, wildflower and rock garden
Growth habit: Clump, erect flower stems
Size of plant (H x W): 1' to 2' x 1' to 2'
Foliage color: Medium green
Time of bloom: Early June-October (frost), peak from late June-early July
Color of bloom: Reddish orange
Size of bloom: 1" to 2.5"

This plant is two-tiered in growth habit. The leaves form a mounded clump. Flowering stalks are erect, with the blooms held well above the foliage. The flowers of 'Mrs. Bradshaw' are double and reddish orange. There is a double yellow cultivar in the trade, Lady Stratheden. The long flower stalks and colorful blooms of either cultivar are excellent for cutting. Deadheading promotes secondary bloom. This species grows best with cool summers and moist soil, high in organic content. Excessive winter moisture can lead to crown rot. The plants at PERC are in full sun and perform reliably over the years with some additional moisture.

G. triflorum Prairie Smoke, Purple Avens, Old Man's Whiskers 🐦 🪶 (11)
Landscape use: Ground cover, wildflower and rock gardens
Growth habit: Creeping
Size of plant (H x W): 1" to 6" x 1' to 2'
Foliage color: Medium green
Time of bloom: Mid-May to June, peak in late June
Color of bloom: Pink to maroon
Size of bloom: Individually 0.5"; inflorescence 1" to 2.5"

This North American native is quite different than 'Mrs. Bradshaw.' The delicate flowers are nodding, bell-shaped and hang from furry stalks. Each flower is ringed by 5 finger-like bracts. The mature fruit is very ornamental. Prairie smoke gets its common name from the pink plumes that twist from each achene fruit.

G. triflorum spreads slowly by rhizomes making a good low growing ground cover. It is easily overtaken by more vigorous neighbors. Use along a path or in a rock garden where the delicate nature of these plants can be appreciated up close. This species is drought tolerant.

Goniolimon tataricum Tatarian Statice, German Statice
(aka *Limonium tataricum*, *Statice tatarica*) ○ ✂ ✿ ❖ (14)
Plumbaginaceae
Landscape use: Border, mass, rock and xeriscape garden, cut and dried flower
Growth habit: Clump, erect flower stalks
Size of plant (H x W): 1' to 2' x 1' to 2'
Foliage color: Dark green, evergreen
Time of bloom: Late June-October (frost), peak in mid-July to mid-August and mid-Sept to frost
Color of bloom: Pinkish-purple
Size of bloom: Individual flower < 0.5", inflorescence >5"

Gypsophila paniculata

Gypsophila repens

Tatarian statice is a popular florist cut and dried flower. It has a basal rosette of dark green, leathery evergreen leaves. The narrowly-winged flower stalks arise from the middle. Panicles of tiny pinkish-purple, tubular flowers are surrounded by silvery persistent sepals that are ornamental long after the petals drop.

G. tataricum thrives in hot climates, full sun and well-drained soils. It has long roots and is difficult to divide or transplant. It is has not been as vigorous at PERC as *Limonium latifolium*, another popular statice plant.

Gypsophila   ◯ ❖
Caryophyllaceae

There are over 100 species of annuals and perennials in this genus. *Gypsophila* means "preference for lime." Sunny locations and alkaline, well-drained soils are ideal conditions for the two species grown with success at PERC. Excess winter moisture can cause stem and crown rot. Try either species in the low to moderate zones of the xeriscape garden. Propagate by sowing seed in autumn or spring or with softwood cuttings in summer. *G. repens* can be divided in the spring.

G. paniculata 'Pink Fairy'   Perennial Baby's Breath ✂ ❀ (4)
Landscape use: Specimen, background, mass, xeriscape garden, cut and dried flower
Growth habit: Clump, erect flower stalk
Size of plant (H x W): 2' to 4' x 2' to 4'
Foliage color: Light green to blue-green
Time of bloom: July-early October, peak from mid-July to early August
Color of bloom: Pale pink
Size of bloom: Individual flower <0.5", inflorescence >5"

Perennial baby's breath is commonly used, either fresh or dried, as a filler in flower arrangements.

The tiny flowers are borne in loose, wide-spreading panicles reaching 4 feet in height. The glaucous green to blue-green leaves are opposite and lanceolate. Nodes are swollen much like those of the florist carnation. The foliage itself is not very ornamental. Plant near showy companions, but allow enough room for the substantial inflorescence.

Perennial baby's breath has white flowers. Pink Fairy is a cultivar with pale pink, double blooms and persistent calyces that remain ornamental. The flower panicles topple over if not staked or supported by companion plants. Cut back after the first bloom to encourage a secondary bloom. *G. paniculata* is tap rooted and can be difficult to divide or transplant.

G. repens   Creeping Baby's Breath
(aka *G. prostrata var. fratensis*, *G. dubia*)   ❧ (14)
Landscape use: Border, xeriscape and rock gardens, ground cover
Growth habit: Creeping
Size of plant (H x W): 1" to 6" x 1' to 2'
Foliage color: Light green to gray, semi-evergreen
Time of bloom: Late May-October (frost), peak from early-late June
Color of bloom: White
Size of bloom: Individual flower <0.5", inflorescence 2.5" to 5"

Creeping baby's breath is a mat-forming ground cover perfect for the front of the border, along a path or spilling over a wall. The leaves are semi-evergreen, linear and somewhat glaucous. Creeping baby's breath blooms heavily in June with sparse bloom the rest of the growing season. Flowers are star-shaped and held in loose panicles. It is a cold hardy native of Europe that requires full sun and sharply-drained soils.

Helianthemum nummularium 'Single Yellow'

Heliopsis helianthoides 'Incomparabilis'

Helianthemum nummularium   Sun or, Rock
(aka *H. mutabile, H. chamaecistus*)   Rose ○ ⋟
Cistaceae
Landscape use: Ground cover, border, mass, rock garden
Growth habit: Mounded clump
Size of plant (H x W): 6" to 1' x 1' to 3'
Foliage color: Varies with cultivar, semi-evergreen
Time of bloom: Late May-July
Color of bloom: Varies with cultivar
Size of bloom: 0.5" to 1"

This species is the most commonly grown of the sun roses. It is a sub-shrub, often evergreen in climates less harsh than ours. The leaves are oblong to lanceolate, opposite and slightly hairy. Foliage color is variable. Some cultivars have gray-green leaves. Stems trail along the ground. The flowers have five petals that surround many showy, yellow stamens. Each flower lasts only one day and close up in cloudy weather. Peak bloom is in June, although flowers are produced in low numbers throughout the summer. Sun roses come in many colors including yellow, pink, orange, and white.

Sun roses can be short-lived. Good drainage is critical. Excess winter moisture leads to crown rot. They prefer neutral to alkaline soils of low fertility and full sun exposures. Light shearing after the first bloom period results in a minor secondary bloom. Mulching in winter prevents winter dessication. They are drought tolerant.

Depending on the source, the following plants are either a cultivar of or share parentage with *H. nummularium*. Of the sun roses trialed at PERC, they have been the most consistent performers.
H. 'Single Yellow'   (12)

The darker green foliage of this sun rose contrasts well with the pale yellow blooms. The paper-thin flower petals are translucent. 'Single Yellow' is more floriferous than 'Wisley Pink,' blooming sporadically into September.
H. 'Wisley Pink'   (5)

This plant combines silvery gray foliage with soft pink flowers. The stamens are a bright yellow contrasting eye.

Heliopsis helianthoides 'Incomparabilis'
(aka *Buphthalmum helianthoides*)   False Sunflower,
Asteraceae (Compositae)   Oxeye
    ○ ✂ ⋟ ⋈ (20)

Landscape use: Background, specimen, mass, wildflower garden and cut flower
Growth habit: Upright, spreading
Size of plant (H x W): 4' x 4' massed
Foliage color: Dark green
Time of bloom: Late June-October (frost), peak from July-August
Color of bloom: Gold
Size of bloom: 2.5" to 5"

Heliopsis spp. are North American natives closely related to the sunflower genus, *Helianthus*. For 20 years, *H. helianthoides* 'Incomparabilis' has spread slowly into an impressive mass of crisp, dark green foliage with golden, zinnia-like blooms, produced abundantly until hard frost. Leaves are ovate to lanceolate, toothed and arranged in opposite pairs. The plant is upright, somewhat coarse and loosely branched. It has not required staking, nor has it been aggressive.

'Incomparabilis' has semi-double flowers with golden ray and disk florets. They are produced on long stalks and make an excellent cut flower. Flowers are long-lived, fading gradually to a tan color. Bees and butterflies find the blooms irresistible.

False sunflower is hardy and has been pest free. It often is listed as a drought tolerant plant. At PERC, it performs best with supplemental watering during our hottest, driest months.

Hemerocallis

Heterotheca villosa

Hemerocallis   Daylily
Liliaceae   ○ ◗ ✂ ❖ ⭐ 🦋 (24)
Landscape use: Border, mass, wildflower, xeriscape
and rock gardens, cut flower
Growth habit: Clump, mounded
Size of plant (H x W): 2′ to 4′ x 2 to 4′ massed
Foliage color: Medium green
Time of bloom: Variable depending on variety
Color of bloom: Yellow
Size of bloom: 2.5″ to 5″

Daylilies are some of the most versatile
perennials, long-lived, adapt to different soil types
and easy to grow even for a novice gardener. Full sun
exposures and regular watering produce the most
blooms. The pale, pastel flowering varieties fade in
full sun at our elevation, and benefit from part shade.
Daylilies form clumps of linear, arching leaves. There
are evergreen varieties suitable for the South. In
Colorado, most daylilies are herbaceous.

Daylilies make excellent cut flowers. Flower
scapes of the most floriferous varieties might produce
10 to 15 flowers each. Individual funnel-form flowers
last only one day. The flower buds and new shoots are
edible and a staple of some oriental cuisines. Breeders
have hybridized daylilies of all colors, except pure
white and blue, and of many forms including diploid
and tetraploid. Dwarf and ever-blooming cultivars
also are available. Choices seem endless and is one of
the reasons this plant is so universal. By planting an
assortment of different cultivars, it is possible to have
flowers from May through October.

At PERC, the longest-lived daylily is of unknown
parentage. It is floriferous, with lemon yellow blooms
that are intensely fragrant. Minor leaf tip burn and
chlorosis are the only two problems noticed with this
plant. Daylilies generally have few problems, with
thrips and aphids as the most notable.

Daylilies are tough and grow in almost any soil,
but do best if it is moist and well drained. They
develop rank growth in rich soil and are smaller with
reduced bloom in xeric conditions. Lift and divide
daylilies after bloom when the clumps become too
large. The swollen, knobby roots are not diseased,
but normal for daylilies. Separate the individual fans
of foliage and cut them back to 1 to 2 inches before
replanting. Daylilies make great gifts to share with
friends and neighbors.

H. 'Butter Curls'   (20)
This medium-sized daylily is 1 to 2 feet high and
1 to 2 feet wide. It has golden yellow flowers. Bloom
begins in July and ends in late August.

H. 'Magic Wand'   (20)
Similar to the above cultivar, but more floriferous
with yellowish-orange flowers.

Heterotheca villosa   Hairy Golden Aster, Hairy
(aka *Chrysopsis villosa*)   False Golden Aster
Asteraceae (Compositae)   ○ ✂ ❖ ⤙ 🦋 (13)
Landscape use: Specimen, background, mass,
wildflower and xeriscape, cut flower
Growth habit: Clump, erect flower stems
Size of plant (H x W): 2′ to 4′ x 2′ to 4′
Foliage color: Medium green
Time of bloom: Mid-August to October (frost), peak
from late September to early October
Color of bloom: Golden yellow
Size of bloom: 1″ to 2.5″

Hairy golden aster is a native of the western and
south central portions of the United States. It is a
large, unrefined plant more at home in a wildflower
garden, meadow, or informal border. Its leaves are
alternate, simple and lance-shaped. The foliage is
slightly hairy and medium to gray-green. *H. villosa*
is a clump former, whose flowering stems elongate
to impressive heights, given good soil and plenty of
water.

In midsummer, its branched flower stems are
covered with bright, golden daisies that are attractive

Heuchera sanguinea

to bees and make nice cut flowers. Due to the weight of the blooms, the plant lodges outwards and would benefit from staking. According to several references, this species varies in height from 8 inches to 5 feet, depending on soil and moisture conditions. Height can be regulated with pinching, much like the true asters.

Hairy golden aster requires full sun and protection from excess winter moisture. It is recommended for low to moderate watering zones in a xeriscape garden. Minor chlorosis, flea beetles, aphids and skeletonizing insects have been the problems noted over the last 13 years.

Heuchera   Alum Root
Saxifragaceae   ◯ ◗ ● ✄ 🌿 ⚘ 🦋
Landscape use: Border, ground cover, mass, rock and woodland gardens, cut flower
Growth habit: Clump, mounded
Size of plant (H x W): 6" to 1' x 1' to 2'
Size of bloom: Individual flowers <0.5", Inflorescence >5"

This genus contains approximately 55 species of evergreen or semi-evergreen perennials native to North America and Mexico. The plants form a mounded rosette of scalloped, heart shaped, or rounded leaves. Flower panicles reach 1 to 1 ½ feet above the foliage and bear masses of nodding, bell-shaped flowers. Alum root is prized as much for its foliage, as for its dainty blooms.

Ideal cultural conditions include moisture retentive soils, high in organic matter. In hot climates and for dark-leaved varieties, part shade to full shade exposures are best. Several of the *Heuchera* spp. at PERC are grown in full sun, and suffer yearly from leaf scorch. Over time, the crown of the plant becomes woody and flowering is reduced. This signals the need for division. Replant non-woody pieces deeply, up to the level of their leaves. Winter mulch prevents

frost heave and protects the crown.

There are many excellent species and hybrid varieties with mottled, prominently veined, and variously colored leaves. Alum root makes a nice groundcover or perennial border edging.

H. micrantha **'Palace Purple'**   Small Flowered Alumroot, Crevice Alumroot
PPY-1991 (8)
Foliage color: Green and purple
Time of bloom: July to mid-September, peak in early September
Color of bloom: White

This species is a native to British Columbia, California, and the Pacific Northwest. A very popular cultivar (although there is still discussion as to its true parentage), 'Palace Purple', has large, maple-shaped leaves of a metallic greenish purple to deep reddish purple. The flowers are white to ivory and are smaller than those of other species. The contrast between the flowers and rich, dark foliage is excellent. Seedling stock of 'Palace Purple' differs in foliage coloration.
H. m. **'Palace Passion'**   (4)
A pink flowering cultivar with the same foliage characteristics as 'Palace Purple.' Peak bloom occurs in mid July.
H. m. **'Chocolate Ruffles'**   (4)
The leaves of this cultivar are ruffled and chocolate-brown on top, with burgundy undersides. Flower stalks are pinkish-purple and bear small white flowers. Bloom begins in June, earlier than the other two cultivars mentioned.

H. sanguinea   Coral Bells 🌱 (14)
Foliage color: Medium green
Time of bloom: June-early October, peak from late June-late July
Color of bloom: Red
Coral bells have scalloped, rounded, medium-

43

Hosta

green basal leaves. The tiny, bell-shaped, red flowers are borne on slender stalks and are attractive to bees and hummingbirds. Bloom is heaviest in mid-summer with sporadic bloom into fall. Flowering can be prolonged with deadheading. This species originated in Mexico and Arizona. It makes an excellent cut flower.

H. Bressingham Hybrids (4)
Seed propagated hybrids sharing parentage with *H. sanguinea* and bred in Blooms Nursery in England. Flowers are in shades of white, pink, and red and plants are of various heights.

Hosta Plantain Lily, Hosta
Liliaceae ◗ ● ✂ ᴥ ℰ
Landscape use: Border, ground cover, specimen, mass, woodland garden, cut flower
Growth habit: Clump, mounded to vase-shaped
Time of bloom: July-September depending on cultivar

Hosta spp. are primarily grown for their foliage. There are hundreds of hybrids and cultivars available, leading to an exciting range of choices in size, foliage color and texture, and flower color. It has been a challenge to grow this normally undemanding plant at PERC. Before the trees developed size, there were no flowerbeds sited in shade. In 1982, *H. tsushimensis* (page 45) was planted in full sun. During the summer of 1999, they were finally dug up and moved to partly shaded areas. Obviously, the plants suffered in our intense sunlight and summer heat. Yet, it was remarkable to note how vigorously the plants had spread from their rhizomes and how many years they had returned undaunted. Hostas are tough, and given the right conditions, perform beautifully with little maintenance.

An ideal spot to plant hostas would be in moisture retentive, organic soil and part to full shade.

They adapt to clay and can compete with the root system of trees. Sunnier sites encourage flowering, often at the expense of the foliage. Shadier sites protect the foliage from sun scorch, especially those with variegated or glaucous leaves.

Hosta leaves are variable. Most often they are long petioled, simple and entire. Shapes range from cordate to ovate to lanceolate. Some varieties have wavy margins or prominent veins. Others, are glaucous, variegated, matte, or shiny. Leaves also vary in size and texture which can range from smooth to puckered. In spring, leaves emerge from the soil tightly rolled like bullets. This is the perfect time to divide a large clump of plants. However, hostas can remain undisturbed for years.

The trumpet-shaped flowers are borne on one-sided racemes held above the foliage. They range in color from white, lavender to violet. Some are fragrant.

Slugs are the primary pest of hostas. Hail, heavy rain and wind can also tatter the foliage and ruin their appearance. The plants are frost sensitive and benefit from a protected spot, especially in the spring and with our variable weather patterns.

H. 'Francee' (6)
Size of plant (H x W): 1' to 2' x 1' to 2'
Foliage color: Variegated medium green and white
Color of bloom: Lavender
Size of bloom: 2.5" to 5"

'Francee' has prominently veined, medium green leaves with a white edge. The heart-shaped leaves, which can reach sizes of up to 1 foot in length, form a tight, vase-shaped clump. At PERC, it is planted at the foot of a small tree where it can receive shade in the afternoon. The lavender flowers are large, showy and hang from a leafy scape reaching three feet. Bloom begins in late July and ends in September, but has not been heavy at PERC. Slugs and sun scorch

Hylotelephium spectabile 'Autumn Glory'

have been minor problems. 'Francee' has spread slowly over the last six years and has been reliable.

H. 'Ginkgo Craig' (6)
Size of plant (H x W): 6" x 6"
Foliage color: Variegated medium green and white
Color of bloom: Violet
Size of bloom: 1" to 2.5"

This dwarf hybrid hosta belongs at the front of the border where the lanceolate, green leaves with irregular white margins can be appreciated. The plant is not vase-shaped like 'Francee,' but lies in a neat mound close to the ground. The flower scape is leafless and reaches 1 foot above the foliage. The violet flowers are smaller and deeper in color than 'Francee.' 'Ginkgo Craig' is floriferous, blooming from late July through September with a late season peak.

H. tsushimensis (17)
Size of plant (H x W): 1' to 2' x 2' to 4'
Foliage color: Medium green
Color of bloom: White
Size of bloom: 2.5" to 5"

This species is native to Japan. The medium-green, heart-shaped leaves are glossy and prominently veined. *H. tsushimensis* forms a vase-shaped clump. The flowers are white and held on stalks reaching 3 feet. The bloom period begins in late July and extends through September with a late season peak.

Hylotelephium Live-forever Stonecrop
(aka *Sedum*) ○ ✿ ❖ 🦋
Crassulaceae
Landscape use: Border, specimen, mass, rock and xeriscape gardens, dried flower
Growth habit: Clump, mounded to erect
Size of plant (H x W): 1' to 2' x 1' to 2'

Foliage color: Grey-green, semi-evergreen
Color of bloom: Pink
Size of bloom: Individually <0.5", inflorescence 2.5" to 5"

These plants often are grouped within the genus *Sedum*. They are succulent plants with unbranched erect stems and fleshy leaves. Drought tolerant, they thrive in well-drained, poor soils and decline with excess winter moisture. Flowers are star-shaped and held in flat topped or domed clusters (much like broccoli) in late summer. Butterflies and bees are attracted to the nectar. The fruit is persistent and showy, turning a bronzy brown.

Although semi-evergreen in nature, removing the old stems each spring reduces the moisture funneled to the crown of the plant. The new foliage emerges in tight rosettes that are reminiscent of rose buds. Division can be done in spring, but is rarely needed. Stem cuttings can be taken in summer.

H. spectabile 'Autumn Glory' Showy
(aka *Sedum spectabile* 'Autumn Glory') Stonecrop (9)
Time of bloom: Late August-early October, peak from early-late September

Showy stonecrop is a native of Japan. It forms a mounded clump of thick stems with fleshy leaves that are either whorled or opposite. The margins are scalloped. It is easy to grow and tolerates almost any soil type as long as it is well drained. The flower is usually pink, but white and red flowering cultivars are available. Showy stonecrop provides an excellent structural element to the border or rock garden and is especially nice massed. The very popular 'Autumn Joy,' is actually a hybrid between this species and *H. telephium* described next.

H. telephium Live-forever, Orpine
(aka *Sedum telephium*) (24)
Time of bloom: Mid-August to mid-October, peak

Hypericum calycinum

Iberis sempervirens

from early-late September

Live-forever stonecrop is a multi-stem, mounded species with fleshy, oval, gray-green leaves. *H. telephium* often is confused with *H. spectabile*. The difference is that the former has leaves that are alternate and toothed. The top of the plant becomes covered with flat heads of rosy pink flowers, changing to coppery red when in fruit. It can be used as a specimen plant or in mass plantings. It tends to spread slowly, dying out in the center when it should be divided.

Hypericum calycinum   Creeping St. Johnswort,
Clusiaceae (Guttiferae)   Aaron's Beard
     ◯ ◗ ☙ ! (14)

Landscape use: Border, groundcover and erosion control
Growth habit: Upright, spreading
Size of plant (H x W): 1' to 2' x 2' to 4'
Foliage color: Blue-green, semi-evergreen
Time of bloom: Mid-July to September
Color of bloom: Yellow
Size of bloom: 1" to 2.5"

Aaron's beard is one of a few plants that can tolerate dry shade. At PERC, this semi-evergreen ground cover is sited in part shade. It spreads from runners and can be aggressive. The leaves are opposite and oblong. They are medium green to blue-green in color and attractive, even after a hard frost. In fall, the foliage develops a rosy tint. This shrubby plant with its smooth blue-green foliage provides a nice contrast to bold companion plants. Cut back in late winter or early spring.

Aaron's beard has been a sparse bloomer at its present site. Given full sun and richer soil expect a show of large yellow flowers. Each flower has five petals and sepals, with a cluster of erect, showy stamens in the center. Plants in the *Hypericum* genus may cause skin allergies in some people.

Iberis sempervirens 'Snowmantle'   Evergreen or
(aka *I. grarrexiana*)   Perennial Candytuft
Brassicaceae (Cruciferae)   ◯ (17)

Landscape use: Border, massed and rock garden
Growth habit: Mounded to spreading
Size of plant (H x W): 6" to 1' x 1' to 2'
Foliage color: Dark green, evergreen
Time of bloom: Late April to mid-June
Color of bloom: White
Size of bloom: Individually >0.5", inflorescence 1" to 2.5"

Evergreen candytuft forms mounds of dark glossy, linear, leathery foliage. It is considered a subshrub and is woody at the base of the stems. It can be used at the front of the perennial border, in rock gardens or raised beds. In spring, sparkling white flower heads cover the plant. The flowers fade to pink as they age. Some cultivars of candytuft also bloom in the fall.

Evergreen candytuft does best in full sun and well-drained, alkaline soil. To keep its compact form, trim half the foliage after flowering. In exposed sites, it may suffer winter burn and should be protected in the winter with some mulch. It is drought tolerant.

I. s. 'Autumn Snow'   (19)

This cultivar boomed from mid-May to mid-June in the spring and again from early September to mid-October in the fall.

I. s. 'Little Gem'   (10)

This compact plant is 6 inches tall and 6 inches to 1 foot wide. It forms a tight mound of dark green foliage and blooms from mid-May to mid-June.

Iris   Iris, Flag, Sword Lily
Iridaceae   ◯ ◗ ✄ 𝒞 ☙ !

Landscape use: Border, specimen, mass, cut flower

Irises have endured as a popular garden plant because of their beautiful flowers, versatile uses and relatively easy care. Conditions in Colorado are

Iris 'Babbling Brook'

Iris 'Stepping Little'

excellent for iris culture. Our alkaline soils, intense sunlight and low humidity reduce the fungi or rot problems frequent in other climates. The iris root borer has not invaded gardens in this region, either.

Irises are divided into two general groups-rhizomatous and bulbous. Those that grow from a rhizomatous rootstock are further grouped according to the presence or absence of a beard. Entire books are dedicated to irises and an in depth discussion is best left to these sources. In general, the flower consists of three upright petals or standards and three drooping petals or falls. The falls may have upright hairs in the center- the beard, or may be beardless, or crested. Leaves are sword-like or grass-like.

Irises have done well at PERC. Leaf spot fungi became a problem in the last few years due to overcrowding in the garden beds. Irises were split up and spread throughout the garden in 1999, to control this problem. The entire plant, especially the rhizome, is poisonous. Some people are sensitive to the plant sap and may develop a rash.

The different species at PERC and their particular traits follow.

I. hybrids   Bearded Iris, Flag ❖
Growth habit: Clump, erect flowering stems
Size of plant (H x W): Varies with cultivar
Foliage color: Light to medium green
Time of bloom: Late May-June; varies with cultivar
Size of bloom: Individually >5"

Bearded irises have been in cultivation for ages. Extensive hybridization has resulted in a wide range of sizes and colors to choose from. Bearded irises have sword-like leaves that extend from a rhizome in a flat fan. Plant rhizomes shallowly, no more than 1 inch below the ground. Rhizomes planted too high may sunburn; those planted too deep are more likely to rot. Well-drained soil is a must with this group of irises, which are drought tolerant. As the clump

matures, flowering lessens and vigor reduces. Lift and divide your irises at this point, preferably after flowering. Discard the older rhizomes and replant the newer, more vigorous pieces. Winter mulch is not necessary and might encourage rot.

Bearded iris come in three basic sizes- dwarf (less than 15 inches), intermediate (15 to 28 inches), and tall (over 28 inches.) The American Iris Society divides these groups further. Colors range from self (all one color) to bicolor to plicata (white flower banded with another color.) Almost every shade is available, except true red. Many of the hybrid bearded irises at PERC were developed by Carl J. Jorgensen, emeritus associate professor of horticulture at Colorado State University. In 1998 and 1999, his field trial plants were moved from south of Prospect Road to PERC. Visiting this field and the PERC perennial garden during peak bloom is an excellent way to see the variety of sizes and flower colors available. Below is a sampling of bearded iris you may wish to consider.

I. 'Babbling Brook'   (20)
An old fashioned tall bearded iris with sky-blue ruffled petals that fade to lavender. This is a fragrant iris.

I. 'Before the Storm'   (5)
A fragrant, tall bearded iris with a deep purple, almost black, flower.

I. 'Stepping Little'   (20)
This is a tall bearded iris with a slight fragrance. The flower is a plicata-white with deep purple bands.

I. 'Summit Angel'   (5)
A fragrant, tall bearded iris with a white flower. Developed by Carl Jorgensen.

I. 'Summit Queen'   (5)
Another Jorgensen introduction with a pastel pink flower.

I. 'Termination Dust'   (5)
A tall bearded iris with a fragrant white flower.

Iris lactea

Iris sibirica

***I.* 'Time Piece'** (5)
A tall bearded iris with a yellow and white bicolor flower.

I. lactea Blue Bouquet Iris
Growth habit: Clump, mounded (4)
Size of plant (H x W): 1' to 2' x 1' to 2'
Foliage color: Medium green to gray-green
Time of bloom: Mid-May to mid-June
Color of bloom: White and blue bicolor
Size of bloom: 2.5" to 5"
   This beardless iris is native to Central Asia, Russia, Mongolia, and the Himalayas. The narrow leaves are grass-like and arch outward giving the plant a mounded appearance. The flowers are exotic and delicate in appearance, with blue standards that are shorter and narrower than the white falls. The flowers are veined and fragrant, but hidden within the foliage. It blooms briefly and modestly, yet the foliage continues to provide a nice structural element to the garden. It is drought tolerant.

I. lactea* var. *oltriensis (8)
   Reaching 3 feet in spread, this variety is larger than the species, blooms a little later and has blue flowers.

I. sibirica Siberian Iris
(aka *I. maritima*) ✿ (18)
Growth habit: Upright, spreading
Size of plant (H x W): 2' to 4' x 1' to 2'
Foliage color: Medium green
Time of bloom: June
Color of bloom: Purple
Size of bloom: >5"
   This iris has slender, grassy foliage held upright or in vase-shaped clumps. It spreads by slender rhizomes. In the fall, the foliage turns a rich brown, which can be left for winter interest. Divide Siberian iris when the clump gradually dies out in the middle.

Although full sun and moist sites are recommended, part-sun and dry conditions are tolerated. Siberian irises perform best with additional moisture in June. These irises also naturalize well near a pond or stream.
   Siberian iris at PERC have deep purple flowers with veined falls. Blue, white, and yellow cultivars are available, as well as bicolor. The flowers are large, showy and beardless. Cut them for flower arrangements or allow the fruit to mature into dark brown capsules that look great in dried arrangements.

Knautia macedonia Knautia, Red Scabiosa
Dipsacaceae ◯ ✂ 🦋 (6)
Landscape use: Border, mass, wildflower garden, cut flower
Growth habit: Upright, spreading
Size of plant (H x W): 1' to 2' x 1' to 2'
Foliage color: Medium green
Time of bloom: Early June-October (frost), peak from early to mid-July
Color of bloom: Red to maroon
Size of bloom: 0.5" to 1"
   Knautia has outstanding wine red flowers held on long wiry stems. Each flower head is domed much like *Scabiosa*, a relative. The plant looks best when allowed to sprawl in amongst its neighbors. It is not as suitable for a formal border, where staking would be a temptation. The rich color of the flowers and the long bloom period make this an outstanding cut flower. Butterflies and bees find it irresistible.
   Knautia forms rosettes of basal leaves, from which branched, slender stems arise. Leaves are simple or divided, with a large terminal lobe. Full sun and hot, dry sites are preferred. Knautia will self-sow in your garden and can become a nuisance. At PERC, chlorosis has been a minor problem.

48

Kniphofia uvaria

Kniphofia uvaria Red-hot Poker, Torch Lily,
(aka *K. alooides, Tritoma uvaria*) Poker Plant
Liliaceae (Asphodelaceae) ◯ ⚔ ❖ 🦋 🌱 (8)
Landscape use: Border, mass, specimen, xeriscape garden and cut flower
Growth habit: Clump
Size of plant (H x W): 2′ to 4′ x 4′ to 6′ massed
Foliage color: Medium green, semi-evergreen
Time of bloom: Early June- July, peak in late June
Color of bloom: Yellow and orange
Size of bloom: Individual flowers 0.5″ to1″, inflorescence >5″

Red-hot poker is a striking plant in bloom. Its torches of drooping, tubular flowers are borne in a terminal raceme, on a leafless stalk reaching 3 to 6 feet. Flowers are scarlet in bud, open to an orange and fade to yellow. They are attractive to hummingbirds and make excellent cut flowers. Deadheading prolongs bloom. *K. uvaria* is the parent plant of many outstanding hybrids, several with softer colors.

Kniphofia spp. forms a basal clump of coarse, linear leaves, with a prominent keel. By midsummer the leaves bend downwards, giving the plant a vase-shaped appearance. It is semi-evergreen along the Front Range. Cut back the foliage in early spring, before new growth begins.

Red-hot poker is considered to a more permanent and reliable perennial. It has been carefree and vigorous at PERC. It prospers and flowers best in full sun and moderately fertile well-drained soil. Excessive winter moisture can be detrimental.

Lamium Deadnettle
Lamiaceae (Labiatae) ◗ ● 🌿 🦋
Landscape use: Ground cover, erosion control, border, woodland garden
Growth habit: Spreading

This genus in the mint family offers several species that are excellent ground covers. Although some also have ornamental flowers, the foliage is the main attraction. Square stems bear opposite, ovate, toothed or wrinkled leaves with colorful patterns. The flowers are two-lipped, the upper lip curved into a helmet. They are arranged in whorls on leafy spikes.

The two species grown at PERC are rhizomatous. They are both excellent nectar sources for bees and beneficial insects. Divide in spring or fall.

L. galeobdolon 'Herman's Pride' Yellow
(aka *Lamiastrum galeobdolon*, Archangel
Galeopsis galeobdolon) (6)
Size of plant (H x W): 6″ to 1′ x 1′ to 2′
Foliage color: Variegated dark green and silver
Time of bloom: Mid-May to late June, peak in late May to early June
Color of bloom: Yellow
Size of bloom: Individual flowers <0.5″; inflorescence 1″ to 2.5″

Herman's Pride is a moderately vigorous cultivar of an otherwise aggressive plant. It forms a dense mat of colorful silver and green leaves. Soft yellow flowers, not particularly showy, are borne in whorls in the leaf axils of elongated flower spikes. 'Herman's Pride' lines the path at PERC, growing in the part-shade of larger companion plants. It is damaged occasionally from skeletonizing insects, but otherwise is pest free.

L. maculatum 'Pink Pewter' Spotted Dead
Nettle (6)
Size of plant (H x W): 1″ to 6″ x 1′ to 3′
Foliage color: Variegated light green and silver, semi-evergreen
Time of bloom: May-October (frost)
Color of bloom: Pink
Size of bloom: Individual flowers 0.5″ to 1″; inflorescence 1″ to 2.5″

The dead nettles have no relationship to stinging

Lamium maculatum 'Pink Pewter'

Lavatera thuringiaca

nettles. They are useful ground covers for shady areas where their variegated foliage and pink, purple or white flowers provide a bright contrast. Although there are several cultivars planted at PERC, Pink Pewter has performed best due to its siting in part shade. ('Beacon's Silver' has struggled in a full sun situation.)

There are several different patterns of variegation possible with *L. maculatum*, depending on the cultivar. 'Pink Pewter' has silvery leaves edged in greenish-gray. The clear pink flowers are especially bright against the foliage. Spotted dead nettles are capable of competing with the roots of trees and can be used in dry shade. A moist, fertile site encourages rapid growth. They are semi-evergreen in Colorado.

Lavandula angustifolia   Lavender
(aka *L. officinalis*)   ○ ✁ ✿ ❖ ✿ (2,12)
Lamiaceae (Labiatae)
Landscape use: Border, mass, cut and dried flower, rock, xeriscape and herb gardens
Growth habit: Mounded
Size of plant (H x W): 1' to 2' x 1' to 2'
Foliage color: Light green to gray, semi-evergreen
Time of bloom: Late June-September, peak from late June to mid-July
Color of bloom: Purple
Size of bloom: Individual flowers <0.5", inflorescence 2.5" to 5"

This shrubby, drought tolerant plant has opposite, light green, linear leaves covered by fine hairs. The foliage is semi-evergreen and aromatic. The stem bases turn woody with age. Flowers are whorled around a spike and are fragrant. Bees are frequent visitors. Lavender has been used for ages for potpourris, sachets and perfumes.

At PERC, lavender has been planted several times with moderate success. The longest-lived clump survived for 12 years, the shortest for two years.

Overwintering lavender can be a challenge in our heavy clay soil. Good drainage is critical, especially in the winter. Poorer soils produce a hardier plant, with a better chance of survival.

Lavatera thuringiaca   Tree Mallow
(aka *L. olbia*)   ○ ✁ (8)
Malvaceae
Landscape use: Specimen, mass, border, background, cut flower
Growth habit: Erect
Size of plant (H x W): 2' to 4' x 3' to 5'
Foliage color: Medium green
Time of bloom: Late June to early August, peak in early to mid-July
Color of bloom: Pink
Size of bloom: 2" to 3"

L. thuringiaca is a shrubby plant closely related to hollyhocks and mallows. The saucer-shaped pink blooms have five showy petals. They are borne in the leaf axils and on loose, terminal racemes. The alternate leaves have three to five lobes and toothed margins.

Tree mallows are easy to grow. Full sun and well-drained, average soils are the only requirements. It does bear a heavy crop of fruit, which can become a nuisance. Deadheading moderates this and produces a bushier, longer-blooming plant.

Leucanthemella serotina 'Herbstern'   Giant
(aka *Chrysanthemum serotinum*,   Daisy, High
C. uliginosum 'Herbstern')   Daisy ○ ☽ ✁ (14)
Asteraceae (Compositae)
Landscape use: Border, mass, background, wildflower garden and cut flower
Growth habit: Upright, spreading
Size of plant (H x W): 2' to 4' x 4' to 6' massed
Foliage color: Medium green

Leucanthemella serotina 'Herbstern'

Leucanthemum x superbum

Time of bloom: Mid-August to early October, peak from early-late September
Color of bloom: White with yellow center
Size of bloom: 1" to 2.5"

This shasta daisy look-alike represents one of two species in this genus. It is a vigorous plant with erect, hairy stems and spreads from rhizomes. The toothed leaves are alternate and lance-shaped to oblong. The flowers are held singly or in loose clusters. The daisy flower of the species has white ray florets and greenish disk florets. 'Herbstern' has a greenish-yellow disk that contrast nicely with the clear white rays.

L. serotina 'Herbstern' has been aggressive at PERC, requiring periodic division to contain its spread. It has been free of disease and insect problems. It is reliably winter hardy.

Leucanthemum x superbum Shasta Daisy
(aka *Chrysanthemum x superbum*, ◗ ◗ ✄ (19)
C. maximum)
Asteraceae (Compositae)
Landscape use: Border, mass, wildflower garden and cut flower
Growth habit: Clump
Size of plant (H x W): 2' to 4' x 2' to 4'
Foliage color: Dark green
Time of bloom: Late June-September, peak from mid-July to early August
Color of bloom: White with yellow center
Size of bloom: 2.5" to 5"

This vigorous perennial forms clumps of glossy, dark green, alternate, and toothed basal leaves. The upper leaves are sessile. Shasta daisies make excellent cut flowers with their long flower stalks and large solitary flowers. Each head has white ray florets and a yellow disk. Cultivars are available with semi-double or double flowers. Deadheading promotes rebloom and pinching produces more compact plants. Lodging

of the flower stems in heavy rain and wind has been a problem at PERC.

Shasta daisies grow best in moderately fertile soil with regular irrigation and good drainage, especially in winter. Division every two or three years in spring keep the plants healthy. The following two cultivars performed well at PERC.

L. x superbum 'Becky' (3)
A tall, self-supporting shasta daisy with large flowers. More floriferous than the species.
L. x superbum 'Esther Read' (3)
This cultivar blooms earlier than the species, beginning in mid-June. The blooms are double and white, with a hint of yellow in the center. 'Esther Read' was the first double shasta daisy to be hybridized.

Liatris Blazing Star, Gay Feather
Asteraceae (Compositae) ◗ ✄ ✿ ⚘ 🦋
Landscape use: Border, mass, wildflower and rock garden, cut and dried flower
Growth habit: Clump, erect flower stems
Size of plant (H x W): 6" to 1' x 6" to 1'
Foliage color: Medium green
Size of bloom: Individual flowers 0.5" to 1", inflorescence >5"

Liatris spp. are native to North America. The tall, dense spikes of fluffy flowers provide a strong vertical accent in the perennial garden. Each flower head opens from the top of the spike downwards, opposite to the majority of spike inflorescence. Gay feather grows from corm-like swollen stems. The leaves are linear and clustered in a basal clump. Leaf arrangement is alternate to whorled. Erect, stiff flowering stems elongate several feet into a peculiar bottlebrush or foxtail-like inflorescence.

Liatris spp. grow best in full sun and well drained, moderate to moist sites. They will not tolerate excessive winter moisture. *L. punctata*, dotted gay

Liatris spicata

Liatris pychnostachya 'Alba'

feather, can be used in xeriscape gardens. Divide the corms every four to five years to maintain vigorous plants.

L. pychnostachya 'Alba'   Kansas Gay feather,
(aka *Laciniaria pychnostachya*)   Button Snakeroot,
          Prairie Blazing Star (8)
Time of bloom: July to mid-September
Color of bloom: White

The Kansas gay feather ranges from Central to Southeastern United States. This species is reported to reach five feet when in flower. 'Alba', the white flowering cultivar at PERC, attained one to 3 feet in bloom. Kansas gay feather has hairy stems with shorter leaves than those at the base. The species has bright purple flowers. Care is similar to the more familiar *L. spicata* described next.

L. spicata   Blazing Star, Gay
          feather
(aka *Laciniaria spicata, Liatris callilepis*)   (20)
Time of bloom: Mid-July to mid-September
Color of bloom: Purple

This native to the Eastern and Southern regions of the United States lacks the hairy stems of the Kansas gayfeather. The flowers are rosy-purple puffs consisting of tubular disk florets surrounded by leafy bracts on spikes approximately 2 feet high. If the central flowering stalk is removed before going to seed, lateral spikes develop. Blazing star self-sows. The tiny seedlings are easy to remove. This plant takes up little room in the perennial border and is an excellent cut or dried flower.

Lilium   Garden Lily
Liliaceae   ○ ✂ 🕯
Landscape use: Specimen, border, mass, wildflower garden and cut flower
Growth habit: Erect

Size of plant (H x W): 1 ½' to 4' x 1' to 2'
Foliage color: Medium green
Time of bloom: Varies with species
Color, size, and height of bloom: Varies with species

Lilies have been in cultivation for centuries. Due to extensive breeding, hundreds of species and hybrids of lilies are available. Lilies grow from scaly bulbs, forming erect plants with narrow, whorled, lanceolate leaves. Although each plant flowers for only one or two weeks, a combination of varieties can be planted to extend bloom from May to October. Flowers come in shades of white, pink, red, orange, yellow, or purple, often with contrasting speckles or throats. The flowers occur in four general types: upright cups, funnel-shaped or trumpets, Turk's cap, with recurved flower segments, and wide-open, flat flowers. Often the anthers are large and showy. Some are very fragrant. Lilies can be used as accent plants, in container gardens, or in mass plantings.

Lilies are easy to grow, most preferring good drainage and slightly acid soil, high in organic matter. They require a cold dormant period to bloom. Three different lilies have done well at PERC, surviving from 19 to 24 years in clay and alkaline soil. The bulbs usually are planted in the fall and divided every six to eight years to prevent overcrowding. They should be fertilized in the spring. Lilies make excellent cut flowers if cut just as the buds begin to swell. Do not remove more than one third of the stem.

L. longiflorum

The popular Easter lily may be planted outdoors and often reflower in the fall and in July or August the year after. Because they are not reliably hardy in zone five, they should be mulched in the winter.

Limonium   Statice
Plumbaginaceae   ○ ✂ ✿ ❖ 🦋
Landscape use: Border, mass, xeriscape and rock gardens, cut and dried flower

Limonium gmelinii

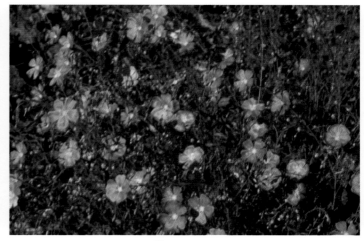

Linum perenne

Growth habit: Clump
Time of bloom: July to mid-October, peak from mid August-early September
Color of bloom: Lavender to purple

Annuals, biennials, perennials and subshrubs make up the 150 species in this genus. Many are semi-evergreen or evergreen. The leathery foliage remains handsome into winter, often turning red in the fall. Statice is a favorite cut or dried flower because of the papery corolla and persistent calyx of a different color. To use as a dried flower, cut the inflorescence just as the flowers begin to open. Dry upside down in a cool place, out of direct sunlight.

The two species of statice grown at PERC are tolerant of our clay loam. Ideal conditions include full sun exposures and fast-draining soils. Propagate statice by spring division, seed, or root cuttings in the winter.

L. gmelinii   Siberian Statice
(aka *Statice gmelinii*)   (8)
Size of plant (H x W): 6" to 1' x 6" to 1'
Foliage color: Medium green, semi-evergreen
Size of bloom: Individual flowers <0.5", Inflorescence 2.5" to 5"

Siberian statice is native to Eastern Europe and Siberia. It is smaller than *L. latifolium* described next, but has the same leathery, basal rosette of leaves. The panicle of flowers is not as wide or held as high and bloom begins later in July. Each flower is darker purple. *L. gmelinii* remains ornamental into late fall.

L. latifolium   Sea Lavender
(aka *L. gerberi, L. platyphyllum,*   (16)
Statice latifolium)
Size of plant (H x W): 1' to 2' x 2' to 4'
Foliage color: Dark green, semi-evergreen
Size of bloom: Individual flowers <0.5",
Inflorescence >5"

Sea Lavender is similar to Tatarian statice (*Goniloimon tataricum*), with a basal rosette of leathery dark green leaves. The inflorescence is an airy, branched panicle that arises from the center, reaching 1 to 3 feet. The tiny flowers consist of a lavender, tubular corolla and a white calyx. Even after the flowers finish, the panicle is showy.

Sea lavender requires little maintenance. It is salt and pollution tolerant and rarely needs division. The inflorescence lodges and can be staked or propped up by neighboring plants.

Linum perenne   Perennial Flax
Linaceae   ◖ ❖ (6)
Landscape use: Border, mass, wildflower, xeriscape and rock gardens
Growth habit: Clump, vase-shaped
Size of plant (H x W): 1' to 2' x 1' to 2'
Foliage color: Blue-green
Time of bloom: Mid-May to October (frost), peaking from early to late June
Color of bloom: Light blue
Size of bloom: 0.5" to 1"

There are over 200 species of flax of varying forms and degrees of hardiness. Most prefer well-drained, moderately fertile soils and full sun exposures. Heavy soil and winter moisture can be detrimental. They are suitable for borders, rock gardens and meadows. Although vigorous growers, they may be short-lived. Self-sowing can perpetuate their presence in your garden, but seedlings are variable.

Perennial flax, *L. perenne*, forms a clump of wiry, arching stems. The linear, grass-like leaves and open habit give it an airy, delicate appearance. The flower buds of flax are rolled up tight, opening to five-petalled, funnel or saucer-shaped blooms. The flowers are various shades of sky blue and about 1 inch wide. White and dwarf cultivars are available. The individual flowers barely last a day, failing by

Lobelia cardinalis

Lotus corniculatus 'Dwarf'

late afternoon, but new flowers are produced in abundance. In cloudy weather the blooms do not open.

Perennial flax needs full sun and good drainage, but appears to thrive in clay soil. It is drought resistant and good for xeriscape use. It self-seeds readily and can fill a large area in a few years. Cut back after bloom to encourage rebloom and to control the seedling population.

Lobelia cardinalis   Cardinal Flower,
(aka *L. fulgens*, *L. graminea*,   Indian Pink
L. splendens)   ○ ◗ ✄ �´ ✹ ! (5)
Campanulaceae (Lobeliaceae)
Landscape use: Border, mass, wildflower garden and cut flower
Growth habit: Erect
Size of plant (H x W): 1' to 2' x 1'
Foliage color: Medium green
Time of bloom: Late July-early October
Color of bloom: Red
Size of bloom: Individual flowers 0.5" to 1", inflorescence >5"

Cardinal flower is an erect native North American species with oblong to lanceolate serrated leaves that often have a purplish cast. The flowers occur on bracted racemes 1 foot or more long. The scarlet flowers are asymmetrical, with a tubular corolla opening into two distinct lips. The upper lip has two lobes; the lower lip has three. These bright, odd flowers add a vivid splash of color to the perennial border.

In nature, *L. cardinalis* is found in wet areas, organic soils and light shade. Growth in full sun is possible, if given enough moisture. Plant cardinal flower near a pond, stream or boggy area. It often self-sows, the mother plant lasting only a few years. Mulch, placed carefully around the crown, improves winter hardiness and protects from frost heave.

Cardinal flower makes good cut flowers if the stems are seared. Hummingbirds find the bright red flower attractive. All fresh tissue is poisonous. When dry the plant has little toxicity. Propagate by seed, cuttings or division.

Lotus corniculatus 'Dwarf'   Dwarf Bird's
(aka *L. ambiguus*, *L. balticus*)   Foot Trefoil
Papilionaceae (Fabaceae)   ○ ◐ (4)
Landscape use: Ground cover, erosion control
Growth habit: Creeping
Size of plant (H x W): 1" to 6" x 1' to 2'
Foliage color: Medium green
Time of bloom: Late May to mid-July
Color of bloom: Yellow
Size of bloom: <0.5"

This prostrate member of the pea family forms a dense, weed-choking mat. It can be used as a ground cover or lawn substitute. The bright green clover-like leaves retain their good looks past the first hard frosts, before going winter dormant in cold climates. The bright yellow flowers have the characteristic pea form and are borne in clusters. The common name of this plant is derived from the fruit, which spreads like a bird's foot. *Lotus* spp. prefer well-drained soil and full sun.

Lupinus   Lupine
Papilionaceae (Fabaceae)   ○ ✄ 🦋 !
Landscape use: Specimen, mass, border, background, wildflower garden, cut flower
Growth habit: Clump

Plants in this genus are nitrogen fixing and have distinct, palmately compound leaves with seven or more leaflets. The handsome mounded clump of foliage with erect flowering stems and racemes of pea-like flowers in many colors make lupine a useful specimen plant for the mid to back border. Because of the large, heavy blooms, lupines may need staking.

Lupinus perennis

Lupinus 'Russell Hybrids'

As cut flowers, they are excellent and rebloom readily if not allowed to go to seed. Although not all lupine species are poisonous, some do contain alkaloids especially in the seeds, pods and young foliage.

L. perennis   Wild or Sundial Lupine ⚓ (5)
Size of plant (H x W): 2' to 4' x 2' to 4'
Foliage color: Medium green
Time of bloom: Late May-August, peak in early June
Color of bloom: Purple and white
Size of bloom: Individual flowers 0.5" to 1", inflorescence >5"

Lupinus perennis is native to Eastern and Central United States, but not as commonly grown as the Russell Hybrids lupine. *L. perennis* makes an excellent accent or specimen plant in wildflower gardens because of its upright column of showy purple and white flowers.

Wild lupine can be short-lived, prefers cool summers and fertile, slightly acidic soils. It needs regular moisture and is stunted in drought conditions. Mountainous areas are more favorable to growth than the Front Range. Mulch in winter to protect the crown. Lodging of the long-flowering stalks and chlorosis have been problems at PERC.

L. Russell Hybrids   (6)
Time of bloom: Late May to early July, peaking in late May and mid-June
Color of bloom: Many; pink and reds at PERC

Russell hybrid lupines were developed by George Russell, a former railroad crossing guard and avid gardener from England. He selected his best seedlings and released them in 1937. They are among the showiest of garden perennials. Large mounds of palmately compound leaves contrast nicely with other garden plants. Almost every flower color is available, as well as bicolors. Earlier plantings at PERC died out after a couple of years. The present specimen has done well for six years, with minor problems from skeletonizing insects, slugs and chlorosis. Full sun or partial shade and well-drained soil is important. Mulch to conserve moisture. Seedlings from this hybrid will be a mixture of colors.

Lychnis chalcedonica   Maltese or Jerusalem
Caryophyllaceae   Cross, Scarlet Lychnis
○ ◗ ✂ 🦋 (12)
Landscape use: Border, mass, wildflower garden, cut flower
Growth habit: Erect
Size of plant (H x W): 1' to 3' x 6" to 1'
Foliage color: Medium green
Time of bloom: June-October (frost), peak from mid-June to early July
Color of bloom: Red-orange
Size of bloom: Individual flowers 0.5" to 1", inflorescence 1" to 2.5"

This stiff, erect plant has opposite, ovate leaves that clasp a hairy, unbranched stem. The terminal clusters contain scarlet red, star-shaped flowers with five notched petals shaped like the arms of a Maltese cross. The genus name is appropriately derived from the Greek word for lamp. *L. chalcedonica* makes an excellent cut flower and is attractive to butterflies. It can self-sow and forms a colony. Original plants tend to be short-lived.

Maltese cross is easy to grow in cool climates and suffers in dry and extended heat. Regular precipitation is necessary or the leaves may brown prematurely. Deadhead to promote rebloom. Lodging and minor chlorosis have been a problem at PERC.

L. 'Molten Lava'   (8)
A cultivar of unknown parentage with shocking orange flowers and purplish green foliage. 'Molten Lava' forms a mounded clump, 6 inches in height and width. A real eye-catcher!

Lychnis chalcedonica

Lysimachia nummularia

Lysimachia nummularia　　　　Moneywort,
Primulaceae　　　　Creeping Jenny
◗ ● ☙ (18)

Landscape use: Ground cover, erosion control, woodland garden
Growth habit: Creeping
Size of plant (H x W): 1" to 6" x 6' to 9'
Foliage color: Medium green
Time of bloom: Early June to early September, peaking in late June and mid-July
Color of bloom: Yellow
Size of bloom: 0.5" to 1"

Moneywort is a useful ground cover for shady areas, spreading quickly by trailing stems that root at the nodes. It can be invasive in moist sites and should be used with caution. The PERC planting is in full sun, an exposure too harsh by midsummer. Regardless, moneywort has spread to well over 9 feet, even with periodic division. The plant is popular for its bright, golden yellow flowers. Each flower is solitary, cup-shaped and borne in the leaf axils. The species name *nummularia* means "coin-like," in reference to the circular, opposite leaves. The glossy green foliage is not evergreen, but turns yellow in the fall and dies back for the winter.

Moneywort is easy to grow and adapts to most situations. Part sun exposures and moist soils are preferred. Full sun resulted in leaf scorch at PERC. Mild chlorosis has been another problem. Due to its aggressive nature, do not plant moneywort near lawns where it can invade and be difficult to remove.

Malva alcea 'Fastigiata'　　Hollyhock or Vervain
(aka *M. fastigiata, M. bismalva*)　　Mallow
Malvaceae　　◗ ◗ (12)

Landscape use: Specimen, border, background
Growth habit: Bushy clump
Size of plant (H x W): 2' to 4' x 1' to 2'
Foliage color: Medium to dark green

Time of bloom: June-September, peaking in late July-early August
Color of bloom: Pink
Size of bloom: 1" to 2.5"

The hollyhock mallow is more upright than the species and forms a woody based, bushy plant. Its foliage is variably shaped with shiny, rounded, and scalloped basal leaves and smaller, more serrated, and palmately divided leaves farther up the stem. The saucer-shaped flowers are borne in terminal racemes and are deep pink with five notched petals. Hollyhock mallow is floriferous, with peak bloom in July. If the plant is not deadheaded, fruit set is abundant and self-sowing can be a problem.

Although, hollyhock mallow is easy to grow, it may be short-lived in overly rich soil. It is drought tolerant and cold hardy. After bloom, cut back the foliage to the base to encourage a new rosette of leaves.

Monarda didyma　　　Beebalm, Bergamot,
　　　　Oswego-tea, Mountain-mint
Lamiaceae (Labiatae)　　◖ ◗ ✄ ☙ ᭪ 🦋 ⚘ (9)

Landscape use: Border, mass, wildflower and herb garden, cut flower
Growth habit: Upright, spreading
Size of plant (H x W): 2' to 4' x 2' to 4'
Foliage color: Medium green
Time of bloom: July-September, peaking from mid July-early August
Color of bloom: Red
Size of bloom: Inflorescence 2.5" to 5"

Beebalm is a North American native with fragrant, hairy, mint-like leaves and a square stem. It is an herb previously used by the American Indians and colonists for tea. The fragrant foliage can be used for potpourris and the nectar rich flowers are a favorite with bees, butterflies and hummingbirds. The flowers are hooded and grow in pincushion-like

56

Monarda didyma

Nepeta x faassenii

heads (called verticillasters) at the top of the stem. Sometimes successive tiers of verticillasters occur on the stem. The native flowers are red, but cultivars are available in many colors.

This species is not drought tolerant. It prefers partial shade and well-drained moist soil, where it can spread vigorously. It can be grown in full sun with sufficient moisture. Beebalm is a good plant for naturalizing in moist areas and makes a splendid cut flower. It often is affected by powdery mildew, although cultivars with mildew resistance are available. It requires division about every three years.

In xeriscape gardens, the lavender-flowered wild beebalm, *M. fistulosa*, is appropriate.

Nepeta x faassenii Catmint
Lamiaceae (Labiatae) ○ ◗ ❖ 🦌 🦋 (20)
Landscape use: Border, mass, rock, herb, wildflower and xeriscape gardens
Growth habit: Spreading, upright to mounded
Size of plant (H x W): 1′ to 2′ x 2′ to 4′
Foliage color: Blue green to gray green
Time of bloom: Late May-October (frost), peaking from early-late June
Color of bloom: Bluish purple
Size of bloom: Individually 0.5″ to 1″, inflorescence 2.5″ to 5″

Catmint is a vigorous, aromatic herb with opposite, heart-shaped, often blue-green leaves. It has been used as a medicinal herb and as a seasoning. Aromatic oil produced from crushed leaves, especially those of *N. cataria* or catnip, is attractive to cats, who often are found rolling in the middle of the plant or chewing on the leaves. The blue to lavender flowers are held in whorls in terminal or axillary racemes. Each flower is tubular with two lips, the top lip having two lobes and the bottom lip having three lobes. Bees are attracted to the flowers.

Nepeta is easy to propagate by division and

requires this frequently to moderate its vigorous growth. Insect and disease problems are not common. Catmints thrive in hot, sunny areas with well-drained soil of moderate to poor fertility. High humidity and wet winter soils are detrimental. They adapt to moist or dry situations and are more erect in dry, poor soils. Cut back after the first bloom to encourage a secondary flowering and more compact growth.

There is some taxonomic confusion in the trade. *N. x faassenii* is a sterile hybrid. It often is offered under the name *N. mussinii*, which is seedling propagated and has a tendency to self-sow in the garden.

N. x f. 'Souvenir d'Andre Chaudron' (4)
This cultivar has the same growth habit as *N. x faassenii* but reaches 1 to 2 feet taller in height and is more appropriate for the middle of the perennial border. The leaves are not as hairy and thus, do not have the grey cast to them. The flowers bloom later, are a deeper blue to purple and held on long interrupted racemes that are very showy. It requires support and is a vigorous spreader, bordering on invasiveness. In some sources this plant is listed as a separate species under the name *N. sibirica* 'Souvenir d'Andre Chaudron.'

Oenothera Evening Primrose,
Onagraceae Sundrops, Suncups
○ ❖ 🦋 🌿

Landscape use: Border, mass, rock, xeriscape and wildflower gardens
Color of foliage: Medium green
Size of bloom: 2.5″ to 5″

This genus of approximately 120 species is native to the temperate areas of North and South America. *Oenothera* means "wine tasting," referring to the ancient Greek practice of serving roots of some species with after dinner wines. Many different species are grown at PERC. In general, flowers are

Oenothera macrocarpa

Oenothera glazioviana

cup or saucer shaped and found in shades of yellow, pink or white. They most often are solitary, large and showy, yet last one day. Sundrops or suncups open their flowers at dawn, evening primroses at dusk.

Oenothera spp. are excellent plants for poor, dry and stony soils. The following species tolerated the heavier clay soil at PERC with success. Many are tap rooted and withstand drought, although periodic deep watering encourages flowering throughout the summer. Excess winter moisture can lead to root rot. Use these plants in full sun exposures in rock gardens, wildflower gardens and perennial borders.

O. glazioviana
(aka *O. erythrosepala, O. blandina*)

Large Flowered Evening Primrose

🌱 (7)

Growth habit: Erect
Size of plant (height x width): 2' to 4' x 2' to 4'
Time of bloom: Mid-June to mid-October
Color of bloom: Yellow

This vigorous species from North America is coarse, hairy and grows erect. Opening in the evening, the scented, yellow flowers contrast with red sepals and red-spotted stems. As they fade in the afternoon, the flowers turn salmon pink and are replaced by a generous supply of blooms nightly.

This species attractive feature is its ability to constantly flower but there are several problems that limit its usefulness. When in bloom, the plants can reach heights of 6 feet, making it more appropriate for the wildflower or naturalized garden. The night blooming *Oenothera* often are pollenized by moths. The sphinx moth is particularly attracted to this plant as is evidenced by the number of horn worms found hidden in the foliage at PERC. Flea beetles have chewed the leaves, but without hampering its growth. Wasps and bees also are frequent visitors.

Large flowered evening primrose is tap rooted and difficult to transplant. It produces an abundance

of seed that is a favorite food for finches. Although short-lived, this plant reseeds itself easily.

O. macrocarpa
(aka *O. missouriensis*)

Ozark Sundrops, Missouri Primrose

🍃🌱 (13)

Growth habit: Spreading
Size of plant (height x width): 6" to 1' x 4' to 6' massed
Time of bloom: Mid-June to mid-October, peak in mid-June to early July
Color of bloom: Yellow

This prostrate, spreading primrose is native to Nebraska, Texas and Missouri, but adapts to the Front Range and mountains of Colorado. Glossy, narrow leaves with a white midrib are held alternately on hairy stems, that often are red tinted. Flowers are lightly scented, delicate looking, and yellow with red spotted sepals. They open in the evening and last through the next day.

Missouri primrose makes an excellent ground cover for poor, dry sites. It blooms modestly throughout the summer. Although hidden by the foliage, the four-winged, capsule fruit also is interesting. Missouri primrose is slow to start growth in the spring.

O. m. 'Fremontii'
(4)

This cultivar has pale yellow flowers, often hidden by the foliage. The leaves are narrower than the species.

O. speciosa 'Siskiyou'
(aka *O. berlandieri, Calylophus berlandieri*)

Compact Mexican Evening Primrose

🍃 (8)

Growth habit: Spreading
Size of plant (height x width): 6" to 1' x 4' to 6'
Time of bloom: Mid-June to late September, peak from late June to late July
Color of bloom: White and pink

Oenothera speciosa 'Siskiyou'

Oxalis crassipes 'Rosea'

Compact Mexican evening primrose spreads from rhizomes into an impressive mass. It is useful as a ground cover or in a wildflower garden, but might be considered too aggressive in a more formal perennial border. Poorer soils keep 'Siskiyou' more compact. The oblong to lance-shaped leaves are slightly toothed and held in basal rosettes. Fall color is red to purple.

This day-flowering species is a reliable bloomer, peaking in late June through July. The flowers are 2 to 2.5 inches wide, smaller than the other species listed. White petals are heavily veined and edged in a pale pink.

***Ophiopogon planiscapus* 'Nigrescens'**   Black
(aka *O. nigresens*, *O. planiscapus*   Mondo Grass
'Niger' or 'Arabicus')   ◑ ◗ ☙ (4)
Convallariaceae (Liliaceae)
Landscape use: Ground cover, mass, accent
Growth habit: Clump, mounded
Size of plant (height x width): 6" to 1' x 6" to 1'
Color of foliage: Purplish black, evergreen
Time of bloom: Late June-July
Color of bloom: White to pale pink
Size of bloom: Individually <0.5", inflorescence 2"

This under used plant looks similar in form to the lilyturf group (*Liriope* spp.) At PERC it is popular with visitors who are surprised by its deep purple-black strap-like, arching leaves that form dainty mounds by a pathway. The flowers are inconspicuous, bell-shaped and held on short terminal racemes often hidden by the foliage.

Although black mondo grass spreads by rhizomes, it is slow growing and does not cover an area quickly. It is most useful as an accent strategically placed near a path or next to chartreuse-leaved plants. Ideal growing conditions include slightly moist, fertile soil, full sun to part shade exposures, and protection from winter wind.

***Oxalis crassipes* 'Rosea'**   Strawberry Wood
Oxalidaceae   Sorrel, Strawberry Oxalis
     ◗ ● (4)
Landscape use: Ground cover, mass, wildflower and woodland gardens
Growth habit: Clump, mounded
Size of plant (height x width): 1" to 6" x 6" to 1'
Color of foliage: Medium green
Time of bloom: June to mid-October, peak in mid-June, August, and late September
Color of bloom: Pink
Size of bloom: 0.5" to 1"

This wood sorrel is an under-utilized plant showing excellent potential for the Colorado Rocky Mountain Front Range. Some species of sorrel are common lawn and greenhouse weeds, which gives the genus a bad reputation. Others are not cold hardy. Strawberry wood sorrel has a clover-like, three-part compound leaf. Each leaflet is shaped like a heart. The pink flower is rolled up tight in bud and in cloudy weather, much like an umbrella. When open, flowers have five petals that hold in clusters above the foliage on slender stalks.

Strawberry wood sorrel does best in humus rich soil with regular precipitation. Part to full shade exposures protect it from overly hot summers. It spreads very slowly at PERC with only a few seedling plants emerging after four years. A winter mulch is beneficial, since this plant is hardy only to Zone 5.

Paeonia   Garden Peony,
Paeoniaceae   Herbaceous Peony
     ◑ ◗ ✂ ❖ ℂ 🦋 (20)
Landscape use: Specimen, mass, border, xeriscape garden, cut flower
Growth habit: Clump
Size of plant (H x W): 2' to 4' x 2' to 4'
Foliage color: Medium to dark green
Size of bloom: > 5"

Paeonia 'Pink Dawn'

Peonies are long-lived, spring to summer blooming perennials that are grouped under two main classifications. Tree peonies are shrubby plants with woody stems. These have not been grown at PERC where the exposed, windy site would consistently damage frost tender new shoots and brittle stems. The second group, herbaceous peonies, have grown successfully for 20 years.

The genus *Paeonia* is an ancient one, dating back to China more than 2,000 years ago. Most modern herbaceous hybrids are derived from *P. lactiflora*. Extensive breeding has resulted in numerous cultivars ranging in colors from white, pink, red, yellow, and bicolor. Flower types can be single, semi-double, double, Japanese, and anemone forms depending on the number of petals or petal-like stamens. Blooms often are fragrant and make excellent cut flowers if cut just as they begin to open. Top-heavy plants need staking, or their weighty blooms bend stems to the ground. By planting early, mid and late blooming cultivars, it is possible to have peonies in bloom for six weeks from late spring to early summer.

Foliage provides another outstanding ornamental feature. The early spring shoots emerge pinkish-purple, unfurling slowly. Mature foliage is glossy, medium to dark-green mounded clumps. Leaves are compound, alternate and often lobed. They make nice additions to flower arrangements. Some cultivars even have reddish fall foliage color.

Peonies grow best in full sun exposures, but the pastel flowered types benefit from part shade. Spring fertilization and a winter mulch is recommended. Tolerant of alkalinity, peonies demand good drainage and deep, fertile soils. Those planted at PERC have done well for 20 years in the heavy clay and poor soils. Several years ago, however, a fungal wilt invaded the thick, woody rootstocks of several plants. When in bloom, water peonies at ground level to prevent flower damage. Peonies are recommended for xeriscape use in the moderate to high water zones.

Plant peonies with permanence in mind. Full bloom occurs within about three years and healthy plants live for more than 20 years. Crowded plants or ones that are no longer blooming heavily may need division. Dig up and divide the tuberous rootstock in late summer or early fall. Replant pieces that have three to five eyes or buds no more than 1 to 2 inches below the surface. Peonies that are planted too deep do not bloom.

The following are only a few of the fine cultivars grown at PERC:

P. 'Charlie's White'
Time of bloom: Early June-early July, peak in late June
Color of bloom: White

Charlie's White has a frilly, double white, slightly fragrant flower. Peak bloom occurs in late June. The plant is sturdy, rarely needing staking. Fall foliage color is reddish purple.

P. 'Pink Dawn'
Time of bloom: June, peaks in early and late June
Color of bloom: Pale pink

Aptly named, this cultivar has a white flower with a pale pink blush. Yellow stamens form a showy central "boss." It is pink in bud and single in form. Peak bloom is early June. Fall foliage color is reddish purple.

P. 'Doreen'
Time of bloom: Early June-early July, peaks in mid- and late June
Color of bloom: Deep pink

This deep pink flowering cultivar has a creamy yellow, ruffled center and a nice fragrance. Peak bloom is late June. Its dark green foliage turns yellow, red and purple in the fall.

P. 'Vivid Rose'
Time of bloom: Early June-late July, peak in mid-June

Papaver orientale

Color of bloom: Pink

This sweet smelling, ruffled pink flower reaches peak bloom in mid-June. Fall foliage color is similar to other varieties.

Papaver orientale   Oriental Poppy
Papaveraceae   ○ ✂ ✿ (20)
Landscape use: Specimen, border, mass, wildflower garden, cut and dried flower
Growth habit: Clump, mounded
Size of plant (H x W): 2' to 4' x 2' to 4'
Foliage color: Medium green
Time of bloom: June-early July
Color of bloom: White, orange, varies with cultivar
Size of bloom: >5"

Oriental poppies are a showy addition to the early summer perennial garden. Their coarse, hairy leaves are long, divided and form a mounded clump. When broken, stems and leaves exude a milky sap. Erect, unbranched flowering stems rise 3 feet to 4 feet above the foliage. Each large flower bud is bristly and nodding, turning upwards as they open. The emerging petals are crinkly. Oriental poppy flowers are as large as peonies, with thin, crepe paper petals and a central showy boss of purple-black stamens. When in bloom, oriental poppies will be the dominant plant in a landscape and look best blended with softer, less striking companion plants.

After blooming, the developing fruit is a showy pod often used in dried flower arrangements. The foliage dies back in the summer and reappears late summer or early fall when nights turn cool again. Plan to have companion plants hide the fading foliage. Oriental poppies require well-drained soils, especially in winter and are drought tolerant. They perform best in full sun to light shade and poorer soils. Fertile soils produce rank growth and lanky flower stems that require staking. Water at ground level when in bloom to prevent flower damage caused by overhead sprinklers.

Oriental poppies respond poorly to transplanting. To propagate, take 4 to 6-inch root cuttings from a dormant plant. If using seed, the daughter plants will vary. At PERC, chlorosis and lodging have been noted as problems.

Penstemon   Beard-tongue, Penstemon
Scrophulariaceae   ○ ◗ ✂ ❖ ⚘ 🦋 ✤
Landscape use: Border, mass, specimen, wildflower, xeriscape and rock garden, cut flower

Penstemon is the largest genus of flowering plants native to North America with many species originating in the western states. The name *Penstemon* is thought to derive from the Greek word *pente* or "five" and *stamon* or "thread" alluding to the fifth sterile stamen or filament found in the flowers. The correct association may actually stem from the Greek word *paene* or "almost." Therefore, *Penstemon* would translate to "almost a stamen." Taxonomists distinguish groups by the shape and hairiness of this filament.

The flower form is distinct. Each tubular corolla has two lips, the uppermost with two lobes and the lowermost with three lobes. Many hybrids are available with white, pink, red, yellow (rare), blue or purple flowers. Hummingbirds are attracted to the nectar and pollinate the red and bright pink varieties. Bees are common pollinators of the white, blue and purple varieties. Within the lower lips and extending into the throat, colored veins or guidelines direct the pollinators to nectar sacs at the base of the flower. These guidelines are distinct, vary and often have interesting patterns.

Growth habits vary from shrubby species, low growing ground covers to upright plants of variable sizes. Most have a basal rosette of opposite, lanceolate leaves from which upright flower stalks arise.

Penstemon digitalis 'Husker Red' (*photos by D. Mizell*)

Different species are evergreen, semi-evergreen, or herbaceous. Leaves may be glaucous, fleshy, needle-like, or hairy–all adaptations to semi-arid and arid climates.

Beard-tongues do best in full sun, although some tolerate part shade. They require well-drained neutral to alkaline soil of average to poor fertility. Planting on slopes or in raised beds helps prevent a tendency to rot if kept too wet in winter. Their reputation for being short-lived derives in part from the excesses of traditional perennial gardens, i.e. overly fertile soils and too much supplemental irrigation. Deadheading after the flowers fade directs plant energy into foliage and root growth, instead of seed production. This aids in plant survival during the winter months.

Many penstemons are excellent rock garden plants. Others perform at their peak in xeriscape gardens where they receive no additional watering. However, not all species are xeric. Investigate the origin of the plant before purchasing penstemons. Purchase species that are suitable for the garden situation you can provide. Hybrids often are the most tolerant for a typical urban garden. The following species performed well at PERC in the traditional perennial garden setting.

P. campanulatus (8)
(aka *P. pulchellus*, *P. campanulata*)
Growth habit: Upright, spreading
Size of plant (H x W): 6" to 1' x 1' to 2'
Foliage color: Medium green to dark green, semi-evergreen
Time of bloom: July-September, peaking in late July
Color of bloom: Purple with white throat
Size of bloom: 0.5" to 1"

The species name of this penstemon means "bell-like", which appropriately describes the shape of the flower. Flower color ranges from violet to purple with a white throat. Plants will reach a height of 18 inches or more when in bloom. The leaves are linear to lanceolate and toothed. This species is native throughout Mexico.

P. digitalis (13)
Growth habit: Upright, spreading
Size of plant (H x W): 1' to 2' x 1' to 2'
Foliage color: Medium green to dark green, semi-evergreen
Time of bloom: June to mid-September, peak from early to late June
Color of bloom: White to pale lavender
Size of bloom: 1" to 2.5"

This widely spread species is the best-known white flowering penstemon. The species name *digitalis* implies a similarity to foxglove most likely due to the large and inflated corolla. Flower color can be variable from white to pale lavender. Some have purple guidelines.

P. digitalis forms a basal rosette of semi-evergreen lanceolate leaves that are a glossy green, often tinged with reddish purple. It tolerates clay loam, heat and humidity.

P. digitalis 'Husker Red' PPY-96 (11)
Dale Lindgren of the University of Nebraska introduced this cultivar, which has reddish purple young leaves that mature to green with a red flush. The plant is vigorous and well suited to a traditional perennial border. Seedlings are variable and may not have the intense reddish foliage that make this selection unique. 'Husker Red' is floriferous and will reach peak bloom several times in the summer. This cultivar was named The Perennial Plant of the Year in 1996.

P. 'Elfin Pink' (19)
Growth habit: Upright, spreading
Size of plant (H x W): 1' to 2' x 2' to 4'
Foliage color: Medium green, semi-evergreen

Penstemon 'Elfin Pink' *Penstemon x mexicali* 'Pikes Peak Purple' *Penstemon pinifolius*

Time of bloom: June-September, peak from mid-June to early July
Color of bloom: Pink
Size of bloom: 0.5" to 1"

'Elfin Pink' is an American hybrid that blooms reliably at PERC. It is carefree and vigorous, spreading into a mass of semi-evergreen glossy leaves. The soft pink flowers have a white throat. Bloom is heaviest in June through early July, with lesser continual bloom throughout the summer.

P. x mexicali **PIKES PEAK PURPLE**™　　PS-1999 (8)
Growth habit: Upright, spreading
Size of plant (H x W): 1' to 2' x 1' to 2'
Foliage color: Medium green, semi-evergreen
Time of bloom: June-October, peak from late June-early July, late July, and late October
Color of bloom: Purple
Size of bloom: 1" to 2.5"

This hybrid, between Mexican and American wild penstemons, has narrow, glossy evergreen leaves. The flowers are a violet purple with a white throat and clustered on stalks reaching two feet tall. PIKES PEAK PURPLE™ can be sited in full sun or part shade and is tolerant of clay loam. Both this cultivar and RED ROCKS™, a selection with rose pink flowers, are Plant Select® introductions for 1999.

P. pinifolius　　　　　　Pineleaf Penstemon
Growth habit: Upright, spreading　　　　　(14)
Size of plant (H x W): 1' to 2' x 1' to 2'
Foliage color: Medium green, evergreen
Time of bloom: June to mid-September, peak from early June-early July
Color of bloom: Scarlet
Size of bloom: 0.5" to 1"

Pineleaf penstemon is a low, shrubby evergreen with a woody base and narrow, needle-like leaves. The small flowers are bright scarlet with a narrow tube-like corolla suitable for hummingbird pollinators. Flowers are borne in profusion in June through early July. Bloom is sporadic and less showy the rest of the summer. It is drought tolerant and requires well-drained sites such as a rock garden or xeriscape garden. Pineleaf penstemon is a native to Arizona, New Mexico and Mexico. It has proven cold hardy at PERC.
P. pinifolius 'Mersea Yellow'　　　　　　(4)
This cultivar is a yellow flowering selection that is not as floriferous as the species.

P. strictus　　　　　　　　Rocky Mountain
Penstemon, Stiff Beard-tongue
Growth habit: Upright, spreading　　　　　(17)
Size of plant (H x W): 1' to 3' x 1' to 2'
Foliage color: Dark green
Time of bloom: Early June-July, peak from mid-June to end of June
Color of bloom: Purple with blue tints
Size of bloom: 0.5" to 1"

This native of Wyoming, Colorado, Utah, New Mexico and Arizona gets its species name from the upright flowering stems. Narrow spikes of deep purple flowers with blue to violet highlights are abundant in June. The flowers are held on only one side of the inflorescence. Smooth basal leaves are spoon shaped and the stem leaves are linear or lanceolate.

Perovskia atriplicifolia　　　　　Russian Sage
Lamiaceae (Labiatae)　　○ ✂ ❀ ❖ 𝒞 🦋 PPY-1995 (14)
Landscape use: Border, background, mass, specimen, wildflower and xeriscape gardens, cut and dried flower
Growth habit: Upright, spreading
Size of plant (H x W): 2' to 4' x 4' to 6' massed
Foliage color: Light green to gray green

Perovskia atriplicifolia

Phlomis russeliana

Time of bloom: July-early October, peak in August-early September
Color of bloom: Lavender blue
Size of bloom: Individually < 0.5", Inflorescence > 5"

This native of Central Asia is a subshrub with many fine ornamental qualities. The stems are downy, white and aromatic. The leaves are opposite, dissected and toothed, with a sage-like aroma that deer find repugnant. The stiff white stems provide an excellent contrast in winter months. Cut back in the spring, just as new foliage emerges to maintain a dense, compact growth habit.

The flowers of Russian sage are whorled and clustered in an airy spike up to 2 feet long. Each tiny flower is two lipped, the upper lip with four lobes. The calyx remains showy after the petals drop. Bees and butterflies find this plant irresistible.

Russian sage needs well-drained soil, especially in winter. It prospers in alkalinity, remaining more compact and upright in full sun and poor soil. It is drought tolerant.

Phlomis russeliana   Sticky Jerusalem Sage
Lamiaceae (Labiatae)   ○ ✂ ❀ (8)
Landscape use: Border, mass, wildflower garden, cut and dried flower
Growth habit: Upright, spreading
Size of plant (H x W): 2' to 4' x 2' to 4'
Foliage color: Medium green, evergreen
Time of bloom: Mid-June to August, peak from late June to mid-July
Color of bloom: Pale yellow
Size of bloom: 1" to 2.5"

When in bloom, sticky Jerusalem sage provides an outstanding architectural presence in the garden. The pale yellow, hooded flowers are held in successively higher whorls (verticillasters) around an erect, unbranched stem, much like beebalm. Each cluster is subtended by leafy bracts. Leave the mature flower

stalks for fall and early winter interest, or cut for dried flower arrangements. Deadheading discourages self-sowing.

The wooly medium green leaves are heart shaped, crinkled and evergreen. Dense hairs on the underside give the leaf a silvery appearance. *P. russeliana* grows best in sunny sites with well-drained, sandy loam but has performed well at PERC. The original clump died out in the center. Newer plants at the margins are more vigorous. Soils low in fertility promote a compact, sturdy plant that does not need staking.

Phlox
Polemoniaceae   ○ ◗ ➷ ✤
Phlox is a diverse genus of approximately 70 species of mostly North American natives. *Phlox* means "flame" suggesting the abundance of brightly colored flowers produced by these versatile plants. The growth habit varies from erect to low growing or cushion forming depending on the species. Most flowers have a tubular base and five flat, ovate to star shaped lobes that are often notched at the tips. Found in terminal clusters, the flowers come in a range of colors from white, pink, magenta, blue or purple. They often are fragrant. Lower leaves are opposite and entire, whereas upper leaves may be alternate. Care differs depending on species.

P. divaricata ssp. *laphamii*   Wild Sweet-William,
                 Woodland Phlox, Wild Blue Phlox ⬥ ⚲ (12)
Landscape use: Border, mass, wildflower and woodland garden, ground cover
Growth habit: Spreading
Size of plant (H x W): 6" to 1' x 1' to 2'
Foliage color: Medium green, semi-evergreen
Time of bloom: Mid-April to early June, peak in mid-late May
Color of bloom: Lavender blue

Phlox divaricata ssp. *laphamii*

Phlox paniculata 'David'

Size of bloom: Individually 1" to 1.5", Inflorescence 2.5" to 5"

This semi-evergreen perennial can be found in humus rich, shady woodland settings in the South and Central United States and Canada. It hugs the ground, spreading from underground stems and above ground prostrate stems that root at the nodes. The oval to lanceolate leaves are opposite and sessile. Place at the front of the border, along a path, or use as a ground cover in shady, moist settings.

Woodland phlox blooms early spring when the soil and temperatures are cool and moisture is plentiful. Its lavender blue flowers are clustered, slightly fragrant and an excellent compliment to early blooming bulbs. The subspecies *laphamii* has a deeper blue flower than the species.

Full to part shade exposures are preferable. At PERC, woodland phlox is planted in the full sun and suffers from the summer heat and minor chlorosis. Divide in the spring or propagate from summer tip cuttings.

P. paniculata   Garden Phlox,
                               Perennial Phlox ✂ ⚭
Landscape use: Border, mass, background,wildflower garden, cut flower
Growth habit: Upright, spreading
Size of plant (H x W): 2' to 4' x 2' to 4'
Foliage color: Medium green to dark green
Time of bloom: July to early October
Color of bloom: Varies with cultivar
Size of bloom: 2.5" to 5"

Perennial phlox is a stiff, upright, native North American species with opposite, lance-shaped leaves. Most of the plants sold are cultivars that vary in height and flower color from bright white, pink, red, salmon, and blue, often with a contrasting eye. The flowers are borne in rounded to pyramidal panicles about 5 inches wide. At PERC, one or more cultivars

were in bloom from early July to frost.

Perennial phlox can be grown in full sun or light shade. It performs best in moist, moderately fertile soil. To prevent seeding and encourage reblooming, remove the flowers as soon as they start to fade. Pinch back the tips of the stem to stimulate side shoots and promote a bushier plant. Divide phlox every three or four years. Although they are good for naturalizing, magenta flowers become dominant. Perennial phlox is fragrant and makes an excellent cut flower. Powdery mildew often is a problem. Refrain from overhead watering and provide good air circulation. Many cultivars are available with good powdery mildew resistance.

P. p. 'David'   (4)
This late blooming, tall cultivar has shown no signs of powdery mildew in the four years it has been evaluated. It is floriferous with pure white flowers.

P. p. 'Franz Schubert'   (10)
This cultivar has a pinkish purple flower and is very vigorous. It has suffered from powdery mildew yearly.

P. subulata   Moss Phlox,
                          Creeping Phlox ❀ ❖ (20)
Landscape use: Border, mass, rock and xeriscape garden, ground cover
Growth habit: Creeping
Size of plant (H x W): 1" to 6" x 1' to 2'
Foliage color: Medium green, evergreen
Time of bloom: Mid-April to mid-June, peak in mid-late May
Color of bloom: Pink or lavender, varies with cultivar
Size of bloom: 0.5" to 1"

Unlike the other two species, *P. subulata* forms a dense mat of evergreen, needle-like leaves. It is useful in rock or xeriscape gardens, at the edge of the border, or draped over rock walls. Blooming before most other perennials, moss phlox is covered with

Phlox subulata 'Emerald Blue'

Physostegia virginiana

star-shaped flowers held in terminal clusters. Each petal is notched. Shear back by half after flowering to encourage a minor rebloom.

Moss phlox requires a sunny spot with good drainage. It suffers from the wind in the winter, often desiccating severely. Shallow rooted, moss phlox benefits from a winter mulch.

P. s. 'Emerald Blue' (4)
This cultivar has light blue flowers.

Physostegia virginiana　　　　Obedient Plant,
(aka Dracocephalum virginianum)　False Dragonhead
Lamiaceae (Labiatae)　　◖◗ ✂ ⚬ 🦋 (17)
Landscape use: Border, mass, wildflower garden, cut flower
Growth habit: Upright, spreading
Size of plant (H x W): 2′ to 4′ x indefinite
Foliage color: Medium green to dark green
Time of bloom: Mid-August to mid-October, peak in mid-late September
Color of bloom: Pink
Size of bloom: Individually 1″ to 2.5″, Inflorescence > 5″

Obedient plant is a native North American species with lanceolate, toothed, bright green leaves. The rosy pink tubular flowers are two lipped and borne in dense terminal and axillary spikes reaching 3 feet. White flowered cultivars are also available. Each flower has a hinged stalk and stays put when moved, thus the name "obedient plant." Flowering peaks in September when many other plants are through blooming.

Obedient plant does well in full sun or partial shade. It is rhizomatous, spreading rampantly in moist soil, less so in dry soil. To keep it under control, divide it frequently or place it in a buried, open bottom pot. Site it next to plants equally as vigorous. It is a good cut flower, attractive to bees and butterflies, and well worth the extra maintenance.

Platycodon grandiflorus　　　　Balloon Flower,
(aka *P. glaucus, Campanula*　　Chinese-bellflower
grandiflorus)　　　　◖◗ ✂ (7)
Campanulaceae
Landscape use: Specimen, border, rock and wildflower gardens, cut flower
Growth habit: Clump, erect to vase-shaped
Size of plant (H x W): 1′ to 2′ x 1′ to 2′
Foliage color: Medium green to blue green
Time of bloom: Late June-September
Color of bloom: Blue
Size of bloom: 1″ to 2.5″

Balloon flower is a long-lived, erect to vase-shaped plant native to Japan, China, and Korea. Its handsome foliage is smooth, medium green to blue-green, with elliptic to lanceolate, toothed leaves. Leaves are whorled on the lower portion of the stem, alternate higher up the stem. Flower buds are inflated like balloons, which open into wide bell or saucer-shaped flowers. Blue, white, and pink single or double flowered cultivars, as well as dwarf forms are available. Blossoms make good cut flowers after the stems are seared. Plants may need staking when in full bloom.

Balloon flowers may live 20 years or more and are drought tolerant once established. They prefer full sun or partial shade in moderately fertile soil that is well drained, especially in winter. The plants take two or three years to become established and give peak performance. The roots are fleshy and the plant fares poorly if disturbed once established. Balloon flowers come up late in spring, and care must be taken to not injure them while cultivating. Propagate by seed or division in early spring.

P. g. 'Komachi' (13)
This cultivar is an oddity. The large blue inflated, balloon-like buds never open but dangle from the plant like Chinese lanterns.

Platycodon grandiflorus

Polygonum affine 'Border Jewel'

Polemonium caeruleum
Polemoniaceae

Jacob's Ladder, Greek Valerian, Charity ○ ◐ ➤ (8)

Landscape use: Border, mass, wildflower and woodland gardens
Growth habit: Mounded clump, upright flowering stems
Size of plant (H x W): 1' to 2' x 1' to 2'
Foliage color: Medium green to dark green
Time of bloom: Late May to mid-August, peak in early June
Color of bloom: Blue
Size of bloom: 0.5" to 1"

Jacob's ladder is an excellent cottage garden or woodland garden plant. Historically, it was used in the medicinal herb garden. The common name, Jacob's ladder, refers to the rungs of alternate leaflets found on pinnately compound leaves that form a mounded basal rosette. The overall effect is delicate and ferny.

The erect flowering stalks reach 1 to 3 feet. They bear clusters of bell-shaped, nodding sky blue flowers with contrasting orange stamens. Pink and white flowering cultivars are available. Jacob's ladder is a modest bloomer from late spring to early summer. It thrives in moist soil and partial shade. If planted in full sun, extra moisture is needed and the foliage may scorch. Deadhead after bloom. Although some members of the genus self-sow to nuisance, no such difficulties have been noted with this species at PERC. Propagate by seed, midsummer stem cuttings, or division.

Polygonum affine 'Border Jewel'
(aka *Persicaria affinis* 'Border Jewel')
Polygonaceae

Knotweed, Himalayan Fleeceflower ○ ◐ ➤ ❖ (9)

Landscape use: Border, mass, ground cover and erosion control, xeriscape garden

Growth habit: Spreading
Size of plant (H x W): 6" to 1' x 2' to 4'
Foliage color: Medium green
Time of bloom: Late May-early October, peak in early August
Color of bloom: Pale pink to white
Size of bloom: Individually <0.5", Inflorescence 2.5" to 5"

This mat-forming perennial is an adaptable ground cover, tolerating moist to dry soil and clay to sandy soils. In fact, its vigorous nature is better contained by drier sites and poorer soils. The shiny, lance-shaped green leaves are slow to emerge in spring. They are semi-evergreen and have a prominent white midvein. In autumn, the foliage turns reddish bronze, coloring especially well in full sun exposures. The pale pink to white funnel-shaped flowers are small and held in tight spikes reaching 1 foot in height. The fruit, which is attractive and persistent, matures to a pinkish-brown.

Grow Himalayan fleeceflower with sufficient moisture if you wish to encourage a dense mat of foliage. Yet, caution is suggested in siting this vigorous plant. It can be grown in full sun to part shade. The winter appearance, a tangled mass of stems after the leaves have fallen, is poor. Old plantings may die out in the middle. Himalayan fleeceflower can be divided in the spring or early fall.

P. a. 'Dimity'   (4)

This carpet-forming cultivar is dense and compact with leathery foliage and pinkish-white flowers that deepen to red with age. The foliage turns a rich red in the fall.

Potentilla recta 'Macrantha'
(aka *P. recta* 'Warrenii,' *P. recta var. warrensii*) ○ ◐ ✿ (17)
Rosaceae

Sulphur Cinquefoil

Landscape use: Border, mass, wildflower and rock garden

Potentilla recta 'Macrantha'

Prunella grandiflora

Growth habit: Clump, mounded
Size of plant (H x W): 1' to 2' x 1' to 2'
Foliage color: Medium green
Time of bloom: June-October (frost), peak in late June
Color of bloom: Yellow
Size of bloom: 0.5" to 1"

Sulphur cinquefoil is a many-branched, mounded plant with coarsely hairy foliage and palmately compound leaves much like a strawberry. The bright yellow flowers are borne in loose clusters and are frequented by bees. Bloom is heaviest in late June. Sporadic bloom continues through the fall. This shrubby plant begins to look unkempt after the first flush of flowers. Cutting back by half encourages new foliage and a tidier appearance.

Sulphur cinquefoil requires full sun and well-drained soil and withstands minor drought. Divide every three years to maintain vigorous, compact plants. At PERC, sulphur cinquefoil has displayed minor chlorosis and a tendency to self-sow. The straight species seeds readily and should not be planted. It is listed on the state of Colorado's noxious weed list. Several prostrate species of *Potentilla* have been grown at PERC for ground covers and are not recommended due to their aggressive nature.

Prunella grandiflora   Large Selfheal, Heal All
Lamiaceae (Labiatae)   ◐ ◗ ☙ ✿ (13)
Landscape use: Border, mass, groundcover, rock and wildflower garden
Growth habit: Spreading
Size of plant (H x W): 6" to 1' x 1' to 2'
Foliage color: Medium green to dark green; semi-evergreen
Time of bloom: Early June-October (frost), peak in late June
Color of bloom: Purple, pink, and white
Size of bloom: 0.5" to 1"

Large selfheal is a favorite of bees. The two lipped flowers are borne on upright spikes. The majority of the flowers at PERC are a rich, deep purple. Some seedling plants have pink or white flowers. The foliage is semi-evergreen. Leaves are opposite and ovate to oblong. They are slightly toothed and sometimes lobed.

Large selfheal can be grown in full sun or part shade. It prospers in most soils. A vigorous spreader, it roots from the nodes, forming an effective groundcover. Plants also self-sow, and should be deadheaded if this is not welcome. The common name alludes to its historical use as a medicinal plant.

Pulmonaria saccharata '**Mrs. Moon**'   Lungwort,
Boraginaceae   Bethlehem Sage
◗ ● ☙ (13)
Landscape use: Border, mass, groundcover, woodland and herb garden
Growth habit: Clump, mounded
Size of plant (H x W): 6" to 1' x 6" to 1'
Foliage color: Variegated dark green and silver; semi-evergreen
Time of bloom: April-early June, peak from late April-early May
Color of bloom: Pink maturing to blue
Size of bloom: Individually 0.5", inflorescence 1" to 2.5"

Among the first to bloom in spring, the lungworts are excellent ground covers for shady spots in the perennial border. Their variously spotted or mottled leaves are bright, interesting, and attractive for most of the year. They form mounded clumps of basal leaves that are slightly hairy and coarse to touch. Lungworts are named for their supposed likeness to a spotted and diseased lung. This seems unfair, since the foliage is the main ornamental feature and the flowers an added bonus.

Flowers are funnel shaped and held in drooping clusters above the rosette of leaves. 'Mrs. Moon' is a

Pulmonaria s. 'Roy Davidson'   *Pulmonaria s.* 'Sissinghurst White'   *Pulsatilla vulgaris*

cultivar with pink buds that open to violet flowers. As the flowers mature they turn a blue to lavender color. All three colors and stages are found simultaneously.

The *Pulmonaria* spp. at PERC are planted at the base of a tree and receive afternoon shade. Although they prefer moist soil, they tolerate dry shade but are not as vigorous. If planted in full sun, the plants require more water and are prone to leaf scorch in midsummer. Divide lungworts in the fall and give them sufficient water until they are established.

P. s. 'Roy Davidson'   (3)

This cultivar has narrow leaves decorated with white to silver splotches. Its deep blue flowers fade to violet. 'Roy Davidson' begins blooming in March and continues through May.

P. s. 'Sissinghurst White'

(aka *P. officinalis* 'Sissinghurst White')   (3)

There is some taxonomic confusion over the origin of this plant. Regardless, it is a strong grower and a heavy bloomer. Of the three lungworts grown at PERC, 'Sissinghurst White' is the largest and most vigorous. It begins blooming in late March. The flowers are a clean white and contrast nicely with the broad, silver spotted leaves.

Pulsatilla vulgaris   European

(aka *P. vulgaris var. serotina,*   Pasque Flower

Anemone pulsatilla, A. serotina)   ○ ◗ ❖ ! (19)

Ranunculaceae

Landscape use: Border, wildflower, xeriscape and rock garden

Growth habit: Clump, mounded

Size of plant (H x W): 6" to 1' x 6" to 1'

Foliage color: Medium green

Time of bloom: April-early June

Color of bloom: Purple

Size of bloom: 2.5" to 3"

This early spring bloomer has showy, cup-shaped nodding flowers that are held singly on downy

stalks. Yellow stamens form a showy central boss. The stamens contain nectar secreting glands, a trait that distinguishes the genus *Pulsatilla* from that of *Anemone*. Flower color is typically purple or violet, but white and pink flowers are possible. The fruit is ornamental, with feathery styles much like those of clematis.

The foliage is a mounded rosette of pinnately divided leaves with fine, silken hairs that glisten. European pasque flower requires full sun or part shade and well-drained alkaline soils. In cooler climates, it is drought tolerant. Use it in a rock garden where its delicate foliage and interesting seed heads provide early season charm. Pasque flower will self sow and can be propagated by root cuttings. It has been known to cause dermatitis upon contact and stomach upset if ingested.

P.v. 'Rubra'   (6)

This cultivar has a dark, burgundy flower.

Rudbeckia fulgida   Orange Coneflower,

var. sullivantii **'Goldsturm'**   Black-eyed Susan

Asteraceae (Compositae)   ○ ◗ ✂ ✿ ❖ ⚘ 🦋 PPY-99 (8)

Landscape use: Border, mass, specimen, wildflower and xeriscape garden, cut and dried flower

Growth habit: Clump, erect flowering stems

Size of plant (H x W): 1' to 2' x 1' to 2'

Foliage color: Dark green to medium green

Time of bloom: Late June to mid-October, peak in mid-July and August

Color of bloom: Golden-yellow to orange-yellow

Size of bloom: 2.5" to 5"

Orange coneflower (often called black-eyed Susan, although that name is more properly applied to *R. hirta*) is an erect flowering plant with a basal clump of ovate to lanceolate dark green leaves. The deep, rich yellow daisy flowers are borne on a long stem and have a bronzy black central cone. Bloom begins in the middle of summer and continues

Rudbeckia fulgida 'Goldsturm'

Ruta graveolens 'Blue Mound'

until frost. Use this plant to introduce a splash of late summer color into the perennial border, for naturalized areas and as a cut flower. The central disk can be used in dried floral arrangements.

Orange coneflowers perform best with full sun and moist average soil. They are recommended for moderate watering zones in xeriscape gardens. Plants grown in rich soil with abundant water tend to become weak stemmed and often need staking. Propagation is best done by division in spring.

The variety *sullivantii* is less hairy than the species with stem leaves becoming progressively smaller higher up the stem. The cultivar Goldsturm remains more compact, reaching 2 feet in height. 'Goldsturm' earned the Perennial Plant of the Year award in 1999.

Ruta graveolens 'Blue Mound'
Rutaceae

Common Rue, Herb of Grace

○ ◗ ✿ ! (17)

Landscape use: Border, mass, specimen, herb garden
Growth habit: Clump, mounded
Size of plant (H x W): 1' to 2' x 1' to 2'
Foliage color: Blue-green, semi-evergreen
Time of bloom: June-August
Color of bloom: Yellow to chartreuse
Size of bloom: 0.5" to 1"

Common rue is a partly woody, rounded plant with pungent, pinnately dissected blue-green leaves. The plant is grown mostly for its foliage, which provides a cool contrast to the typical green foliage of many perennials. The greenish-yellow flowers are not very showy and are held in loose clusters above the foliage. The cultivar Blue Mound has a larger, deeper blue leaf than the species. It is also more drought tolerant.

Common rue can be grown in full sun or part shade. It requires well-drained soil and tolerates alkalinity and poor fertility. Common rue can also be used as a low hedge in the herb or knot garden. Cut back every year to keep it compact. Some people are allergic to the plant sap and foliage and may develop a rash, particularly in hot weather.

Salvia
Lamiaceae (Labiatae)

Sage

○ ✂ 🦋

Landscape use: Border, mass, specimen, herb and wildflower garden, cut flower
Growth habit: Clump
Size of bloom: Individually 0.5" to 1", inflorescence > 5"

Salvia, the largest genus in the mint family, includes many fine perennials as well as tender species used as bedding plants. The name is derived from the Latin *salvare* meaning to "save" or "heal." *S. officinalis*, common sage, has both culinary and medicinal uses. Members of the sage genus are beautiful ornamentals. They make effective foliage plants with their thick, wrinkled, often woolly leaves. Some are aromatic. Their colorful two-lipped flowers are arranged in spikes, racemes or panicles. The upper lip is helmet shaped or erect, the lower lip flat to spreading. Sage requires well-drained, ordinary soil and sunny sites. Excess winter moisture is detrimental. Bees are very fond of this genus.

S. argentea
Silver Sage ✿ PS-1997 (4)

Size of plant (H x W): 6" to 1' x 1' to 2'
Foliage color: Grey, semi-evergreen
Time of bloom: Late June to mid-July
Color of bloom: White

Silver sage is aptly named. Its large wrinkled leaves are covered with dense white to silver hairs. The foliage, which grows in a basal rosette, is the main ornamental feature. The white flowers are borne in open panicles reaching 2 to 3 feet tall. Once the plant begins to flower, it loses its neat appearance and becomes rangy. Many people choose to cut off the flowering stalks. This preserves the compact growth

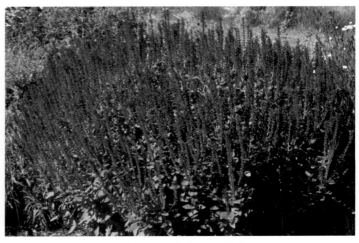

Salvia argentea   *Salvia pratensis*   *Salvia x superba* 'May Night'

habit and increases the longevity of this often short-lived perennial. Silver sage is tap rooted and drought tolerant. It grows best in full sun and tolerates poor soil if well drained. In 1997, silver sage was added to the Plant Select® program.

S. pratensis   Meadow Clary,
                                                    Meadow Sage (24)
Size of plant (H x W): 6" to 1' x 1' to 2'
Foliage color: Medium green to dark green
Time of bloom: Late May to mid-October, peak in early June
Color of bloom: Purple

The somewhat hairy, wrinkled leaves of meadow clary are oblong to lanceolate and toothed. They form a low basal rosette. Flower stalks can reach 2 feet in height. The deep purple, hooded flowers open from the bottom of the inflorescence upwards. The stalks tend to lodge. Meadow clary self-sows and is good for naturalized areas. It is drought tolerant. S. pratensis is sometimes sold as *S. haematodes*.

S. x sylvestris 'May Night'   Perennial Sage,
(aka *S. nemorosa* 'May Night,'   Violet Sage
S. x superba 'May Night')   PPY-1997 (19)
Size of plant (H x W): 1' to 2' x 1' to 2'
Foliage color: Medium green
Time of bloom: Early June-September, peak from late June-early July
Color of bloom: Indigo blue

This dwarf cultivar of perennial sage was developed by the German horticulturist Karl Foerster who introduced it in 1956. The flower buds are pinkish purple and the flower is indigo blue. Reddish purple calyxes remain ornamental even after the flowers fade. Deadheading encourages a minor rebloom.

Perennial sage is a many-stemmed, rounded plant with oblong to lanceolate toothed leaves. At

PERC, 'May Night' reaches 3 feet in bloom. It is planted in a partly shaded bed and would most likely remain more compact in full sun. By midsummer, the lower leaves on the stems drop, giving the plant a leggy appearance that would be better hidden by companion plants.

Santolina chamaecyparissus   Lavender Cotton
(aka *S. incana*)   ○ ☙ ❖ ℃ (6)
Asteraceae (Compositae)
Landscape use: Border, mass, herb, xeriscape and rock garden
Growth habit: Clump, mounded subshrub
Size of plant (H x W): 1' to 2' x 1' to 2'
Foliage color: Grey-green, evergreen
Time of bloom: Late June to mid-August, peak in early August
Color of bloom: Yellow
Size of bloom: 0.5"

Lavender cotton provides a striking grey contrast in the rock, xeriscape, or herb garden. Stems are woody at the base and the finely divided leaves are aromatic. *Santolina* leaves have been used as an air freshener and insect repellent since medieval times. It is purportedly deer resistant and can be sheared for use as a hedge in knot gardens.

The button-like yellow flowers are secondary to the foliage in importance. In some years, the plant has not bloomed at PERC. Lavender cotton requires well-drained soils that do not retain winter moisture. Plant it in rock gardens, on slopes, or raised beds in dry, poor soils for the best performance. It is tolerant of heat, wind and alkalinity. Although evergreen, lavender cotton has shown some dieback during the winter and may not survive a really harsh winter. The species *S. virens* (aka *S. rosmarinifolia*) has a similar appearance but with bright green leaves and a strong scent. It is not as cold hardy as *S. chamaecyparissus*.

Santolina chamaecyparissus

Scabiosa columbaria 'Pink Mist'

Scabiosa columbaria 'Butterfly Blue' — Pincushion
Dipsacaceae — Flower, Small Scabious
○ ◗ ✄ ☙ PPY-2000 (4)
Landscape use: Border, mass, cut flower
Growth habit: Clump, mounded
Size of plant (H x W): 1' to 2' x 1' to 2'
Foliage color: Medium green to blue-green
Time of bloom: Late June-October (frost), peak in early July and early August
Color of bloom: Lavender blue
Size of bloom: 1" to 2.5"

Pincushion flower forms a basal mound of opposite, simple or variably divided leaves from which erect flowering stalks arise. The leaves on these stalks are divided into long fingers. One of the most floriferous perennials, pincushion flower blooms for most of the summer beginning in mid June. Each flower is actually comprised of many florets, the outer ones larger and somewhat frilly, and the small tubular inner ones clustered into a dome or pincushion.

'Butterfly Blue' is a compact cultivar with pastel blue to lavender flower heads and blue-green foliage. It did not need staking at PERC. Bees and butterflies were attracted to the flowers. Pincushion flower does best in cool, humid climates with alkaline soils. It tolerates our intense sun with regular irrigation. To promote flowering, divide plants every few years and remove flowers as they fade. This cultivar has been named the Perennial Plant of the Year for year 2000.

S. columbaria 'Pink Mist' (4)
This is the pink flowered version of 'Butterfly Blue."

Sedum — Stonecrop, Live-forever
Crassulaceae — ○ ☙ ❖ ☙
Landscape use: Border, mass, ground cover, erosion control, rock and xeriscape gardens

Sedum is a diverse genus comprising over 400 species of plants. In the wild they are often found on rocky sites and poor, dry soils. Their fleshy, succulent foliage is attractive for months. This is, in some species, their main ornamental value. They can be creeping, mat-forming, rosette-forming, or upright plants. The flowers are borne in terminal clusters of short spikes or flat heads. Five-petalled, star-shaped flowers may be yellow, white, or shades of pink, red, or purple. Bloom period ranges from May through October. If protected, many are evergreen. All require good drainage and are drought tolerant.

Sedums are used widely in rock and xeriscape gardens or as a ground cover in a mass planting. The best performing species, out of the many grown at PERC, are discussed in more detail in the following descriptions.

S. aizoon — Aizoon Stonecrop (20)
(aka *S. maximowiczii, S. woodwardii*)
Growth habit: Upright, spreading
Size of plant (H x W): 6" to 1' x 2' to 4'
Foliage color: Medium green
Time of bloom: Mid-June to July, peak in late June to early July
Color of bloom: Yellow
Size of bloom: Individually 0.5" to 1", inflorescence 2.5" to 5"

Aizoon stonecrop is an upright species with bright-green toothed leaves and branching clusters of bright yellow flowers. Unlike many other stonecrops, it is herbaceous. At PERC it blooms from early June through July, with persistent russet brown seed heads following in August. Once the fruit matures, the plant becomes open and sparse. Aizoon stonecrop spreads vigorously, therefore divide every three years.

S. kamtschaticum 'Floriferum' — Kamschatka
(aka *S. k. 'Weihenstephaner Gold, ' S. floriferum*) — Stonecrop ✿ (20)
Growth habit: Spreading

Sedum aizoon

Sedum kamtschaticum 'Floriferum'

Sedum spurium 'Dragon's Blood'

Size of plant (H x W): 6" to 1' x 2' to 4'
Foliage color: Medium green, semi-evergreen
Time of bloom: Early June to mid-August
Color of bloom: Yellow
Size of bloom: Individually 0.5" to 1", inflorescence 2.5" to 5"

Kamschatka stonecrop is a carpeting, semi-evergreen species from China, East Siberia, and Japan. The glossy, scalloped leaves form miniature rosettes and look good throughout the growing season. Bright yellow, star-shaped flowers are borne in loose, flat, four-branched cymes. Equally attractive are the bronzy red seed capsules.

S. k. 'Variegatum' (20)
This attractive cultivar has pink-tinged green leaves with a cream margin. The deep yellow flowers age to crimson, providing a striking contrast to the foliage. Peak bloom occurs in late June.

S. nevii (14)
Growth habit: Creeping
Size of plant (H x W): 1" to 6" x 2' to 4'
Foliage color: Light green, semi-evergreen
Time of bloom: June to mid-July, peak in mid-July
Color of bloom: White
Size of bloom: Individually <0.5", inflorescence 1" to 2.5"

S. nevii is a low-growing ground cover whose main ornamental feature is its foliage. The light green leaves are crowded into dense rosettes, which provide an interesting color and textural contrast in the border. The flowers, which are not very showy, are white with dark purple anthers that cast a faint, pinkish overall tint. This sedum prospered in light shade at the base of larger companion plants.

S. spectabile- see *Hylotelephium spectabile*

S. spurium 'Dragon's Blood' Two-row Sedum ✿ (20)

Growth habit: Spreading
Size of plant (H x W): 6" to 1' x indefinite
Foliage color: Medium green with red tints, evergreen
Time of bloom: Late June-early October, peak in late July
Color of bloom: Pink
Size of bloom: Individually 0.5" to 1", inflorescence 2.5" to 5"

Two-row sedum is a vigorous, spreading species with round, coarsely toothed leaves that are green, bronzy, or red depending on the cultivar. This species makes an excellent evergreen ground cover. The ½ inch pink or red flowers are borne in flat clusters. White flowered cultivars also are available. 'Dragon's Blood' has pink flowers and red-tinted mature foliage. The bronzy-red fruit is also ornamental and the foliage turns red in the fall. Many cultivars have done well at PERC.

S. s. var. album (12)
A white-flowering variety with lighter green foliage with a peak bloom from mid to late July.

S. s. 'Bronze Carpet' (20)
This plant is similar to 'Dragon's Blood' but has rosy-pink flowers and bronzy foliage. It blooms earlier in June and is more floriferous than 'Dragon's Blood.'

S. s. 'Red Carpet' (20)
A cultivar with red flowers, fruit and red foliage throughout the season. It is a striking plant when in bloom. It bloomed or was in fruit at PERC from late June to mid-August, and its appearance was good to excellent throughout the period.

S. telephium - see Hylotelephium telephium

73

Sedum spurium 'Red Carpet'

Sempervivum

Sempervivum   Hen and Chicks,
Crassulaceae   Houseleek
                                          ○ ◗ ⚘ ❖

Landscape use: Border, rock and xeriscape garden, ground cover
Growth habit: Clump, mounded
Size of plant (H x W): 1" to 6" x 1" to 6"
Foliage color: Light green to blue-green, evergreen
Time of bloom: Late June-August
Color of bloom: Pink, yellow or white
Size of bloom: Individually 0.5" to 1", inflorescence 2.5" to 5"

Houseleeks or hen and chickens are best known for their tight, basal rosettes of fleshy leaves. These evergreen, low-growing perennials were grown on the roofs of houses in ancient Rome to ward off witches and natural disasters. Today, they are used in rock gardens, xeriscape gardens or tucked in cracks of a wall or walkway. All species of *Sempervivum* require full sun to part shade and do best in well-drained, poor and rocky soil.

Houseleeks spread slowly. The generic name means "live forever," which raises false expectations except in a broad sense. In fact, after the plant flowers, the original rosette dies. The many offset rosettes that are produced on lateral runners, however, live on. The flower cluster is a flat, terminal panicle of star-shaped flowers on a long stalk. Colors range from pink, purple, yellow, and white. The inflorescence is odd-looking, but note-worthy since the houseleeks do not flower until maturity.

Many species and hybrids are available. The following list are a few that have done well at PERC.
S. arachnoideum   (8)
Cobweb houseleek has tight, basal rosettes of fleshy leaves about 3/4 inch across. The tips of the leaves are connected with many cobwebby gray hairs. For most of the year, the plant is barely 1 inch high but from late June through July it sends up a tall stalk

on which is produced a flat head of 1 inch deep pink flowers.
S. tectorum 'Atropurpureum'   (12)
This species has bristle-tipped thick succulent leaves tinged with reddish purple. The cultivar Atropurpureum planted at PERC has dark violet colored foliage and a pink flower cluster held on a 10 inch to 12-inch stalks. It bloomed from mid July through early September.

Sidalcea 'Party Girl'   Prairie Mallow,
                        Checker Mallow, False Mallow
Malvaceae   ○ ◗ ✂ ⚘ 🦋 (8)
Landscape use: Border, mass, background, wildflower garden, cut flower
Growth habit: Upright, spreading
Size of plant (H x W): 2' to 4' x 2' to 4' (massed)
Foliage color: Medium green
Time of bloom: July-October (frost), peak in late July
Color of bloom: Pink
Size of bloom: 0.5" to 1"

Prairie mallow is a handsome plant in leaf or in flower. The basal leaves are shiny and either rounded or palmately lobed. Erect flowering stems reaching 4 feet high bear leaves that are divided into finger-like lobes. The flowers are borne in terminal racemes and resemble miniature hollyhock flowers. 'Party Girl' has silky pink petals and a white central eye.

Prairie mallow is native to the western United States with species found in various habitats from mountain streamsides, woodlands, to prairies. It is rhizomatous and has spread into an impressive mass at PERC where it receives regular moisture. Deadheading after the first flowering encourages a neater appearance and rebloom. To propagate, lift and divide or start from seed.

Sidalcea 'Party Girl'

Solidago virgaurea 'Peter Pan'

Solidago virgaurea 'Peter Pan' — European Goldenrod
Asteraceae (Compositae)

◯ ◗ ✂ ❖ ✈ (16)

Landscape use: Border, mass, wildflower and xeriscape garden, cut flower
Growth habit: Upright, spreading
Size of plant (H x W): 2' to 4' x 4' to 6' (massed)
Foliage color: Medium green
Time of bloom: Mid-July to mid-October, peak in mid-August
Color of bloom: Golden yellow
Size of bloom: Individually < 0.5", inflorescence > 5"

European goldenrod is an upright rhizomatous plant with arching stems and bright green, simple, toothed leaves. The small golden yellow flowers are crowded together into dense, panicle-like clusters 6 inches long or more. The cultivar Peter Pan reaches 3 feet tall and when in bloom is covered by bees and wasps. After bloom, the developing fruit remains showy. To control self-sowing deadhead before the seed matures.

Many hybrid goldenrods are available, most of them derived from North American species. Wild species can be invasive. Hybrids do not spread as freely but still require forethought before placement in the border. Goldenrods prefer full sun and moist soil, yet are adaptable to dry watering regimes. The taller ones may need staking. Goldenrods do not cause hay fever. They are insect-pollinated and do not release pollen into the air.

X *Solidaster luteus* 'Lemore' (4)

This intergeneric hybrid between *Solidago canadensis* and *Aster ptarmicoides* was discovered in France nearly one hundred years ago. It is not as vigorous or coarse as the goldenrods but is very similar in appearance otherwise. Lemore is a cultivar with sprays of pale yellow flowers in August. It has stayed a compact size of 1 to 2 feet in height and width and has not required staking.

Stachys byzantina — Lambs'-Ears, Woolly Betony
(aka *S. lanata, S. olympica*)
Lamiaceae (Labiatae)

◯ ◗ ✂ ✿ ⚘ ❖ ✈ (19)

Landscape use: Border, mass, ground cover, xeriscape garden, cut and dried flower
Growth habit: Upright, spreading
Size of plant (H x W): 6" to 1' X indefinite
Foliage color: Grey, semi-evergreen
Time of bloom: Late June to mid-September
Color of bloom: Pink
Size of bloom: Individually < 0.5", inflorescence > 5"

Lambs'-ears is used mainly for its foliage where its thick, wooly leaves provide an interesting contrast in color and texture. These lance-shaped leaves are covered with fine white hairs and the velvety appearance gives this plant its common name. Lambs'-ears is vigorous and can be used as edging or to fill a large area.

In summer, whorls of tubular pink flowers are borne on spikes 1 foot or taller. The elongated flowering stalks also are wooly and provide a dramatic vertical accent. Flowers can be used in fresh or dried arrangements and are attractive to bees. Some people prefer removing the flower spikes to enhance the foliage effect. Nonflowering forms such as 'Silver Carpet' also are available. If allowed to flower, deadheading moderates its tendency to self-sow.

Lambs'-ears requires good drainage especially in the winter. It is tolerant of drought and is recommended for low to medium watering zones in a xeriscape garden. Full sun exposures and poor, well-drained soils produce the most compact growth. Propagate this plant through seed, cuttings or division.

Stachys byzantina

Teucrium chamaedrys

Teucrium   Germander
Lamiaceae (Labiatae)   ◯ ◗ ⇜ 🦋
Landscape use: Border, mass, ground cover, herb
garden
Growth habit: Spreading, mounded
Size of plant (H x W): 6" to 1' x 4' to 6'
Foliage color: Dark green, evergreen
Time of bloom: Mid-July to September
Color of bloom: Purplish pink
Size of bloom: < 0.5"

This genus contains evergreen and deciduous
shrubs, sub-shrubs, and perennials. The two species
grown at PERC have handsome, evergreen foliage
every bit as ornamental as the flowers. Shearing
back after bloom encourages a tighter plant. Provide
germanders with full sun to part shade and well-
drained soil. They adapt to poor soils. In exposed
sites, protect the evergreen foliage from drying winter
winds with evergreen boughs. Propagate by seed or
spring division.

T. canadense   Wild Germander,
                                American Germander ⇜ (20)
This North American perennial herb has thick,
shiny dark green leaves held on stiff, usually
unbranched, square stems. The leaves are opposite
and have notched to scalloped margins. It is
rhizomatous, spreading effectively into a neatly
mounded clump that can be used to edge a path.
Purplish pink flowers are found midsummer in loose
terminal clusters. Each flower is bell-shaped with two
lips. As with many plants in the mint family, bees find
the flowers irresistible.

T. chamaedrys   Common Germander,
                                Wall Germander (20)
Wall germander differs from its North American
counterpart in several ways. This easily sheared,
shrubby European and southwestern Asian species

has been traditionally used as a low hedge in knot
gardens. The leaves are slightly aromatic when
crushed and shaped somewhat like oak leaves,
hence the species name *chamaedrys* or "ground oak."
The flowers are slightly larger than *T. canadense*. All
other general characteristics are similar to those of *T.
canadense*.

Thalictrum aquilegiifolium   Columbine
Ranunculaceae   Meadow Rue
                                                ◯ ◗ ✂ (24)
Landscape use: Border, mass, wildflower and
woodland garden, cut garden
Growth habit: Clump, erect flowering stems
Size of plant (H x W): 2' to 4' x 1' to 3'
Foliage color: Gray-green to blue-green
Time of bloom: Mid-May to June, peak in early June
Color of bloom: Pink to lavender
Size of bloom: Individually 0.5" to 1", inflorescence
2.5" to 5"

Columbine meadow rue gets its name from its
delicate gray-green compound foliage that resembles
columbine (*Aquilegia* spp.). It is clump forming;
somewhat rounded in appearance with erect
flowering stems reaching 3 feet high. The flowers are
unusual with reduced petals and showy sepals and
stamens. Plants are male or female (dioecious), the
male having the showiest flowers. Flowers are small
but are clustered in fluffy balls that form heads up to
4 inches across. The usual color is pink to lavender,
but a white cultivar also is available.

This species can be grown in full sun or partial
shade and requires moist soil. It does better if the
soil is high in organic matter, yet over fertilization
produces weak stem growth. It produces good cut
flowers and can be naturalized. It has died back in
the heat of midsummer at PERC, but produces fresh
foliage as autumn approaches. Divide in spring.

Thymus pseudolanuginosus

Thymus serpyllum 'Coccineus'

Thymus   Thyme

Lamiaceae (Labiatae)   ○ ◗ ⚘ ❖ 🝆 🦋

Landscape use: Ground cover, erosion control, rock, herb and xeriscape garden
Growth habit: Creeping
Size of plant (H x W): 1" to 6" x 2' to 4'
Size of bloom: < 0.5"

There are many wonderful thymes to choose from. Excellent drainage, alkaline soils, hot, dry climate and low humidity are perfect conditions for growth. *Thymus* is derived from the Greek *thyo* meaning "to perfume." The aromatic foliage and essential oils of this genus are used in cooking, as potpourri, sachets, disinfectants, deodorants, mouthwashes, toothpastes and other products. Ancient Egyptians used thyme in their embalming fluid. Thymes are nectar rich and an important bee plant.

T. pseudolanuginosus   Woolly Thyme (6)
Foliage color: Gray-green, evergreen
Time of bloom: Sparse to no bloom at PERC
Color of bloom: Pink to lavender

Woolly thyme is an evergreen ground cover with prostrate stems that root at the nodes. The stems and tiny leaves are woolly. Most of the year, the foliage color is a soft, gray-green. When the weather turns cold the foliage takes on a plum coloration. Due to its creeping growth habit, woolly thyme makes an excellent filler between flagstones in a walkway. It tolerates moderate foot traffic. Its usefulness as a ground cover makes up for the sparse bloom of pale pink to lavender flowers.

Woolly thyme is drought tolerant and has low to moderate water needs. It desiccates in the winter if not periodically watered. Root rot is a problem in heavy, wet soils. Although it performs best in full sun, woolly thyme tolerates partly sunny exposures.

T. serpyllum 'Coccineus'   Mother-of-Thyme, Creeping Thyme (18)
Foliage color: Dark green, evergreen
Size of plant (H x W): 1" to 6" x 2' to 4'
Time of bloom: Mid-June to October, peak from late June to mid-July
Color of bloom: Dark violet

There are many cultivars of mother-of-thyme with growth habits from shrubby to creeping. 'Coccineus' is a creeping form whose usefulness as a ground cover rivals *T. pseudolanuginosa*. The visual effect is quite different, however. 'Coccineus' has dark green aromatic leaves that produce a tight mat of foliage. It has bloomed reliably at PERC with peak bloom in late June through mid July. The tiny violet flowers borne on roundish spikes about 1 inch long are striking against the dark foliage.

This species can be grown in full sun or in light shade in sandy, well drained to dry soil. It spreads slowly and is frequently used in rock gardens, as edging, as a ground cover, and among paving stones. It tolerates limited foot traffic, can be mowed and can be used as a lawn substitute.

Tradescantia   Spiderwort, Spider-lily,
Commelinaceae   Trinity Flower ○ ◗ ⚘ 🦋

Landscape use: Border, wildflower and woodland garden
Growth habit: Upright, spreading
Size of plant (H x W): 2' to 4' x 1' to 2'
Foliage color: Light green to medium green
Size of bloom: Individually 0.5" to 1", inflorescence 1" to 2.5"

The two spiderworts grown at PERC are native species that share the same genus as the popular houseplant known as wandering Jew and Moses-in-the-cradle. The long, strap-like leaves become somewhat unkempt and sprawling by midsummer. The flowers are saucer shaped with three petals and

Tradescantia virginiana 'Red Cloud'

Tricyrtis hirta

sepals and stamens with hairy filaments (hence the common name trinity flower.) Blossoms are borne in a terminal umbel above leafy bracts shaped somewhat like a canoe.

T. ohiensis   Ohio Spiderwort (17)
Time of bloom: Late June-September, peak in mid-July
Color of bloom: Blue to purple

Ohio spiderwort blooms heaviest in July. Each blue to purple flower lasts one day, but is continuously replaced. Cut back as soon as the foliage becomes ratty for a fall rebloom. Although suggested for boggy areas and pool sides, spiderwort performed well in the bright sun and heavy clay at PERC. In fact, less water and poorer soils produce a denser, neater clump of foliage. Divide every three to four years in the spring or fall.

T. virginiana 'Red Cloud'   Virginia Spiderwort
(aka *T. x andersoniana*,   (13)
T. Andersoniana Group)
Time of bloom: Late May-September, peak in early June
Color of bloom: Magenta

This species is native to the eastern United States. There is some confusion over the name, due to reports of interspecific hybridization that has not been conclusively documented. There does appear to be considerable variation within the species. Flower colors can range from white to shades of blue and purple. Red Cloud is a cultivar with bright magenta flowers and hairy magenta stamens. It blooms well in July, but becomes rank and unkempt in appearance afterwards. After cutting back, the fresh linear leaves form a tidier clump. Rebloom occurs in autumn. *T. virginiana* is rhizomatous and can spread vigorously in moist soil.

Tricyrtis hirta   Hairy Toad Lily
(aka *T. japonica*)   ◗ ● ✂ (6)
Liliaceae
Landscape use: Specimen, border, wildflower and woodland gardens, cut flower
Growth habit: Upright, spreading
Size of plant (H x W): 1' to 2' x 1' to 2'
Foliage color: Medium green to dark green
Time of bloom: September to frost
Color of bloom: White with purple spots
Size of bloom: 1" to 2.5"

Although not a heavy bloomer (its flowers often are nipped by frost along the Colorado Front Range) the hairy toad lily is unforgettable in bloom. The white star-shaped flowers are variably spotted with purple. They are thick and waxen in appearance, almost looking unreal. The stamens and stigmas are fused into a central column. The six tepals (a combination of both petals and sepals) are slightly recurved at the tips.

Hairy toad lily is a native of Japan where it is found in humus rich, shady woodlands. At PERC, it grows in partial shade at the base of taller plants that provide some protection. The upright stems bear alternate, fleshy leaves that clasp the stem. The leaf veins are parallel and deeply set. Stems and leaves are covered in soft hairs. The foliage and flowers are frost tender and often damaged by early fall frosts. Provide *T. hirta* with sufficient moisture and humus-enriched soil. Although it grows slowly following disturbance, it can be divided in spring or propagated by seed.

Trollius x cultorum 'Golden Queen'   Globeflower
(aka *T. ledebourii*)   ◗ ● ✂ (6)
Ranunculaceae (Helleboraceae)
Landscape use: Specimen, border, wildflower and woodland gardens, cut flower
Growth habit: Clump, erect flowering stems
Size of plant (H x W): 6" to 1' x 6" to 1'

Trollius x cultorum 'Golden Queen'

Veronica allioni

Foliage color: Medium green
Time of bloom: June- July, peak in early June
Color of bloom: Orangish-yellow
Size of bloom: 1" to 2.5"

The globeflower lends itself to the traditional perennial border as well as the pools and bogs of its native habitat. It has handsome, palmately divided and toothed leaves with globe-shaped or cup-shaped bright yellow to orange flowers held on erect stems. At PERC, it is planted in part shade. Full sun exposures are possible if given plenty of moisture. Globeflowers perform best with moisture retentive, rich soils.

'Golden Queen' has vivid orangish-yellow flowers that are held on stalks reaching 2 feet high. It makes an excellent cut flower. Deadheading prolongs the bloom, which peaks in early June.

Veronica   Speedwell, Bird's-eye
Scrophulariaceae   ○ ◗ ▧
Landscape use: Border, mass, ground cover, rock gardens

This variable genus contains over 250 species of plants that range from erect to prostrate in form. The leaves are opposite on the main plant and often alternate or whorled on the flowering stalks. In the PERC perennial garden, many speedwells grow successfully. They are generally non-temperamental given well-drained ordinary soil and sunny to lightly shaded exposures. Some are drought tolerant. Divide speedwells every few years to encourage compact, vigorous growth.

Although blue is the predominant color, white and pink flowering cultivars are available. Deadheading as soon as the first blooms fade encourages rebloom. Each flower generally is smaller than 0.5 inch but may be clustered in axillary or terminal racemes. The flower is a short tube with four or five spreading lobes and only two stamens. Petals

fall quickly after the flowers are picked, giving rise to the name speedwell or good-bye.

V. allioni   Swiss Mat Speedwell ❧ (12)
Growth habit: Creeping
Size of plant (H x W): 1" to 6" x 2' to 4'
Foliage color: Medium green, semi-evergreen
Time of bloom: Late May-early July, peak in early-mid-June
Color of bloom: Purplish blue
Size of bloom: Individually <0.5", inflorescence 2.5" to 5"

This species forms an effective ground cover of shiny, lanceolate leaves on prostrate stems. It is useful in the front of the border, walls, rock gardens, and slopes. It is vigorous and spreads indefinitely if not lifted and divided periodically. Flowering peaks in June when the plant is covered with intense purplish blue flowers in upright racemes that continue to elongate as flowers open from the bottom upwards. Plant this species in full sun. It is moderately drought tolerant and purportedly deer resistant. Cut back after bloom.

V. austriaca ssp. *teucrium*   Hungarian
'Royal Blue'   Speedwell (17)
(aka *V. teucrium*)
Growth habit: Upright, spreading
Size of plant (H x W): 1' to 2' x 4' to 6' (massed)
Foliage color: Medium green
Time of bloom: Late May to mid-July, peak in late June
Color of bloom: Deep blue
Size of bloom: Individually < 0.5", inflorescence 2.5" to 5"

This long-lived speedwell has grown into an impressive mass at PERC from five original plants. The leaves are slightly toothed, ovate at the base and lanceolate and sessile at the top of the stems. It grows

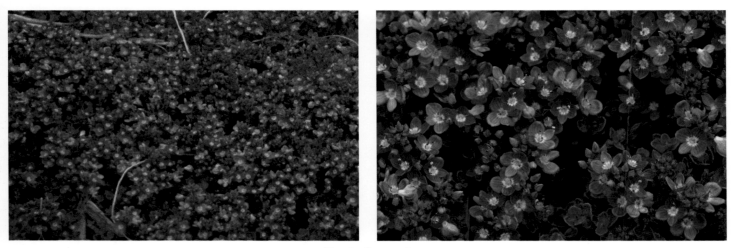

Veronica liwanensis

upright initially, then begins to sprawl outwards. Provide the plant with support if you find this unattractive and shear back hard after bloom.

The deep blue flowers are produced on loose axillary racemes unlike *V. spicata* that form terminal racemes. It reblooms moderately in the fall.

V. incana 'Minuet'   Silver Speedwell,
(aka *V. spicata subsp. incana,*   Woolly Speedwell (14)
Pseudolysimachion incanum)
Growth habit: Spreading
Size of plant (H x W): 1" to 6" x 1' to 2'
Foliage color: Gray-green
Time of bloom: Late June to mid-October
Color of bloom: Pink
Size of bloom: Individually <0.5", inflorescence >5"

This species is an excellent choice for the rock garden or xeriscape garden. It is similar to *V. spicata* described later, but has grayish-white hairs covering the leaves. Even when not in bloom, the silvery foliage provides a soft contrast to the typical green of other plants. *V. incana* is intolerant of excess moisture and performs best in full sun and low humidity. The species has blue flowers. Minuet is a bright pink flowering cultivar whose flower stalks reach 1 foot in bloom.

V. liwanensis   Turkish Veronica
     ❧ PS-1997 (4)

Growth habit: Creeping
Size of plant (H x W): 1" to 2" x 2' to 4'
Foliage color: Medium green, evergreen
Time of bloom: Late May to early September
Color of bloom: Light blue
Size of bloom: < 0.5"

Turkish veronica's shiny ovate leaves produces a low mat of evergreen foliage that turns purplish in the hot sun. An adaptable species, it grows well in clay, loam, or sand with either moderate to dry watering regimes. It is useful as a ground cover, between flagstones, or in a rock garden. The light blue flowers have a white central eye and are produced on racemes reaching three inches tall. Turkish veronica is one of the most popular Plant Select® introductions.

V. pectinata   Comb Speedwell,
     Blue Woolly Veronica ❧ ❖ (13)
Growth habit: Creeping
Size of plant (H x W): 1" to 6" x 2' to 4'
Foliage color: Light green to gray-green, evergreen
Time of bloom: April to mid-October, peak in late May
Color of bloom: Purplish blue
Size of bloom: Individually <0.5", inflorescence 1" to 2.5"

Blue woolly speedwell has many different characteristics that make it easy to identify. The prostrate stems bear wedge-shaped leaves that are deeply lobed. The plant is covered with fine hairs giving it a gray cast. It is drought tolerant. Use it to sprawl over a wall or between stones. This species is vigorous and requires division or periodic shearing to contain.

The purplish blue flowers have a white center and four lobes. Blue woolly speedwell is one of the first veronicas to bloom in the spring. It even-blooms sporadically during a warm winter.

V. peduncularis 'Georgia Blue'   (4)
(aka *V. p.* 'Oxford Blue')
Growth habit: Spreading to mounded
Size of plant (H x W): 6" to 1' x 1' to 2'
Foliage color: Medium green to dark green with purple tints, semi-evergreen
Time of bloom: Mid-May to mid-July, fall rebloom
Color of bloom: Deep blue
Size of bloom: < 0.5"

V. peduncularis has bluntly-toothed lanceolate

Veronica spicata 'Icicle'   *Veronica spicata* 'Red Fox'   *Veronica* 'Sunny Border Blue'

to ovate leaves held on wiry reddish purple stems. The foliage can have a slight purplish cast and colors a rich reddish purple in the fall. It forms a dense mound, but spreads through branching rhizomes.

The deep blue flowers with white centers are found in loose axillary racemes. They tremble in the breeze. 'Georgia Blue' is more vigorous than the species. At PERC, this it is planted next to tall grasses that shade it considerably. The bloom has been sparser than if planted in full sun.

V. spicata   Spike Speedwell
(aka *Psuedolysimachion spicatum*)   (20)
Growth habit: Upright to mounded
Size of plant (H x W): 6" to 1' x 1' to 2'
Foliage color: Medium green
Time of bloom: Mid June- October, peak in late June-mid July
Color of bloom: Blue
Size of bloom: Individually <0.5", inflorescence >5"

Spike speedwell gets its name from the long, terminal flower racemes. The upright growth habit and dense, spiky flower clusters create a strong vertical accent. The species has medium green leaves with rounded teeth and blue flowers. It performs best in full sun. A fungal leaf spot or mildew can develop or the lower leaves may drop in shady, crowded conditions. For a range of sizes and flower colors, there are many cultivars and hybrids to choose from.
V. s. 'Icicle'   (4)
This floriferous white flowering cultivar bloomed from July through mid-October at PERC. The flower spikes reach two to three feet in height.
V. s. 'Red Fox'   (12)
Deep pink flowers cover this cultivar from late June through mid-October. It is more compact than 'Icicle' reaching one foot in bloom.
V. s. 'Rosea'   (8)
This light pink flowering cultivar blooms from

late June through early October and is similar to 'Red Fox' in habit.

V. 'Sunny Border Blue'   ✄ PPY-1993 (8)
Growth habit: Upright
Size of plant (H x W): 1' to 2' x 1' to 2'
Foliage color: Dark green
Time of bloom: Late June to early October, peak in mid-July to early August
Color of bloom: Dark purplish blue
Size of bloom: Individually <0.5", inflorescence >5"

This hybrid resulted from a cross between *V. spicata* and *V. longifolia*. It was introduced in 1947 by Sunny Border Nurseries in Connecticut and was named the Perennial Plant of the Year in 1993 for its deep green crinkly leaves and dark violet blue flowers. At PERC it has minor problems with mildew and loses the lower leaves on the stems during the summer. Plant other perennials or annuals in front to hide the bare stems. It is very showy when in bloom.

***Veronicastrum virginicum* 'Album'**   Culver's Root,
(aka *Veronica virginica*,   Bowman's Root,
Leptandra virginica)   Black Root, Tall Speedwell
Scrophulariaceae   ◐ ◗ ⚘ 🦋 (4)
Landscape use: Specimen, background, border, wildflower gardens
Growth habit: Clump, erect flowering stems
Size of plant (H x W): 2' to 4' x 1' to 2'
Foliage color: Dark green
Time of bloom: July-October (frost)
Color of bloom: White
Size of bloom: < 0.5"

This veronica look-alike provides a bold vertical accent in the perennial garden. The foliage is toothed, lance shaped, and held in horizontal whorls of three to five leaves around the stem. In bloom, long terminal racemes of tiny white or pale lavender flowers with prominent stamens look somewhat like

Veronicastrum virginicum 'Album'

Yucca glauca

an elaborate candelabra. The plant can reach heights of 6 feet in bloom. Album is a cultivar with white flowers and dark green foliage.

V. virginicum is native to the Northeastern United States and Canada where it is found in woodlands and meadows. At PERC, it is sited in a south facing bed under an immature tree that casts light shade. It is adaptable to most soils as long as they are well drained. Regardless of its size, it rarely needs staking. Bees are fond of the flowers.

Yucca
Agavaceae   ○ ❖ ⬟

Landscape use: Specimen, rock and xeriscape gardens
Growth habit: Clump, erect flowering stems
Size of plant (H x W): 2' to 4' x 2' to 4'
Foliage color: Blue-green to gray-green, evergreen

Yuccas are rosette forming evergreen perennials with sword-shaped leaves that often are spine tipped. Their symmetrical form and rounded growth habit make them an excellent specimen plant for a dry border, rock garden or xeriscape garden. Grouped, they create an effective barrier to discourage traffic. Tap rooted and drought tolerant, these plants thrive in sandy poor soils and hot, dry climates. The species at PERC adapted well to the heavier clay and are long-lived. Seed propagation is slow. Separating the off-shoots from the base of the main plant is the easiest way to propagate yuccas.

Y. filamentosa
Spanish Bayonet, Adam's Needle (18)
Time of bloom: July to early August, peak in late July
Color of bloom: White to cream
Size of bloom: 1" to 2.5"

Adam's needle is native to the Southeastern United States. Its name is derived from the curly threads that hang from the margins and tips of each leaf. The erect panicle reaches three to six feet tall and holds nodding, bell-shaped creamy white flowers in midsummer. Several plants have survived in what is now a partly shaded bed, but they have not bloomed. Fruit is rare in cultivation since the main pollinator is the yucca moth.

Y. glauca
Soapweed, Small Soapweed, Soapwell (19)
Time of bloom: Mid June-late July, peak in late June
Color of bloom: Greenish white to cream
Size of bloom: 2.5" to 5"

This clump former has slender, rigid, sharply pointed blue-green leaves that are painful to work around. It is native to Western and Central regions of the United States and to parts of Canada. It is reliably cold hardy. The inflorescence is shorter than *Y. filamentosa*, reaching three feet high. The greenish white flowers may have a rosy brown tint to them.

Best Performing Ornamental Grasses

Ornamental grasses have become popular additions to the garden for many reasons. Although lacking in the brightly colored flowers of traditional perennials, grasses provide a wide range of foliage colors and textures, come in a variety of sizes and growth habits, and provide a sense of line and movement unrivaled by the standard perennial choices. Often the foliage is the main ornamental feature. Fall colors can match the hues of the changing deciduous trees and the winter presence helps provide continual interest and structure to the otherwise sleeping garden. When in bloom, ornamental grasses provide color, height, texture, and contrast with inflorescences that can be used as cut flowers, dried for arrangements, or left to ripen for the birds.

The ornamental grasses featured in this publication belong to the family Poaceae (Gramineae.) There are several characteristics to consider when choosing the right ornamental grass for your garden. Cool-season grasses will grow best at temperatures of 60° to 70° F. Growth begins either in fall or early spring and slows or stops altogether in hot temperatures. These grasses often bloom in the spring and require more moisture than warm season grasses. Warm-season grasses thrive in temperatures between 80° and 95° F. Flowering times occur late in the summer, early in autumn, or not at all in areas with a short growing seasons. The foliage often turns brilliant colors in the fall and is dormant in the winter.

Grasses may either be spreading or clumping. Spreading grasses will cover an area by producing stolons above ground or rhizomes under the ground. This quality is important when desiring a ground cover. However, given the right conditions, spreading grasses can become invasive. Clumping grasses or bunch grasses come in various forms from tufted to arching. They remain in separate bunches and grow in width from the crown. Unless planted very close together, bunch grasses will not create a turf or close-knit ground cover.

The following ornamental grasses have performed reliably at PERC:

Andropogon gerardii

Calamagrostis x acutiflora 'Overdam'

Andropogon gerardii   Big Bluestem,
Turkey Foot ○ ◗ ✂ ✿ ❖ ⚰ (6)

Landscape use: Specimen, border, background, mass, wildflower and xeriscape gardens, cut and dried flower
Growth habit: Erect clump, warm-season grass
Size of plant (height x width): 2' to 4' x 1' to 2'
Color of foliage: Medium to blue-green
Time of bloom: Late August to early October
Color of bloom: Purplish-red maturing to reddish brown

This North American native was one of the primary forage grasses found in the tall grass prairies. The foliage is held erect in full sun and will become lax and weeping in part shade. It can reach sizes well over four feet high if given plenty of moisture and a long growing season. At PERC, big bluestem grew to three or four feet with flowering stalks reaching six feet in height. The foliage color may be variable, with some plants showing strong blue coloration. The tips of the leaves are tinted purple in summer.

By late August or early September, big bluestem sends up a unique three-parted inflorescence resembling the toes of a turkey foot. The blooms are purplish-red and have orange stamens. Fall coloration is excellent with the foliage turning a rich copper to purplish red. The dormant winter foliage is tan.

Big bluestem grows best in full sun with adequate moisture. It can tolerate periods of drought but is not recommended for low watering zones in the xeriscape garden. Clay soils do not present a problem as long as they are adequately drained and moderately fertile. No winter injury, disease, or insect problems were experienced at PERC.

Calamagrostis   Reed Grass
○ ◗ ✂ ✿

Landscape use: Specimen, border, background, massed, cut or dried flower
Size of plant (height x width): 2' to 4' x 1' to 2'

This genus includes approximately 250 species originating from the temperate northern hemisphere. Although the native habitat of many reed grasses is moist, even marshy, meadows and woodlands the three grasses of merit trialed at PERC have required no special care. The two described in detail have survived the minimum three years required for this publication.

Reed grasses should be cut back to the crown late winter or early spring. They can be propagated by division most successfully in the spring.

C. x acutiflora 'Overdam'   Feather Reed Grass (5)
Growth habit: Erect, clumping cool-season grass
Color of foliage: Variegated, medium green with cream stripes
Time of bloom: June
Color of bloom: Pinkish green maturing to a gold

This variegated feather reed grass is vertical in habit, making an excellent accent plant or, when massed, a natural screen. The medium textured green leaves are striped with cream. Colorado's climate of low humidity and cool summer nights preserves the strong contrast in leaf colors.

The flowers are held erect in slender spikes, which emerge open and feathery then tighten into narrow seedheads. The maturing fruit is golden brown and persists into winter. The stiff, narrow flowering stalks provide an especially dramatic "exclamation point" to the winter landscape.

Along the Front Range of the Colorado Rocky Mountains, Overdam feather reed grass prospers in locations partially shaded from the hot sun. It has been tolerant of the heavy clay soils at PERC.

Calamagrostis brachytricha

Festuca cinerea

Overdam feather reed grass is purportedly less vigorous than the species. At PERC, no problems have been noted in the five years it has been grown.

Another excellent cultivar of feather reed grass is Karl Foerster. It is not variegated but has deep green foliage. It was named the perennial plant of the year for 2001. At the time of this publication, 'Karl Foerster' had been at PERC for only 2 years.

C. brachytricha   Fall-blooming Reed Grass, Korean Feather Reed Grass (4)
(aka *Stipa brachytricha, Achnatherum brachytricha*)
Growth habit: Upright, arching warm-season grass
Color of foliage: Medium green
Time of bloom: September
Color of bloom: Pinkish green, maturing silver
Korean feather reed grass is tolerant of partially shady sites, making this an especially versatile ornamental grass. It grows into an upright clump with arching leaves. Unlike Overdam feather reed grass, the pinkish green flowers stay open and feathery, eventually maturing to silver. They are excellent as fresh or dried cut flowers. Bloom time is late in the summer to early fall.

Korean feather reed grass turns yellow in the fall and is winter dormant. It is reliably cold hardy. In full sun and hot climates, this species requires adequate moisture weekly.

Deschampsia caespitosa   Tufted Hair Grass, Tussock Grass ○ ◗ ⨯ (8)
Landscape use: Border, massed, wildflower gardens
Growth habit: Tufted to mounded cool-season grass
Size of plant (height x width): 1' to 2' x 1' to 2'
Color of foliage: Medium green
Time of bloom: Mid-June to July
Color of bloom: Greenish yellow maturing to gold
This cool-season grass is tolerant of moist, partly shady sites and heavy soils. It forms a dense mound of foliage that is a favorite snack of rabbits. The flowers appear in June and extend a foot higher than the foliage. The inflorescence matures to a golden color, remaining attractive until shattered by snow.

Although native to portions of North America, those sold in the nursery trade are most likely to be of European origin. There are several cultivars available which provide a range of flower colors and one, Northern Lights, has variegated foliage. Tufted hair grass grows poorly in hot, dry sites.

Festuca   Fescue
                                         ○ ◗ ⨯
Landscape use: Ground cover, border, mass
Growth habit: Mounded tuft, cool season grass
Color of foliage: Blue-green to blue-gray, evergreen
This genus contains many fine grasses perfect for a ground cover, border along a pathway, or accent plant. Authorities often disagree upon the origin and nomenclature of the many species and cultivars available. Seed propagation produces much variability in foliage color and size further complicating the distinctions for nurseries and consumers. The cultivars are best propagated by division to preserve the special traits they claim.

The ornamental fescues are densely tufted. These cool season evergreen grasses prosper in the spring and fall and often look shabby in the heat of summer. In hot weather, fescue can go dormant. Growth begins again in the fall. Old clumps tend to die out in the center and may need replanting every three to four years. By late winter, fescue can be sheared back to reshape. This genus requires regular moisture, but well drained soils and can tolerate light shade.

Helictotrichon sempervirens

Miscanthus sinensis 'Gracillimus'

F. amethystina **'Superba'**   Sheep's Fescue, Large Blue Fescue, Tufted Fescue (11)

Color of bloom: Pink, maturing tan

Sheep's fescue shares many of the same features as blue fescue described next and can be used in the garden under the same circumstances. The foliage is blue-gray and slightly weeping. The flowers of the cultivar Superba emerge pink and are held on purplish stalks reaching two feet tall. This color combination remains showy for several weeks. The foliage takes on shades of orange and red in the fall.

F. cinerea   Blue Fescue, Garden Fescue, Gray Fescue (6)
(aka *F. ovina, F. glauca, F. ovina* var. *glauca*)
Size of plant (height x width): 6" to 1' x 6" to 1'
Time of bloom: Mid-May to June
Color of bloom: Green, maturing tan

The finely textured leaves of blue fescue range from blue-green to blue-gray depending on the parentage. Many cultivars are available with distinct leaf colors that are maintained by vegetative propagation.

Blue fescue blooms in late spring to early summer. The inflorescence, which is not particularly showy, matures to a tan color. In fact, you may wish to remove the flowering stalks to preserve the neat appearance and emphasize the foliage color of the plant. Try blue fescue in containers for a dramatic accent plant.

Helictotrichon sempervirens   Blue Oat Grass, Blue Avena Grass
(aka *Avena sempervirens*)
◖ ◗ (12)
Landscape use: Specimen, border, background, mass
Growth habit: Clumping, cool season grass
Size of plant (height x width): 2' to 4' x 2' to 4'
Color of foliage: Blue-green to blue-gray

Time of bloom: End of May- June
Color of bloom: Blue-green, maturing golden brown

The intensely blue-green to blue-gray foliage of this grass makes it an excellent specimen or accent plant. The foliage is sharply pointed and held in a stiff mound that remains attractive nearly year round. The flowers are showy through June, and are held two feet above the foliage. Upon maturity the seed heads are golden brown. The inflorescence shatters, however, scattering seed throughout the garden. Seedlings are easy to locate and pull out if unwanted.

Ideal growing conditions include fertile, well-drained soils, and cool, wet springs. At PERC, blue oat grass is grown in full sun with no special care.

Miscanthus sinensis **'Gracillimus'**   Eulalia Grass,
(aka *Eulalia japonica* var. *gracillima*)   Japanese Silver Grass
◖ ◗ ✂ ❀ (14)
Landscape use: Specimen, border, background, mass, fresh cut or dried flower
Growth habit: Clumping, erect to vase-shaped warm season grass
Size of plant (height x width): 4' to 6' x 2' to 4'
Color of foliage: Medium green
Time of bloom: Late September-October
Color of bloom: Pink, maturing silver

This Japanese silver grass cultivar has grown into an imposing mass at PERC. Although it does not bloom reliably, requiring a long hot season for flower formation, the foliage makes an attractive screen or accent. The clump is strongly erect at the base and arches outward at the top. The medium textured foliage is green with a silver midrib. In the fall, the leaves turn golden with orange and red highlights before bleaching to a straw color. The individual leaves can be cut to add to fresh or dried flower arrangements. They twist as they dry.

Flowers of the Japanese silver grass are pink and

Panicum virgatum

Pennisetum alopecuroides 'Hameln'

very showy. Their ornamental value extends into the winter, when the mature seed heads fade to silver. This grass reaches heights of six feet at PERC and requires a sharp blade or sturdy string trimmer to cut back in the early spring. In overly moist, fertile soils it can become floppy in growth habit. Division of a large, mature clump should be done in the spring, although this is no simple task.

Panicum virgatum   Switch Grass
○ ☽ ✂ ✿ ⚲ (15)

Landscape use: Specimen, border, background, mass, wildflower garden, cut and dried flower
Growth habit: Erect to vase shaped clump, warm season grass
Size of plant (height x width): 4' to 6' x 2' to 4'
Color of foliage: Medium green
Time of bloom: End of July to August
Color of bloom: Pinkish green maturing to tan

Switch grass is native to the North American tall grass prairies. It is a warm season clumping grass with an upright to vase shaped form that becomes more lax in shade. The open panicles of pinkish to purplish green flowers hover delicately over the foliage and wave dramatically in the wind. Several cultivars are now available that offer variations in color from the steel blue leaves of 'Heavy Metal' to the reddish orange fall color found in 'Haense Herms.'

Switch grass is adaptable and easy to grow. It grows best in full sun and moist, fertile soil but can tolerate soil extremes. The fall foliage color is golden yellow. In winter the dormant foliage is beige. Lodging is a common problem noted at PERC. Cut back in late winter or early spring before the new growth begins. Propagate by spring division or seed.

Pennisetum alopecuroides 'Hameln'   Dwarf
(aka *P. japonicum*)   Fountain Grass
○ ☽ ✂ ✿ (8)

Landscape use: Specimen, border, mass, wildflower and meadow gardens, fresh cut or dried flower
Growth habit: Mounded clump, warm season grass
Size of plant (height x width): 1' to 2' x 1' to 2'
Color of foliage: Medium green
Time of bloom: Mid-August to September
Color of bloom: Greenish white, maturing to tan

The fountain grasses are warm season clumping grasses whose common name is derived from its floriferous nature ("fountain of flowers.") *P. alopecuroides* is the most commonly grown cold hardy species. The cultivar Hameln grown at PERC is a dwarf form reaching two feet in height. It is fine textured and mounded in growth habit. The flowers are greenish white, dense, and cylindrical. They are excellent for fresh or dried use.

Dwarf fountain grass requires regular moisture to perform well. It is hardy to zone 5 or 6, but has overwintered consistently at PERC with winter mulch. The fall color is gold.

P. alopecuroides 'Little Bunny'   (8)
This cultivar is smaller than Hameln reaching 10-12" in height.

Saccharum ravennae   Hardy Pampas Grass, Plume
(aka *Erianthus ravennae*)   Grass, Ravenna Grass
○ ☽ ✂ ✿ (6)

Landscape use: Specimen, border, background, cut or dried flower
Growth habit: Upright to mounded, clumping warm-season grass
Size of plant (height x width): 4' to 6' x 2' to 4'
Color of foliage: Light green
Time of bloom: Mid to late August
Color of bloom: Pinkish green, maturing silver

Hardy pampas grass is a coarse textured warm

Schizachyrium scoparium

season grass. The pale green to gray-green leaves have a central white stripe. At PERC, in the shade of two crab apple trees, the clump has only grown to four feet in height. Along the front range and in full sun, this grass can reach 6 feet with flowering stalks up to 10 feet. There are few grasses hardy to this region that will achieve these proportions. Use S. ravennae as a substitute for the true but tender pampas grass, *Cortaderia selloana*.

Hardy pampas grass flowers late summer to early fall after a long, hot growing season. The stout flower stalks bare silky pinkish green blooms that mature to a translucent silver. The inflorescence can be used fresh or dried if cut before fully expanded. The flower stalks turn burgundy and the foliage shows tints of purple and orange in the fall. The winter presence of the flowers and foliage remains excellent.

Although drought tolerant once established, hardy pampas grass performs best with regular watering. It requires full sun for the most upright growth and consistent flowering. Grown with too much water and fertility, this grass will become lanky and unkempt. Cut back each spring before new growth begins. Divide the clump when the center dies out or start over with new plants since it is difficult to lift a grass this size.

Schizachyrium scoparium   Little Bluestem, Prairie
(aka *Andropogon scoparius*)   Beard Grass, Broom
Sedge ◯ ◗ ❖ ⤙ (6)

Landscape use: Specimen, border, mass, wildflower and xeriscape gardens
Growth habit: Erect clump, warm season grass
Size of plant (height x width): 2′ to 4′ x 1′ to 2′
Color of foliage: Medium green
Time of bloom: Mid-August to September
Color of bloom: Pinkish green, maturing tan

This grass, native to the open, dry prairies of North America, is an excellent choice for the Front Range. It is tolerant of a wide range of growing conditions and soil types. The fine textured foliage is medium green, but some seedlings may be blue-green. The leaf tips are often tinted purple.

Little bluestem flowers in late summer to early fall. The flower stalks extend a foot or more above the foliage. At PERC bloom was often curtailed by early snowstorms or frosts. The fall color of this grass, however, make it worthwhile for the perennial garden. With cool nights the foliage turns orange, red and purple.

Little bluestem performs best in full sun with average soil and good drainage. It tends to be short lived in xeriscape or drier meadow gardens.

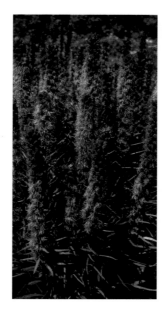

GLOSSARY

Achene ❧ The small, dry, indehiscent (non-splitting) fruit of a plant in which the seed is only attached to the ovary wall in one place. The sunflower is an example of an achene fruit.

Background plant ❧ Landscape use: A larger sized plant that can be used at the back of the perennial border.

Basal ❧ Located at the base of an organ or structure.

Biennial ❧ A plant that lives for two growing seasons only, dying after reproducing in the second season.

Border-Landscape use ❧ A permanent planting bed that is traditionally , but not n ecessarily, long and narrow. Borders may consist of herbaceous perennials or a mixture of herbaceous and woody plants.

Boss ❧ A dense cluster of stamens.

Bract ❧ A modified leaf associated with a flower or group of flowers.

Calyx ❧ The name for the sepals either referred to collectively or when structurally combined.

Chlorosis ❧ The yellowing of plant parts (most often the leaves) which is often a symptom of mineral deficiency or disease. At PERC, chlorosis is most often associated with lack of iron, although magnesium, manganese, and zinc deficiencies can also result in chlorosis.

Clasping ❧ A term indicating that the leaf is stalkless and partially surrounds (clasps) the stem.

Clump ❧ The growth habit of a plant which grows from the crown in a distinct bunch. Not spreading.

Compound ❧ A term used to describe a leaf divided into two or more distinct parts (leaflets) or a flower made up of florets (little flowers). See floret, pinnate, and palmate for further definition.

Cordate ❧ Heart-shaped. Used to describe a leaf with a lobed, rounded base and a pointed tip.

Corolla ❧ The name for the petals either referred to collectively or when structurally combined.

Corymb ❧ A type of inflorescence made up of many flowers held in a flat topped or rounded cluster. In contrast to the umbel, the flower stalks (pedicels) are of varying lengths. The corymb differs from the cyme in that it is indeterminate in growth with the outer flowers opening up first.

Creeping ❧ The growth habit of a plant which grows near ground level often forming a mat.

Crown ❧ The basal portions of a herbaceous plant, usually where the aerial stems and the roots meet.

Crown rot ❧ Rot of the crown caused either by bacteria or fungi and often initiated due to poor cultural practices.

Cultivar ❧ The shortened term meaning "cultivated variety." A cultivar has one or more traits that are distinctly different from the species and is produced through the propagative efforts of man.

Cut flower-Landscape use ❧ The flowers can be cut fresh and used in arrangements. They may be fragrant, long lasting, or especially showy.

Cyme ❧ A type of inflorescence made up of many flowers held in a flat topped or rounded cluster. In contrast to the umbel, the flower stalks (pedicels) are of varying lengths. The cyme differs from the corymb in that it is determinate in growth with the central flowers opening up first.

Determinate ❧ A description of growth habit in which the terminal flower opens first ending further elongation of the inflorescence.

Divide ❧ A propagation method in which a plant is split into several pieces each with its own root system and shoot.

Dieback ❧ Death of a shoot usually from the tip downwards caused by disease, mechanical or insect damage, or cultural difficulties.

Diploid ❧ Having two sets of chromosomes.

Dried flower ❧ The flowers or fruit can be cut and dried for

arrangements or left on the plant to provide winter texture and interest in the garden.

Erect ❧ The growth habit of a plant that is upright and vertical in appearance; perpendicular to the gound. Often used interchangeably with "upright."

Erosion control-Landscape use ❧ The plant spreads through rhizomes or stolons and can cover an area rapidly enough to prevent soil erosion from wind or water.

Floret ❧ A small flower most often found in the family Compositae (Asteraceae) or in a dense inflorescence. The typical daisy flower of an aster, sunflower, or mum is composed of outer ray florets which are petal-like and the disk florets which are tubular, reduced, and usually arranged in the center.

Glaucous ❧ Used to describe the blue-green to blue-grey appearance of a leaf that is covered with a waxy coating or fine bloom that is easily rubbed off.

Ground cover-Landscape use ❧ Typically a low-growing plant that spreads by rhizomes or stolons and is used to cover bare ground and/or suppress weeds.

Herb garden-Landscape use ❧ A plant that is either used for medicinal or culinary purposes, or one that lends itself to use in a herb garden through historical reference.

Hybrid ❧ The progeny resulting from the cross of two distinct and dissimilar parental lines.

Indeterminate ❧ A description of growth habit in which the lowest flowers open first and elongation of the inflorescence continues until conditions are no longer satisfactory.

Inflorescence ❧ A cluster of flowers and their accessory parts that is found in a distinct arrangement such as a par icle, umbel, cyme, corymb, spike, or raceme.

Involucre ❧ A group of bracts or small leaves underneath a flower or inflorescence.

Keel ❧ The prominent ridge found on the underside and middle of some leaves (much like the keel of a boat) or the fused lower petals of the flowers typical of the pea family.

Lanceolate ❧ Used to describe a leaf that is lance or sword-shaped, i.e. the leaf is longer than its width and has a pointed tip.

Lodge ❧ To fall over.

Mass-Landscape use ❦ Planting in multiple numbers to increase the visual effect of a plant in the garden.

Melt-out ❦ The disintegration of a spreading plant most often beginning in the center and due to over watering or poorly drained soils.

Mounded ❦ The growth habit of a plant which is full at ground level and rounded at top, i.e. semi-circular in silhouette.

Nodes ❦ The region of a stem where one or more leaves are attached.

Ovate ❦ Used to describe a leaf that is egg-shaped with the broadest part found below the middle of the leaf and about 1.5 to 2 times as long as it is broad.

Palmate ❦ A term indicating that the leaflets of a compound leaf radiate from a single point. When using to describe the lobes in a single leaf, the term indicates that the indented part points towards the leaf stalk or petiole much like fingers on a hand.

Panicle ❦ An inflorescence arrangement that is a much branched raceme and is indeterminate in growth.

Perennial ❦ A plant that lives for three or more growing seasons.

Picotee ❦ A color combination in which the outer edge of the flower is a contrasting color to the inner portion of the flower.

Pinnate ❦ A term indicating that the leaflets of a compound leaf are arranged in rungs along a central axis. The leaflets may be opposite each other or alternate to each other.

Pistil ❦ The female reproductive organ of a flower consisting of the ovary, style, and stigma.

Raceme ❦ An inflorescence arrangement in which each flower is attached to a central stalk by an individual flower stalk or pedicel. A raceme is indeterminate in growth.

Rhizomatous ❦ Producing or possessing rhizomes.

Rhizome ❦ A horizontal stem that has nodes and buds, grows underground or at ground level and will send up aerial shoots.

Rock garden-Landscape use ❦ Plants that are useful in a rock garden are often but not always compact, perform best with stony, well drained soil, or are found naturally in rocky environments.

Rosette ❦ The growth habit characterized by the leaves radiating from the crown of the plant instead of from an upright network of stems.

Scape ❦ The leafless stalk of a flower or inflorescence arising most often from a rosette of leaves.

Sepal ❦ The individual component of the calyx. A petal-like or sometimes leaf-like structure of a flower, which is found underneath the petals and may or may not be brightly colored.

Sessile ❦ Stalkless.

Sheath ❦ The basal part of the leaf that surrounds a stem in a grass or a tubular, elongated structure that surrounds another plant part.

Shear ❦ To cut back hard.

Simple ❦ Opposite to "compound" when describing a leaf or flower arrangement. One leaf that may or may not be lobed but is not divided into separate leaflets or an unbranched flower arrangement.

Specimen-Landscape use ❦ A plant that can be used singly as a focal point due to size and/or unique features.

Spike ❦ A unbranched inflorescence with each flower directly attached (sessile) to the central stalk. The growth is indeterminate.

Spreading ❧ The growth habit of a plant, which grows outward in size through vegetative means such as stolons or root suckers.

Stigma ❧ The top portion of the pistil, which receives the pollen.

Stolon ❧ The prostrate or trailing above ground stem of a plant that roots at the nodes and sends up shoots. A runner.

Style ❧ The part of the pistil that connects the ovary with the stigma.

Subtend ❧ Inserted below a different organ.

Succulent ❧ Fleshy and thickened.

Sucker ❧ An adventitious shoot arising from the root system of a plant.

Taxa ❧ The plural form of taxon, the general term for a taxonomic group or unit.

Trifoliate ❧ Having three leaflets.

Tetraploid ❧ Having four sets of chromosomes.

Tuber ❧ A short, thick underground stem most often used for storage of food.

Tuberous ❧ Bearing tubers.

Umbel ❧ A flat-topped or rounded inflorescence arrangement in which the flowers are held on pedicels of approximately the same length and that arise from the same point.

Upright ❧ The growth habit of a plant that is erect and perpendicular to the ground. Often used interchangeably with "erect."

Variegated ❧ Marked irregularly with different colors, usually green and cream or green and white.

Vase-shaped ❧ The growth habit of a plant in which the base is narrow and the top flares outward.

Verticillaster ❧ A flower cluster commonly found with mints that appears to be a whorl but is actually a pair of dense cymes at the base of opposite leaves.

Whorl ❧ A circular arrangement of flowers or leaves in which three or more attach to the same node on the stalk or stem.

Wildflower garden-Landscape use ❧ Plants useful in wildflower gardens are usually but not necessarily native. Often these plants are important nectar plants for bees, butterflies, hummingbirds, and beneficial insects. They may be less suited to traditional perennial gardens due to a tendency to self-sow, a sprawling habit, unkempt appearance, or association with natural habitats. Or they may require a specific habitat that the gardener imitates from nature.

Woodland garden-Landscape use ❧ Plants that grow best in part shade to full shade exposures as an understory to trees and shrubs. These plants often perform best in humus rich, moist soils.

Xeriscape ❧ The term trademarked by and used with permission from the Denver Water Department to describe the use of plants adapted to dry sites in a landscape plan to conserve water and reduce maintenance.

Xeriscape garden-Landscape use ❧ A collection of plants that are adapted to drier conditions and arranged in compatible watering zones. A garden installed using the seven principles of xeriscape: plan and design, create practical turf areas, use appropriate plants and zone the landscape according the their water needs, improve the soil when necessary, mulch, irrigate efficiently, and maintain the landscape.

APPENDIX 1
AVERAGE BLOOM TIMES OF FLOWERING PLANTS

The following charts illustrate the average bloom times for most of the plants highlighted in this publication. Flowering data is collected yearly on the percent bloom covering a given species every week of the growing season beginning in April and ending with the first killing frost. An average was calculated and the percentages converted to a color value. Low bloom, the stage where the foliage is still predominant, is shown as the color green and represents 1-33 % plant coverage when in flower. Medium bloom is shown as the color gold and represents 34-66 % plant coverage. Purple represents the most bloom coverage from 67-100 %. The numerical average is shown in the charts so that the reader can distinguish between the slight bloom of 1% shown in green to that of 33% also in green etc.

The charts are first segregated by color of flower and then by approximate size of the plant when in bloom. This will allow homeowners, plant enthusiasts, and designers to search for a plant to fit a specific niche in their garden beds. The month and the week of the year is given as a guideline. The exact bloom date will vary with site, weather, and cultural conditions. Yet, the bloom pattern of each taxa is well represented by these charts.

After the scientific name a number is given in parentheses that represents the number of years that went into the average (not necessarily the number of years the plant has survived.) When two numbers are shown, the first number given represents how many different locations that taxa was planted at PERC.

Average Bloom Times for White Flowering Plants at PERC

Scientific Name / weeks of the year	April				May				June					July				August				September					October			
	14	15	16	17	18	19	20	21	22	23	24	25	26	27	28	29	30	31	32	33	34	35	36	37	38	39	40	41	42	43
Very Short Plants: 1"-6"																														
Galium odoratum (12) sweet woodruff														10	5															
Gypsophila repens (5) creeping baby's breath								30	33	75	86	77	67	59	28	26	30	26	24	20	39	33	33	33	30	33	30	5	5	
Iberis sempervirens 'Little Gem' evergreen candytuft						25	15	46	36	47	48	25																		
Ophiopogon planiscapus 'Nigrescens' (4) black mondo grass													60	40	43	9	25													
Sedum nevii (6) stonecrop									27	24	47	65	65	58	70	25														
Short Plants: 6"-12"																														
Anemone sylvestris (6) snowdrop anemone			40	60	43	55	73	48	32	23	23	3	10	1	23	10	10	7	8	8	11	8	8	11	12	12	15	13		
Aster 'White Fairy' (6) aster																		10	15	30	23	45	65	61	80	65	13	15		
Campanula carpatica 'White Clips' (6) Carpathian harebell												4	9	21	37	43	52	64	44	28	23	13	15	7	5	4	4			
Cerastium tomentosum 'Silver Carpet' (6) snow-in-summer								13	33	47	59	44	30	32	4	7	4													
Dianthus plumarius (6) cottage pink									26	63	92	94	69	50	26	17	15	10	4											
Heuchera micrantha 'Palace Purple' (4) small flowered alumroot														10	10	33	65	50	43	39	30	100	43	25						
Heuchera micrantha 'Chocolate Ruffles' (4) small flowered alumroot												60	25	20	28	50	10	32	40	7			5	40	40	50				
Iberis sempervirens 'Autumn Snow' evergreen candytuft						75	53	27	25	28	20	10																		
Iberis sempervirens 'Snowmantle' (6) evergreen candytuft				20	35	42	48	51	46	20	18																			
Oenothera speciosa 'Siskiyou' (5) compact Mexican evening primrose												50	43	71	95	83	88	36	24	18	11	11	18	25	10	10				
Polygonum affine 'Border Jewel' (5) knotweed								10	18	27	40	50	29	39	23	44	65	69	60	54	52	38	44	37	21	17	5			
Pulmonaria sacch. 'Sissinghurst White' (2) lungwort	80	100	75	50	50	20	50	30																						
Sedum spurium var. *album* (6) two-row sedum													30	38	91	74	68	40	18	15										

☐ = 1-33% bloom coverage   ▨ = 34-66% bloom coverage   ▦ = 67-100% bloom coverage

Average Bloom Times for White Flowering Plants at PERC

Medium Sized Plants: 1'-3'

Scientific Name / common name	April				May				June					July				August				September					October			
weeks of the year	14	15	16	17	18	19	20	21	22	23	24	25	26	27	28	29	30	31	32	33	34	35	36	37	38	39	40	41	42	43
Achillea ptarmica 'The Pearl' (5) / sneezewort											13	30	35	83	80	85	76	79	60	32	15	10	13	10	10	5	5	5		
Aster novi-belgii 'White Opal' (6) / New York aster																					20	55	92	88	50	39	5			
Anaphalis margaritacea (6) / pearly everlasting																10	25	25	47	82	100	83	74	81	88	87				
Aquilegia 'Dove' (4) / columbine								63	80	77	88	48	10	10																
Boltonia asteroides 'Snowbank' (4) / boltonia																		10	8	7	8	23	37	73	91	95	94	55	20	
Centranthus ruber 'Albus' (7) / white Jupiter's beard							10	15		29	64	88	100	66	40	19	13	9	12	14	33	22	32	41	37		33	21	20	5
Clematis recta (6) / bush clematis												50	88	100	50	20	20	10	40	50	50	40	10	5	5					
Dicentra spectabilis 'Alba' (5) / white bleeding heart							30	24	50	76	66	19	27	10																
Echinacea purpurea 'White Swan' (4) / white coneflower											5	5	10	33	67	75	87	83	90	83	80	60	30	50	42	31	10			
Filipendula vulgaris (4) / meadowsweet										10	50	77	47	10																
Hosta tsushimensis (2-11) / hosta																	10	15	46	45	54	66	52	43	31	80				
Iris lactea (3) / blue bouquet iris						12	35	43	47	23	4																			
Iris 'Stepping Little' (5) / bearded iris									38	44	23	50																		
Leucanthemum x superbum 'Esther Read' (2) / shasta daisy											50	88	100	100	50	20	20	10	40	50	50	40	10	5	5					
Liatris pychnostachya 'Alba' (6) / Kansas gayfeather														5	10	12	33	49	47	45	35	15	5							
Lilium species (6) / lily													10	80	73	40	75													
Paeonia 'Charlie's White' (6) / garden peony									33	36	51	100	10																	

Legend:
= 1-33% bloom coverage   = 34-66% bloom coverage   = 67-100% bloom coverage

Average Bloom Times for White Flowering Plants at PERC

Medium Sized Plants: 1'-3'

Scientific Name	April				May				June					July				August				September					October			
weeks of the year	14	15	16	17	18	19	20	21	22	23	24	25	26	27	28	29	30	31	32	33	34	35	36	37	38	39	40	41	42	43
Papaver orientale (2-12) oriental poppy									7	21	58	53	43	10																
Penstemon digitalis (6) beard-tongue									10	100	43	86	66	53	10	10		10	10	50	15	15	10							
Penstemon 'Husker Red' (6) beard-tongue									10	40	48	75	58	72	20	60	40	90	40	9										
Tricyrtis hirta (6) hairy toad lily																							15	17	22	28	15			
Veronica spicata 'Icicle' (4) spike speedwell														4	68	70	63	75	65	53	60	38	35	35	38	30	10			
Yucca filamentosa (6) Adam's needle														40	53	58	83	40												
Yucca glauca (2-11) soapweed											30	86	38	50	30	10														

Tall Plants: >3'

Scientific Name	April				May				June					July				August				September					October			
weeks of the year	14	15	16	17	18	19	20	21	22	23	24	25	26	27	28	29	30	31	32	33	34	35	36	37	38	39	40	41	42	43
Boltonia asteroides 'Snowbank' (4) boltonia																		10	8	7	8	23	37	73	91	95	94	55	20	
Centranthus ruber 'Alba' (7) white Jupiter's beard							10	15	29	64	88	100	84	66	40	19	13	9	12	14	33	22	32	41	41	37	33	21	20	5
Gaura lindheimeri (4) whirling butterflies															5	5	8	5	28	33	52	60	78	85	90	85	63	45	23	
Leucanthemella serotina 'Herbstern' (5) giant daisy																			4	14	34	81	91	81	68	48	10			
Leucanthemum x superbum (6) shasta daisy													7	45	73	89	93	82	54	40	32	10	5	5	5	5				
Paeonia 'Charlies White' (6) garden peony									51	36	33	100	10																	
Papaver orientale (2-12) oriental poppy									7	21	58	53	43	10																
Phlox paniculata 'David' (3) garden phlox																	18	57	70	65	39	40	28	18	28	32	20			
Veronicastrum virginicum 'Album' (4) culver's root														5	20	18	37	55	63	40	38	5	8	4	60	60	60	50	20	
Yucca filamentosa (6) Adam's needle														40	53	58	83	40												

■ = 1-33% bloom coverage   ■ = 34-66% bloom coverage   ■ = 67-100% bloom coverage

Very Short Plants: 1"- 6"																														

Average Bloom Times for Yellow and Orange Flowering Plants at PERC

Scientific Name / weeks of the year	April 14	15	16	17	May 18	19	20	21	June 22	23	24	25	26	July 27	28	29	30	Aug 31	32	33	34	Sept 35	36	37	38	39	Oct 40	41	42	43
Anthemis marschalliana (6) — Marshall chamomile								52	60	75	47	82	67	43					10	10										
Delosperma nubigenum (2-9) — yellow ice plant								8	20	38	26	24	20	28	10	25	10													
Lotus corniculatus 'Dwarf' (3) — dwarf bird's foot trefoil								20	35	52	40	25	8	10	10				10											
Lychnis 'Molten Lava' (6) — lychnis												70	61	36	25	38	50	30	17	10	10	10	10							
Lysimachia nummularia (6) — moneywort											10	25	73	66	75	69	40	10	10	10	10	4								
Short Plants: 6"- 12"																														
Alchemilla mollis 'Auslese' (2) — lady's mantle											75	70	73	50	43															
Aurinia saxatilis 'Compacta' (5) — dwarf basket-of-gold							63	93	35	10	10																			
Gaillardia x grandiflora 'Goblin' (2-8) — blanket flower												32	35	63	70	90	85	45	49	52	50	40	35	24	15	8	7	8	9	
Helianthemum 'Single Yellow' (6) — sun rose								8	30	38	68	74	66	44	13	13	12	25	10	7	8	5	5	5						
Lamium galeobdolon 'Herman's Pride' (6) — yellow archangel						30	70	83	72	61	50	25																		
Oenothera macrocarpa 'Fremontii' (4) — Ozark sundrops											50	51	36	80	25	10	18	20	19	8	13	10	5	5	3					
Oenothera macrocarpa (2-12) — Ozark sundrops													18	68	48	37	36	30	25	20	18	12	11	15	16	19	8	10		
Sedum aizoon (5) — aizoon stonecrop											25	39	70	90	28	18	8													
Sedum kamtschaticum 'Floriferum' (5) — Kamschatka stonecrop										59	55	40	13					4	4	4	4									
Sedum kamtschaticum 'Variegatum' (6) — Kamschatka stonecrop									10	27	52	87	61	51	45	10	10	10	10	4										

■ = 1-33% bloom coverage ■ = 34-66% bloom coverage ■ = 67-100% bloom coverage

Medium Sized Plants: 1'-3'

Average Bloom Times for Yellow and Orange Flowering Plants at PERC

Scientific Name / weeks of the year	April				May				June					July				August				September					October			
	14	15	16	17	18	19	20	21	22	23	24	25	26	27	28	29	30	31	32	33	34	35	36	37	38	39	40	41	42	43
Achillea filipendulina 'Coronation Gold' (6) fernleaf yarrow									10	19	36	68	63	87	94	82	98	87	78	64	56	39	31	22	17	18	15	12	9	
Achillea 'Moonshine' (6) yarrow									10	21	56	78	83	94	98	100	83	64	48	38	25	15	15	8	9	9	7	8		
Agastache rupestris (3) sunset hyssop																10	10	20	25	25	40			80	90	88	20	25		
Alchemilla mollis (6) lady's mantle									75	100	93	100	97	88	78	56	70	10												
Aurinia saxatilis 'Compacta' (5) dwarf basket-of-gold							63	93	35	10	10	10																		
Coreopsis verticillata (6) threadleaf coreopsis													19	64	94	93	72	52	21	12	12	7	12	8	10					
Coreopsis verticillata 'Moonbeam' (6) threadleaf coreopsis															30	64	61	73	61	63	60	60	58	54	50	28	10			
Digitalis grandiflora (5) large yellow foxglove											40	54	57	30	17	18	15	10	10											
Gaillardia x grandiflora 'Goblin' (2-8) blanket flower											32	35		63	70	90	85	45	49	52	50	40	35	24	15	8	7	8		
Geum chiloense 'Mrs. Bradshaw' (2-12) geum									28	63	73	68		73	38	33	16	11	11	9		18	16	20	9	8	8			
Hemerocallis 'Butter Curls' (6) daylily														25	24	60	36	27	28	9										
Hemerocallis 'Magic Wand' (5) daylily														30	34	70	48	30	40											
Hypericum calycinum (6) creeping St. Johnswort															10	10	11	14	15	25	8	7	10	10						
Kniphofia uvaria (13) red-hot poker										17	51	67	62	46	26	34	11													
Papaver orientale (2-12) oriental poppy									7	21	58	53	43	10																
Penstemon pinifolius 'Mersea Yellow' (5) yellow pineleaf penstemon									45	55	70	83	65	67	60	8	10	5	4	20	30									
Potentilla recta 'Macrantha' (2-12) sulphur cinquefoil									1	28	36	79	65	34	12	10	10	10	18	5	14	19	23	22	30	27	22	26	10	

Average Bloom Times for Yellow and Orange Flowering Plants at PERC

Medium Sized Plants: 1'- 3'

Scientific Name / common name	April				May				June					July				August				September					October			
weeks of the year	14	15	16	17	18	19	20	21	22	23	24	25	26	27	28	29	30	31	32	33	34	35	36	37	38	39	40	41	42	43
Rudbeckia fulgida sullivantii 'Goldsturm' (4) / orange coneflower													4	40	95	40	55	100	90	90	100	52	50	32	55	33	25	28		
Santolina chamaecyparissus (5) / lavender cotton													10	20		33	43	75	50											
Solidago virgaurea 'Peter Pan' (6) / European goldenrod															10	20	42	60	86	88	51	48	24	15	15	10	5	10		
x *Solidaster* 'Lemore' (3)																		25	53	57	40	10								
Trollius x cultorum 'Golden Queen' (6) / globeflower									10	70	34	30	50	40	30	30	20													

Tall Plants: > 3'

Scientific Name / common name	April				May				June					July				August				September					October			
weeks of the year	14	15	16	17	18	19	20	21	22	23	24	25	26	27	28	29	30	31	32	33	34	35	36	37	38	39	40	41	42	43
Achillea filipendulina 'Parker's Variety' (5) / fernleaf yarrow												20	36	63	76	83	90	88	88	79	84	78	59	42	40	30	13	15		
Alcea rugosa (4) / hollyhock																30	47	37	53	35	40	28	28	28	23	19	8			
Centaurea macrocephala (6) / globe centaurea												10	37	53	37	42	37	15	10											
Coreopsis verticillata (6) / threadleaf coreopsis													19	64	94	93	72	52	21	12	12	7	12	8	10					
Gaillardia aristata (4) / blanket flower												20	45	30	50	75	67	57	47	55	65	50	50	55	43	35	8	30		
Heliopsis helianthoides 'Incomparabilis' (6) / false sunflower												16	54	88	98	98	93	81	79	72	70	63	49	46	26	13	9	4		
Hemerocallis sp. (6) / daylily									5	10	55	55	28	38	35	59	53	20	4	10										
Heterotheca villosa (6) / hairy golden aster																				15	25	18	41	58	81	89	89	71	40	20
Kniphofia uvaria (13) / red-hot poker											17	51	62	46	26	34	11													
Oenothera glazioviana (6) / large flowered evening primrose											4	4	8	17	65	49	62	65	58	53	60	41	35	29	43	26	30	30		
Papaver orientale (2-12) / oriental poppy									7	21	58	53	43	10																
Phlomis russeliana (6) / sticky Jerusalem sage											8	48	91	78	70	15	4	5	5	10	25									

☐ = 1-33% bloom coverage   ☐ = 34-66% bloom coverage   ☐ = 67-100% bloom coverage

99

Average Bloom Times for Red Flowering Plants at PERC

Short Plants: 6"-12"

Scientific Name / weeks of the year	April 14	15	16	17	May 18	19	20	21	June 22	23	24	25	26	July 27	28	29	30	Aug 31	32	33	34	Sept 35	36	37	38	39	Oct 40	41	42	43
Gaillardia x grandiflora 'Goblin' (2-8) / blanket flower												32	35	63	70	90	85	45	49	52	50	40	35	24	15	8	7	8	9	
Heuchera sanguinea (5) / coral bells									10	33	33	63	68	95	93	83	53	18	15	17	23	23	20	17	15	15	10			
Pulsatilla vulgaris 'Rubra' (6) / European pasque flower	80	50	55	38	61	100	58	20	8	10																				
Sedum spurium 'Red Carpet' (6) / two-row sedum												90	85	88	60	65	63	32	25											

Medium Sized Plants: 1'- 3'

Scientific Name / weeks of the year	April 14	15	16	17	May 18	19	20	21	June 22	23	24	25	26	July 27	28	29	30	Aug 31	32	33	34	Sept 35	36	37	38	39	Oct 40	41	42	43
Achillea millefolium 'Red Beauty' (6) / common yarrow												25	50	100	60	80	75	89	78	73	78	47	47	31	38	53	75	50		
Aster novi-belgii 'Winston S. Churchill' (4) / New York aster																					10	40	38	57	87	90	75	57	60	10
Knautia macedonia (6) / knautia										10	15	34	48	70	77	77	64	53	43	42	37	41	38	39	46	32	28	14	10	
Lobelia cardinalis (4) / cardinal flower																	10	35	37	40	53	50	65	55	37	35	30			
Lupinus Russell Hybrids (6) / lupine								70	61	54	70	30	13	10					10	25	10									
Lychnis chalcedonica (6) / Maltese cross									60	65	93	92	91	69	11	55	25	18	6	8	8	13	14	25	16	30	7			
Monarda didyma (6) / beebalm														10	37	68	72	82	59	42	35	15	18	8	7	4				
Penstemon pinifolius (6) / pineleaf penstemon								1	9	71	84	78	87	77	58	57	51	40	21	19	20	7	10	10						

Tall Plants: > 3'

Scientific Name / weeks of the year	April 14	15	16	17	May 18	19	20	21	June 22	23	24	25	26	July 27	28	29	30	Aug 31	32	33	34	Sept 35	36	37	38	39	Oct 40	41	42	43
Centranthus ruber (7) / Jupiter's beard							10	15	29	64	88	100	84	66	40	19	13	9	12	14	33	22	32	41	41	37	33	21	20	5

☐ = 1-33% bloom coverage ☐ = 34-66% bloom coverage ☐ = 67-100% bloom coverage

100

Average Bloom Times for Pink Flowering Plants at PERC

Very Short Plants: 1"- 6"

Scientific Name / weeks of the year	April				May				June					July				August				September					October			
	14	15	16	17	18	19	20	21	22	23	24	25	26	27	28	29	30	31	32	33	34	35	36	37	38	39	40	41	42	43
Armeria maritima (6) — sea thrift							5	19	44	76	66	58	46	25	12	18	17	22	24	23	17	23	11	11	11	6	8	10		
Dianthus gratianopolitanus 'Tiny Rubies' (5) — Cheddar pink							50		40	74	81	58	49	22	4	5	4													
Geum triflorum (6) — prairie smoke						10	5	54	58	57	45	67	10																	
Lamium maculatum 'Pink Pewter'(6) — spotted dead nettle					4	4	4	10	5	35	41	65	57	46	23	9	7	8	10	15	15	25	8	6	8	8	8	4		
Oxalis crassipes 'Rosea' (4) — strawberry wood sorrel									20	30	100	57	63	45	28	40	55	100	86	86	80	55	43	55	58	68	50	32	40	
Phlox subulata (5) — moss phlox			15	18	42	58	76	75	53	33	40	30																		
Sempervivum arachnoideum (5) — hen and chicks												20	90	80	100	45	10													
Sempervivum tectorum 'Atropurpureum' (5) — hen and chicks															10	10	48	50	46	29	43	10								

Short Plants: 6"- 12"

Scientific Name / weeks of the year	April				May				June					July				August				September					October			
	14	15	16	17	18	19	20	21	22	23	24	25	26	27	28	29	30	31	32	33	34	35	36	37	38	39	40	41	42	43
Callirhoe involucrata (6) — purple poppy mallow									8	8	13	24	50	87	88	96	85	77	54	34	29	31	18	22	22	22	15	11		
Dianthus caryophyllus (6) — clove pink										35	56	74	53	10	8	10	10	10	4	4										
Dianthus nardiformis (5) — garden pink												4	22	30	40	38	41	42	48	36	27	24	23	25	22	24	20	10		
Geranium x oxonianum 'A.T. Johnson' (4) — cranesbill									20	53	60	70	70	90	53	57	43	40	23	38	30	12	15	25	18	23	10			
Geranium macrorrhizum 'Bevans Variety' (6) — bigroot geranium									5	38	31	38	28	10	10				10	5	5	10								
Helianthemum 'Wisley Pink' (3) — sun rose								4	17	70	37	25	10	20	5	5	4													
Heuchera micrantha 'Palace Passion' (3) — small flowered alumroot															30	90	48	15	17	25	10	10	20	60	30					
Oenothera speciosa 'Siskiyou' (5) — compact Mexican evening primrose											50	43	71	95	83	88	36	24	18	11	11	18	25	10	10					
Polygonum affine 'Border Jewel' (5) — knotweed								10	18	27	40	50	29	39	23	44	65	69	60	54	52	38	44	37	21	17	5			

■ = 1-33% bloom coverage   ■ = 34-66% bloom coverage   ■ = 67-100% bloom coverage

Average Bloom Times for Pink Flowering Plants at PERC

Short Plants: 6"- 12"

Legend:
- ▢ = 1-33% bloom coverage
- ▨ = 34-66% bloom coverage
- ▰ = 67-100% bloom coverage

Scientific Name	April				May				June					July					Aug.			Sept.					Oct.			
weeks of the year	14	15	16	17	18	19	20	21	22	23	24	25	26	27	28	29	30	31	32	33	34	35	36	37	38	39	40	41	42	43
Pulmonaria saccharata 'Mrs. Moon' (6) lungwort	20	45	70	68	45	36	27		32	8																				
Sedum spurium 'Bronze Carpet' (5) two-row sedum										25	100	100	10	55	37	70	75	77	39	15	12	13	25	15	10	10	10	10		
Sedum spurium 'Dragon's Blood' (6) two-row sedum													4	25	63	55	78	52	26	17	7			10		7	4			
Stachys byzantina (6) lambs'-ears												28	25	33	37	44	51	26	15	15	9	8	10	5						
Teucrium canadense (6) wild germander														8	20	21	28	29	35	23	26	23	15	12	15	7				
Teucrium chamaedrys (4) common germander																30	50	56	27	30		10	10	10						
Veronica incana 'Minuet' (6) silver speedwell													15	67	78	88	55	55	37	22	11	18	10	8	10	5	4	4		
Veronica spicata 'Red Fox' (6) spike speedwell													25	18	43	82	63	51	43	42	33	29	23	14	16	20	12	10		
Veronica spicata 'Rosea' (5) spike speedwell													10	31	53	73	76	74	43	38	25	24	15	11	9	7	5			
Medium Sized Plants: 1'- 3'																														
Acanthus balcanicus (4) bear's breeches													45	75	80	88	70	55	30	15	20	8	8	10						
Achillea millefolium 'Rosea' (6) common yarrow											8	23	55	97	73	69	83	75	56	53	46	38	28	15	10	8	13	18		
Aquilegia 'Robin' (6) columbine						25	25	45	56	62	72	37	29	25	18	10	10													
Aster novi-belgii 'Finalist' (6) New York aster																						11	59	98	89	81	69	25	5	
Centaurea dealbata 'Rosea' (6) knapweed										15	55	68	63	53	30	25	11	15	8	10	10	18	18	18	14		8	10		
Coreopsis rosea (2)																4	18	10	20	40	50	80	45	40	35	50	10			
Dianthus barbatus (4) sweet-william									10	33	100	92	97	100	53	25	20	10	20	20	20									
Dianthus caryophyllus (6) clove pink										35	56	74	53	10	8	10	10		4	4				15	10	9	9	5		

Medium Sized Plants: 1'- 3'

Average Bloom Times for Pink Flowering Plants at PERC

Scientific Name	April				May				June					July				August				September					October			
weeks of the year	14	15	16	17	18	19	20	21	22	23	24	25	26	27	28	29	30	31	32	33	34	35	36	37	38	39	40	41	42	43
Dicentra spectabilis (5) bleeding heart								32	64	78	63	25	15	10																
Echinacea purpurea 'Bright Star' (6) purple coneflower												10	23	55	68	84	93	84	79	54	41	33	18	8	10					
Geranium sanguineum (6) bloody cranesbill								10	20	39	48	58	68	70	28	33	18	12	13	14	15	13	16	15	13	17	12	20		
Hylotelephium spectabile 'Autumn Glory' (5) showy stonecrop																					10	40	84	83	72	48	20			
Hylotelephium telephium (5) live-forever																				10	15	46	88	77	92	100	20	4	40	
Lavatera thuringiaca (4) tree mallow										18	36			81	90	82	58	35												
Malva alcea 'Fastigata' (5) hollyhock mallow									10	10	20	30	38	29	38	60	75	70	45	33	15	12	10	8	8					
Paeonia 'Doreen' (6) garden peony										51	71	42	100	25																
Paeonia 'Pink Dawn' (6) garden peony									23	90	66	60	75																	
Paeonia 'Vivid Rose' (6) garden peony										10	75	41	48	37	10	25														
Penstemon 'Elfin Pink' (6) beard-tongue									12	51	89	80	88	75	12	24	12	16	13	12	12	8	10	10	8	6				
Physostegia virginiana (5) obedient plant																				10	13	29	54	69	75	59	45	13		
Scabiosa columbaria 'Pink Mist' (2-6) pincushion flower										15	60	88	79	70	62	42		56	59	53	43	35	25	18	10	20	17	15	30	
Stachys byzantina (6) lambs'-ears												28	25	33	37	44	51	26	15	15	9	8	10	5						
Thalictrum aquilegiifolium (6) columbine meadow rue							10	27	82	75	63	41	30																	
Tradescantia virginiana 'Red Cloud' (5) Virginia spiderwort								20	47	90	48	20	25	10	45	20	10	25	18	18	35	35	30	18	23	20				
Veronica spicata 'Red Fox' (6) spike speedwell												25		18	43	82	63	51	43	42	33	29	23	14	16	20	12	10		
Veronica spicata 'Rosea' (5) spike speedwell													10	31	53	73	76	74	43	38	25	24	15	11	9	7	5			

▨ = 1-33% bloom coverage   ▨ = 34-66% bloom coverage   ▨ = 67-100% bloom coverage

103

Average Bloom Times for Pink Flowering Plants at PERC

Tall Plants: > 3'

Scientific Name	April				May				June					July				August				September					October			
weeks of the year	14	15	16	17	18	19	20	21	22	23	24	25	26	27	28	29	30	31	32	33	34	35	36	37	38	39	40	41	42	43
Agastache barberi (2-5) giant hummingbird mint													46	40	98	88	79	82	61	44	25	23	23	9	10	9	7	9	13	15
Agastache rupestris (3) sunset hyssop																10	10	20	25	25	40			80	90	88	20	25		
Anemone hupehensis 'Prince Henry' (6) Japanese anemone																			13	20	30	21	38	48	79	95	65	17		
Anemone tomentosa (5) grapeleaf anemone																20	29	49	80	93	98	75	45	38	7	4	4			
Dictamnus albus 'Purpureus' (6) gas plant						10	45	77	84	94	51	31	23	10																
Epilobium angustifolium (6) fireweed											12	58	70	73	46	30	26	29	26	30	55	38	25	7	5	20	20			
Eupatorium maculatum (6) Joe-pye weed																		40	58	63	70	70	81	58	50	5				
Gysophila paniculata 'Pink Fairy' (4) perennial baby's breath													15	51	80	75	75	90	63	38	42	40	30	20	18	13	5			
Malva alcea 'Fastigata' (5) hollyhock mallow									10	10	20	30	38	29	38	60	75	70	45	33	15	12	10	8	8	8				
Monarda fistulosa (6) wild beebalm																	20	58	100	86	48	40	25							
Paeonia 'Doreen' (6) garden peony										51	71	42	100	25																
Paeonia 'Pink Dawn' (6) garden peony									23	90	66	60	75																	
Paeonia 'Vivid Rose' (6) garden peony										10	75	41	48	37	10	25														
Sidalcea 'Party Girl' (5) prairie mallow														25	19	50	70	63	65	36	20	25	18	15	10	8	10	10	9	

■ = 1-33% bloom coverage   ■ = 34-66% bloom coverage   ■ = 67-100% bloom coverage

104

Average Bloom Times for Blue and Purple Flowering Plants at PERC

Very Short Plants: 1"- 6"	April				May				June					July				August				September					October			
Scientific Name / **weeks of the year**	14	15	16	17	18	19	20	21	22	23	24	25	26	27	28	29	30	31	32	33	34	35	36	37	38	39	40	41	42	43
Ajuga pyramidalis 'Metallica Crispa' (5)					5	15	51	68	37	45	25			8	8	7	7	8	8	6	6	7	6	5	5	5	7	8		
upright bugleweed																														
Ajuga reptans 'Bronze Beauty' (6)					4	25	22	16	15	10	5				10	10	10	10	10	8	8	8	8	13	13	9	8	13		
common bugleweed																														
Campanula cochlearifolia (6)											10	10	24	35	30	24	28	32	22	33	33	21	11	11	8	7	7	4		
fairies' thimbles																														
Phlox subulata 'Emerald Blue' (4)				10	67	100	90	43	15	5					9	10				9	9									
moss phlox																														
Thymus serpyllum 'Coccineus' (6)											21	56	85	88	79	65	28	14	8	10	14	15	8	13	13	20	20	5		
creeping thyme																														
Veronica allioni (6)								12	52	76	95	46	44	33																
Swiss mat speedwell																														
Veronica liwanensis (3)					5	5	20	62	58	23	7	4	4	5	5	5	5	5	5	5	5	5								
Turkish veronica																														
Veronica pectinata (6)	20		43	25	32	63	77	94	45	16	11	13	16	20	15	13	8	7	6	8	7	8	6	7	5	10	7	8		
comb speedwell																														
Short Plants: 6"- 12"																														
Campanula carpatica (6)												10	15	42	68	54	48	49	26	17	14	8	10	5						
Carpathian harebell																														
Campanula rotundifolia (6)										8	35	58	87	94	59	66	33	27	19	18	14	11	15	19	16	20	18	18		
Scotch bluebell																														
Gentiana septemfida (6)													18	100	50	31	44	66	46	43	20	10	5							
crested gentian																														
Geranium himalayense (6)								7	19	37	69	74	72	70	10	26	12	10	7	7	7	9	9	11	11	15	4	4	4	
bigroot geranium																														
Hosta sieboldii 'Ginkgo Craig' (6)																	10	60	37	46	20	38	30	40	60	100				
hosta																														
Limonium gmelinii (5)															40	40	18	50	68	81	75	75	57	53	62	62	28	60	60	
Siberian statice																														
Penstemon campanulatus (6)														25	63	65	77	54	55	53	31	27	18	18	15	10				
beard-tongue																														
Phlox divaricata ssp. laphamii (6)			10	10	59	63	84	67	35	27																				
wild sweet-William																														

= 1-33% bloom coverage   = 34-66% bloom coverage   = 67-100% bloom coverage

Average Bloom Times for Blue and Purple Flowering Plants at PERC

Short Plants: 6"- 12"

Scientific Name	April				May				June					July				August				September					October			
weeks of the year	14	15	16	17	18	19	20	21	22	23	24	25	26	27	28	29	30	31	32	33	34	35	36	37	38	39	40	41	42	43
Prunella grandiflora (6) large selfheal																											40	40	10	
Pulmonaria saccharata 'Roy Davidson' (2) lungwort	80	80	40	40	40	33	15		4																					
Pulsatilla vulgaris (2-8) European pasque flower	40	10	25	50	50	67	33	10	10																					
Salvia pratensis (6) meadow clary								17	53	69	50	50	26	13	7	25	4	4	4	4	4	4	4	10	9	9	4	9		
Teucrium canadense (6) wild germander														8	20	21	28	29	35	23	26	23	15	12	15	7				
Teucrium chamaedrys (4) common germander																30	56	50	27	27	30	10	10	10						
Veronica peduncularis 'Georgia Blue' (4) speedwell							25	30	23	20	20	40	50	13	10					4	7	7	7	10	10	16	4	13	10	

Medium Sized Plants: 1'- 3'

Scientific Name	April				May				June					July				August				September					October			
weeks of the year	14	15	16	17	18	19	20	21	22	23	24	25	26	27	28	29	30	31	32	33	34	35	36	37	38	39	40	41	42	43
Aquilegia 'Bluebird' (2-9) columbine								47	50	54	68	42	17	12	9		8													
Brunnera macrophylla (2-10) Siberian-bugloss					17	28	36	53	60	42	19	7	4	5	5							30								
Campanula glomerata 'Superba' (5) clustered bellflower											15	73	75	76	34	23	4	10	10	7	7	10		4						
Campanula persicifolia (6) peach-leaved bellflower											51	72	70	66	53	65	35	23	19	21	18	16	18	23	13	25	18	20		
Centaurea montana (11) mountain-bluet						10	15	38	54	49	54	67	38	23	9	25	15	15	15	8	9	8	13	8	7	9	7	7		
Ceratostigma plumbaginoides (6) plumbago																		4	8	9	19	30	44	50	54	53	27	14		
Clematis heracleifolia (4) tube clematis																			4	25	58	80	25	10	13	10				
Clematis intergrifolia (5) solitary clematis								8	34	91	65	85	82	76	72	69	48	43	23	18	8	8	25	10						
Geranium platypetalum (7) broad-petaled geranium									33	82	69	52	32	25	5	5	5	5	10	10	10									
Goniolimon tataricum (3-16) tatarian statice									10	20	30	60	34	36	49	70	71	80	70	70	51	60	66	78	72	70	70	70	75	

█ = 1-33% bloom coverage █ = 34-66% bloom coverage █ = 67-100% bloom coverage

Medium Sized Plants: 1'- 3'

Average Bloom Times for Blue and Purple Flowering Plants at PERC

Scientific Name / weeks of the year	April				May				June					July				August				September					October			
	14	15	16	17	18	19	20	21	22	23	24	25	26	27	28	29	30	31	32	33	34	35	36	37	38	39	40	41	42	43
Hosta fortunei 'Francee' (6) hosta																	15	18	39	49	30	25	20	10	3					
Iris 'Babbling Brook' (5) bearded iris							10		70	41	27	35																		
Iris lactea var. *oltriensis* (6) blue bouquet iris								25	62	54	37	37	10	10																
Iris lactea (3) blue bouquet iris						12	35	43	47	23	4																			
Iris 'Stepping Little' (5) bearded iris									38	44	23	50																		
Lavandula angustifolia (2) lavender												50	75	75	75	75	43	50	63	50	25	25	25	25	25					
Liatris spicata (2-5) blazing star															10	35	48	55	40	25	5	5	5	5						
Limonium latifolium (6) sea lavender														20	40	30	26	48	63	82	72	69	44	25	18	20	10	10		
Linum perenne (5) perennial flax							40	47	56	95	95	73	46	18	8	30	37	15	22	16	22	10	18	15	13	8	10	10		
Lupinus perennis (7) wild lupine								6	46	76	57	28	35	10	5	20	10	10	10	10	30		20	30	30	30	9			
Nepeta x faassenii (6) catmint								10	46	75	82	93	85	72	46	34	22	18	12	12	9	15	14	15	22	20	15	12	4	4
Penstemon campanulatus (6) beard-tongue														25	63	65	77	54	55	53	31	27	18	18	15	10				
Penstemon x mexicali Pikes Peak Purple (6) beard-tongue										10	48	68	96	88	58	70	31	40	36	45	35	44	41	48	53	57	48	40	80	80
Penstemon strictus (6) beard-tongue										38	75	68	72	58	13	8	9													
Phlox paniculata 'Franz Schubert' (5) garden phlox														5	37	60	48	32	55	57	52	40	37	15	10	10	7			
Platycodon grandiflorus (2-8) balloon flower													25	28	33	47	63	36	60	24	28	18	18	25	25	25				
Platycodon grandiflorus 'Komachi' (6) balloon flower																18	37	61	62	70	71	45	34	14	10	7				

= 1-33% bloom coverage   = 34-66% bloom coverage   = 67-100% bloom coverage

Average Bloom Times for Blue and Purple Flowering Plants at PERC

Month groupings: **April** (wks 14–17), **May** (18–21), **June** (22–26), **July** (27–30), **August** (31–34), **September** (35–39), **October** (40–43)

Medium Sized Plants: 1'–3'

Scientific Name / weeks of the year	14	15	16	17	18	19	20	21	22	23	24	25	26	27	28	29	30	31	32	33	34	35	36	37	38	39	40	41	42	43
Polemonium caeruleum (6) Jacob's ladder								50	69	58	50	23	18																	
Salvia pratensis (6) meadow clary								17	53	69	50	50	26	13	7	25	4	4	4	4	4	4	4	10	9	9	4	9		
Salvia x sylvestris 'May Night' (5) perennial sage										15	40	58	83	69	46	43	35	19	16	18	31	11	8	8	7	9				
Scabiosa columbaria 'Butterfly Blue' (2-5) pincushion flower												15	53	70	48	48	52	80	32	32	25	23	18	13	12	12	15	24		
Tradescantia ohiensis (6) Ohio spiderwort													4	40	65	75	58	40	40	27	32	26	17	23	18	15	20			
Tricyrtis hirta (6) hairy toad lily																								15	17	22	28	15	15	
Veronica austriaca teucrium 'Royal Blue' (5) Hungarian speedwell								10	36	55	66	76	68	38	13	25					9	10	10	10	10	8	9			
Veronica spicata (6) spike speedwell											17	65	89	85	69	50	52	54	34	27	31	26	31	31	15	8	12	15	20	
Veronica 'Sunny Border Blue' (5) speedwell													25	19	54	87	87	86	48	36	33	23	22	16	16	8	5			

Tall Plants: > 3'

Scientific Name / weeks of the year	14	15	16	17	18	19	20	21	22	23	24	25	26	27	28	29	30	31	32	33	34	35	36	37	38	39	40	41	42	43
Baptisia australis (3-17) blue false indigo				5	10	10	16	28	43	69	40	33		25																
Echinops ritro 'Taplow Purple' (6) globe thistle													37	41	69	85	73	44	30	10	10	15	18	28	11	16	13			
Echinops ritro (6) globe thistle														10	25	38	73	88	76	81	64	54	31	17	19	8	4	4	4	
Iris sibirica (5) Siberian iris									5	28	30	27	50																	
Nepeta x faassenii 'Souv. d'Andre Chaudron' (4) catmint											10	50	97	88	58	60	60	65	60	50	20	13	13	10	6					
Perovskia atriplicifolia (6) Russian sage														3	10	28	53	77	85	88	79	51	35	27	16		5			

Legend:

■ = 1–33% bloom coverage ■ = 34–66% bloom coverage ■ = 67–100% bloom coverage

APPENDIX 2
PLANT LISTS

Use as Cut Flower

Acanthus balcanicus
Achillea spp.
Agastache spp.
Alcea spp.
Alchemilla mollis
Anaphalis margaritacea
Andropogon gerardii
Anemone spp.
Aquilegia spp.
Armeria maritima
Aster spp.
Baptisia australis
Boltonia asteroides 'Snowbank'
Calamagrostis x acutiflora 'Overdam'
Calamagrostis brachytricha
Campanula glomerata 'Superba'
Campanula persicifolia
Centaurea spp.
Centranthus ruber
Chrysanthemum x morifolium
Coreopsis verticillata
Dianthus barbatus
Dianthus caryophyllus
Dianthus hybrids
Dianthus nardiformis
Dicentra spectabilis
Dictamnus albus 'Purpureus'
Echinacea purpurea
Echinops spp.
Eupatorium maculatum
Filipendula vulgaris
Gaillardia spp.
Gaura lindheimeri
Geranium spp.
Geum chiloense 'Mrs. Bradshaw'
Goniolimon tataricum
Gypsophila paniculata 'Pink Fairy'
Heliopsis helianthoides 'Incomparabilis'
Hemerocallis hybrids
Heterotheca villosa
Heuchera spp.
Hosta spp.
Iris spp.
Knautia macedonia
Kniphofia uvaria
Lavandula angustifolia
Lavatera thuringiaca
Leucanthemella serotina 'Herbstern'

Leucanthemum x superbum
Liatris spp.
Lilium spp.
Limonium spp.
Lobelia cardinalis
Lupinus spp.
Lychnis chalcedonica
Miscanthus sinensis 'Gracillimus'
Monarda didyma
Paeonia spp.
Papaver orientale
Pennisetum alopecuroides 'Hameln'
Penstemon spp.
Perovskia atriplicifolia
Phlomis russeliana
Phlox paniculata
Physostegia virginiana
Platycodon grandiflorus
Rudbeckia fulgida var. sullivantii 'Goldsturm'
Saccharum ravennae
Salvia spp.
Scabiosa columbaria 'Butterfly Blue' and 'Pink Mist'
Sidalcea 'Party Girl'
Solidago virgaurea 'Peter Pan'
X Solidaster luteus 'Lemore'
Stachys byzantina
Thalictrum aquilegiifolium
Tricyrtis hirta
Trollius x cultorum 'Golden Queen'
Veronica 'Sunny Border Blue'

Attracts Bees and Butterflies

Achillea spp.
Agastache spp.
Ajuga spp.
Alcea spp.
Anaphalis margaritacea
Anemone spp.
Aquilegia spp.
Aster spp.
Campanula spp.
Centaurea spp.
Centranthus ruber
Ceratostigma plumbaginoides
Dianthus spp.
Dictamnus albus 'Purpureus'
Echinacea purpurea
Echinops spp.
Epilobium angustifolium

Eupatorium maculatum
Gaillardia spp.
Gaura lindheimeri
Geranium spp.
Heliopsis helianthoides 'Incomparabilis'
Heterotheca villosa
Heuchera sanguinea
Hylotelephium spp.
Iris spp.
Knautia macedonia
Kniphofia uvaria
Lamium spp.
Lavandula angustifolia
Liatris spp.
Limonium spp.
Lupinus spp.
Lychnis chalcedonica
Monarda didyma
Nepeta spp.
Oenothera spp.
Paeonia spp.
Penstemon spp.
Perovskia atriplicifolia
Phlox spp.
Physostegia virginiana
Potentilla recta 'Macrantha'
Prunella grandiflora
Rudbeckia fulgida var. *sullivantii* 'Goldsturm'
Salvia spp.
Scabiosa columbaria 'Butterfly Blue' and 'Pink Mist'
Sedum spp.
Sidalcea 'Party Girl'
Solidago virgaurea 'Peter Pan'
X Solidaster luteus 'Lemore'
Stachys byzantina
Teucrium spp.
Thymus spp.
Tradescantia spp.
Veronica spp.
Veronicastrum virginicum 'Album'

Attracts Hummingbirds

Agastache spp.
Aquilegia spp.
Centranthus ruber
Heuchera sanguinea
Kniphofia uvaria
Lobelia cardinalis
Monarda didyma
Penstemon 'Elfin Pink'
Penstemon x mexicali RED ROCKS™
Penstemon pinifolius

Use as Dried Flower or Ornamental Fruit

Acanthus balcanicus
Achillea spp.
Agastache spp.
Anaphalis margaritacea
Andropogon gerardii
Baptisia australis
Calamagrostis x acutiflora 'Overdam'
Calamagrostis brachytricha
Centaurea macrocephala
Clematis spp.
Dictamnus albus 'Purpureus'
Echinacea purpurea
Echinops spp.
Goniolimon tataricum
Gypsophila paniculata 'Pink Fairy'
Hylotelephium spp.
Iris sibirica
Lavandula angustifolia
Liatris spp.
Limonium spp.
Miscanthus sinensis 'Gracillimus'
Papaver orientale
Pennisetum alopecuroides 'Hameln'
Perovskia atriplicifolia
Phlomis russeliana
Pulsatilla vulgaris
Rudbeckia fulgida var. *sulllivantii* 'Goldsturm'
Saccharum ravennae
Sedum kamtschaticum cvs.
Sedum spurium cvs.
Stachys byzantina

Use as a Ground Cover or for Ornamental Foliage

Ajuga spp.
Alchemilla mollis
Anemone sylvestris
Armeria maritima
Bergenia spp.
Brunnera macrophylla
Callirhoe involucrata
Campanula carpatica
Campanula cochleariifolia
Cerastium tomentosum 'Silver Carpet'
Ceratostigma plumbaginoides
Delosperma nubigenum
Dianthus gratianopolitanus 'Tiny Rubies'
Festuca spp.
Galium odoratum
Geranium spp.
Geum triflorum
Gypsophila repens
Helianthemum nummularium

Heuchera spp.
Hosta spp.
Hypericum calycinum
Lamium spp.
Lotus corniculatus 'Dwarf'
Lysimachia nummularia
Nepeta spp.
Oenothera macrocarpa
Oenothera speciosa 'Siskiyou'
Ophiopogon planiscapus 'Nigrescens'
Phlox divaricata ssp. *laphamii*
Phlox subulata
Polygonum affine 'Border Jewel' and 'Dimity'
Prunella grandiflora
Pulmonaria spp.
Ruta graveolens 'Blue Mound'
Salvia argentea
Santolina chamaecyparissus
Sedum spp.
Sempervivum spp.
Stachys byzantina
Teucrium spp.
Thymus spp.
Veronica allioni
Veronica liwanensis
Veronica pectinata
Veronica peduncularis 'Georgia Blue'

Poisonous or May Cause Dermatitis

Anemone spp.
Baptisia australis
Chrysanthemum x morifolium
Clematis spp.
Dicentra spectabilis
Dictamnus albus 'Purpureus'
Digitalis spp.
Gaillardia spp.
Hypericum calycinum
Iris spp.
Lobelia cardinalis
Lupinus spp.
Pulsatilla vulgaris
Ruta graveolens 'Blue Mound'

Plants that Prefer Part or Full Shade

Ajuga spp.
Alchemilla mollis
Anemone spp.
Aquilegia spp.
Bergenia spp.
Brunnera macrophylla
Dicentra spectabilis
Digitalis grandiflora
Galium odoratum

Heuchera spp.
Hosta spp.
Lamium spp.
Lobelia cardinalis
Lysimachia nummularia
Oxalis crassipes 'Rosea'
Phlox divaricata ssp. *laphamii*
Polemonium caeruleum
Prunella grandiflora
Pulmonaria spp.
Thalictrum aquilegiifolium
Tricyrtis hirta
Trollius chinensis 'Golden Queen'

Fragrant Flower or Foliage

Achillea spp. (foliage)
Agastache spp.
Anemone sylvestris
Anthemis marschalliana (foliage)
Centranthus ruber
Chrysanthemum x morifolium
Clematis heracleifolia
Clematis recta
Dianthus barbatus
Dianthus caryophyllus
Dianthus gratianopolitanus 'Tiny Rubies'
Dianthus hybrids
Dianthus plumarius
Dictamnus albus 'Purpureus' (foliage)
Filipendula vulgaris
Galium odoratum
Geranium macrorrhizum (foliage)
Hemerocallis (select cultivars only)
Hosta spp. (select cultivars only)
Iris spp. (select cultivars only)
Lilium spp.
Monarda didyma (foliage)
Nepeta spp.
Oenothera glazioviana
Oenothera macrocarpa
Paeonia spp. (select cultivars only)
Perovskia atriplicifolia (foliage)
Phlox paniculata (select cultivars)
Santolina chamaecyparissus (foliage)
Thymus spp. (foliage)

Xeric or Drought Tolerant

Achillea spp.
Agastache barberi
Agastache rupestris
Anaphalis margaritacea
Andropogon gerardii
Anthemis marschalliana
Armeria maritima

Aurinia saxatilis 'Compacta'
Baptisia australis
Callirhoe involucrata
Campanula rotundifolia
Centranthus ruber
Cerastium tomentosum 'Silver Carpet'
Coreopsis verticillata
Delosperma nubigenum
Dianthus nardiformis
Dianthus plumarius
Dictamnus albus 'Purpureus'
Echinacea purpurea
Echinops spp.
Epilobium angustifolium
Gaillardia spp.
Gaura lindheimeri
Geranium sanguineum
Geum triflorum
Goniolimon tataricum
Gypsophila spp.
Helianthemum nummularium
Hemerocallis spp.
Heterotheca villosa
Hylotelephium spp.
Iberis sempervirens 'Snowmantle'
Iris (German Bearded)
Knautia macedonia
Kniphofia uvaria
Lavandula angustifolia
Liatris punctata
Limonium spp.
Linum perenne
Malva alcea 'Fastigiata'
Monarda fistulosa
Nepeta x faassenii
Oenothera spp.
Paeonia spp.
Papaver orientale
Penstemon spp.
Perovskia atriplicifolia
Phlomis russeliana
Phlox subulata
Platycodon grandiflorus
Polygonum affine 'Border Jewel' and 'Dimity'
Pulsatilla vulgaris
Rudbeckia fulgida var. sullivantii 'Goldsturm'
Ruta graveolens
Salvia argentea
Salvia pratensis
Salvia x sylvestris 'May Night'
Santolina chamaecyparissus
Schizachyrium scoparium
Sedum spp.
Sempervivum spp.
Solidago virgaurea 'Peter Pan'

Stachys byzantina
Thymus spp.
Veronica allioni
Veronica liwanensis
Veronica incana 'Minuet'
Veronica pectinata
Yucca spp.

Author's Favorites

Acanthus balcanicus
Anemone hupehensis var. japonica 'Prince Henry'
Anemone tomentosa
Baptisia australis
Calamagrostis brachytricha
Centranthus ruber
Clematis heracleifolia
Clematis integrifolia
Clematis recta
Dictamnus albus 'Purpureus'
Gaura lindheimeri
Heliopsis helianthoides 'Incomparabilis'
Ophiopogon planiscapus 'Nigrescens'
Phlomis russeliana
Platycodon grandiflorus
Pulsatilla vulgaris
Tricyrtis hirta
Veronicastrum virginicum 'Album'

Old Faithfuls
(survived 15 years or more)

Achillea filipendulina 'Parker's Variety'
Achillea x filipendulina 'Coronation Gold'
Achillea 'Moonshine'
Ajuga reptans 'Bronze Beauty'
Anaphalis margaritacea
Anemone tomentosa
Baptisia australis
Campanula carpatica
Campanula rotundifolia
Centaurea macrocephala
Centaurea montana
Centranthus ruber
Cerastium tomentosum 'Silver Carpet'
Chrysanthemum x morifolium 'South Pass'
Clematis integrifolia
Coreopsis verticillata
Dianthus caryophyllus
Dicentra spectabilis
Dictamnus albus 'Purpureus'
Echinops ritro
Epilobium angustifolium
Galium odoratum
Geranium sanguineum
Heliopsis helianthoides 'Incomparabilis'

Hemerocallis spp.
Hosta tsushimensis
Hylotelephium telephium
Iberis sempervirens 'Snowmantle'
Iris hybrids
Iris sibirica
Leucanthemum x superbum
Liatris spicata
Limonium latifolium
Lysimachia nummularia
Nepeta x faassenii
Paeonia spp.
Panicum virgatum
Papaver orientale
Penstemon 'Elfin Pink'
Penstemon strictus
Phlox subulata
Physostegia virginiana
Potentilla recta 'Macrantha'
Pulsatilla vulgaris

Ruta graveolens 'Blue Mound'
Salvia pratensis
Salvia x sylvestris 'May Night'
Sedum aizoon
Sedum kamtschaticum 'Floriferum'
Sedum kamtschaticum 'Variegatum'
Sedum spurium 'Dragon's Blood'
Sedum spurium 'Bronze Carpet'
Sedum spurium 'Red Carpet'
Solidago virgaurea 'Peter Pan'
Stachys byzantina
Teucrium canadense
Teucrium chamaedrys
Thalictrum aquilegiifolium
Thymus serpyllum 'Coccineus'
Tradescantia ohiensis
Veronica austriaca ssp. *teucrium* 'Royal Blue'
Veronica spicata
Yucca filamentosa
Yucca glauca

APPENDIX 3
FEATURED PLANTS FROM FIRST PUBLICATION NOT FOUND IN THIS REVISION

The following plants were featured and recommended in the original 1989 publication "Flowering Herbaceous Perennials for the High Plains." They have not been included in this revision for the various reasons listed below. This does not necessarily reflect their suitability for garden use along the Rocky Mountains and High Plains region.

Plant and Reason not Included

Aconitum napellus   Monkshood
Insufficient data; died out in 1992 due to herbicide damage and not replaced

Aegopodium podagraria   Bishop's
                                                    Goutweed
Combined score 5.76; notoriously invasive and difficult to remove once established; excellent for erosion control

Arabis caucasica   Rock-cress
Combined score 3.25; original planting failed to over winter after 4 yrs.; replacement failed to establish

Artemisia spp.   Sage
All species scored beneath the cut off score of 6.0 most

likely because they are used for their excellent foliage and have inconspicuous flowers

Asclepias tuberosa   Butterfly Weed
Original plants died of unknown causes after 6 yrs.; replacement plants failed to overwinter consistently

Aster alpinus   Dwarf Alpine Aster
Lack of data; died out in 1990 of unknown causes and not replaced

Aster x frikartii 'Wonder of Staffa'   Frikart's
                                                    Aster
Lack of data; failed to over winter in 1992 and was not replaced

Aubrieta deltoidea   False Rock-cress
Combined score 4.60; original planting dead of unknown causes in 1992

Campanula poscharskyana   Serbian
                                                    Bellflower
Died of unknown causes; original 1987 planting survived for 7 yrs, replacement survived for 2 yrs.

Coreopsis lanceolata   Lance Coreopsis, Tickseed
Lack of data; original planting failed to over winter after 4 yrs.

Dianthus anatolicus
Combined score 6.14; lack of current data; died in 1995 of unknown causes

Erigeron **spp.**   Fleabane
Low combined score of 4.64; long-lived species with minor problems with chlorosis and lodging; many fine cultivars are available in the nursery trade

Eupatorium coelestinum   Hardy Ageratum, Mist Flower
Lack of current data; 3 plantings failed to overwinter but survived an average of 6 yrs.

Helianthemum apenninum   Silver Sun Rose
Lack of current data; 2 plantings failed to overwinter in 1992

Hibiscus grandiflorus **'Pink Marvel'**   Rose Mallow
Exact identity unknown; current plant at PERC a possible seedling of original plant that performed well

Linaria vulgaris   Toadflax, Butter-and-eggs
Currently on state noxious weed list

Lysimachia punctata   Yellow Loosestrife, Circle Flower
Plant of merit with combined score of 5.5; flowers not very showy; plant overly vigorous and slightly chlorotic

Lythrum virgatum **'Morden Pink'**   Morden Pink Loosestrife
Straight species considered a noxious weed; use of this cultivar strongly cautioned although performance has been outstanding

Myosotis scorpioides   Dwarf Forget-me-not
var. *semperflorens*
Lack of current data; original planting died of unknown causes after 11 years

Oenothera serrulata   Toothleaved Evening Primrose
Lack of data; 1987 planting failed to overwinter in 1992

Oenothera tetragona   Common Sundrops
Lack of current data; original planting replaced with cultivar 'Sonnenwende' which has a score of 5.80

Penstemon perfoliatus   Beardtongue
Data and identity of plant questionable

Penstemon hirsutus **'Pygmaeus'**   Dwarf Hairy Beardtongue
Died in 1992 of unknown causes

Polygonum cuspidatum   Knotweed
var. *compactum*
Aggressive spreader; combined score 5.93

Saponaria ocymoides   Soapwort
Failed to overwinter in 1991; lack of current data

Scabiosa caucasica   Pincushion Flower
Current plant a seedling of original that died out in 1992; data incomplete

Sedum acre   Goldmoss Stonecrop
Data mixed up with that of other sedums in area; long lived garden worthy plant that can be invasive

Sedum rosea **var.** *integrifolia*   King's Crown Roseroot
Combined score of 4.86; overly shady and crowded location; plant quality poor after bloom

Sedum reflexum **'Blue Spruce'**
Tiny original planting overrun by more aggressive sedums; score of 5.40

Thalictrum minus   Low Meadow Rue
Garden worthy foliage plant that received low scores for inconspicuous flowers

Thermopsis montana   Golden Banner
Low combined score (4.21) a reflection of its tendency to go summer dormant

Veronica prostrata   Harebell Speedwell Rock Speedwell
Lack of bloom lowered score (5.13); died in 1997

APPENDIX 4
TAXA NOT INCLUDED IN THIS PUBLICATION

The following taxa have not performed as well at PERC as those featured in this publication, yet have survived for many years. In some cases the plant is considered to have little ornamental value or may receive low scores based on inconspicuous or short-lived flowers. In other cases, the plant may have performed less than optimally due to cultural circumstances. Not including these plants in this publication does not necessarily mean that the plant will not perform satisfactorily at a different location or under different cultural conditions.

Acaena microphylla   New Zealand burr (13)
Aggressive ground cover useful for erosion control; inconspicuous flowers; minor chlorosis

Achillea tomentosa   Woolly yarrow (6)
Aggressive in 1994 but by 1996 was crowded out by more vigorous perennials; moved to new site in 1999 and bloomed briefly that year

Allium cernuum   Wild onion (9)
Over run by more vigorous neighbors; small plant easily overlooked when in bloom

Amsonia illustris   Blue stars (4)
Fair flower aesthetics; light blue flowers look faded in strong sunlight, would perform better in part shade

Aralia racemosa   Spikenard (10)
Insect and winter crown damage; sun scorch; died in 1998

Arrhenatherum elatius **var.**   Variegated oat grass (11)
bulbosum **'Variegatum'**
Rated good for plant aesthetics, poor for flower aesthetics; aggressive nature; severe lodging

Artemisia ludoviciana   Prairie sage (12)
Aggressive; inconspicuous flowers; lodging; not showy

Astilbe arendsii **'Snowdrift'**   False spirea (11)
Lacks vigor in our dry, heavy soils; heat stress and chlorosis

Astrantia major **'Margery**   Greater masterwort (15)
Fish'
Garden worthy plant requiring more shade; flowers more interesting than showy; problems with vigorous nature and chlorosis

Carex buchananii   Leatherleaf sedge (5)
More interesting than showy, foliage plant with unusual russet brown color; lacks bloom, would perform better with more moisture

Carex ornithodpoda **'Variegata'**   Bird's foot sedge (14)
Rated fair to excellent for foliage effect; problems with leaf scorch and lodging; lacks bloom

Chelone obliqua   Rose turtlehead (14)
Rated high for flower aesthetics and fair for foliage; problems with aggressive nature, chlorosis, insects, and lodging

Crambe cordifolia   Colewort (4)
Has not bloomed; leaves damaged by chewing insects

Doronicum caucasicum   Leopardsbane (13)
Problems with chewing insects, chlorosis, leaf spot and poor vigor; two plantings died out after 10 years

Dryopteris erythrosora   Japanese shield fern (9)
Good plant aesthetics but lacks vigor; would perform better in moist soil; some leaf scorch

Duchesnea indica   Mock strawberry (12)
Effective ground cover for erosion control; notoriously aggressive; some chlorosis and scorch

Elymus canadensis   Canadian wild rye (10)
Aggressive grass that tends to lodge; mixed with Elymus glaucus and hard to identify now

Elymus glaucus   Blue wild rye (10)
Aggressive plant whose identity is now questionable

Epimedium alpinum **'Rubrum'**   Red barrenwort (14)
Lacks vigor in our dry, heavy soils; leaf scorch and chewing insects affect appearance

Epimedium grandiflorum   Longspur barrenwort (13)
Problems with chewing insects, heat stress, chlorosis, and leaf spot; failed to overwinter in 1995

Eriogonum umbellatum **var.**   Sulphur flower (12)
subalpinum
Very small plant more appropriate for rock garden; lacks vigor and flowers; suffers from chlorosis and winter dieback

Fragaria vesca 'Variegata'   Strawberry (8)
Lacks vigor and flowers; sun scorch; crowded out by more vigorous neighbors

Houttuynia cordata 'Cameleon'   Houttuynia (5)
Failed to bloom until fifth year; lacks vigor; problems with insects and chlorosis; needs more moisture

Iris missouriensis   Missouri flag (17)
Lack of bloom and tip scorch; would perform better in a moist site

Jasione laevis   Shepard's scabious (4)
Very chlorotic and over run by more vigorous perennials nearby

Leontopodium alpinus   Edelweiss (6)
More interesting and unusual than showy; problems with insect damage and lack of vigor

Liatris punctata   Snakeroot (8)
Poor vigor; chewing insects; late to emerge in spring; performs better in sandier soil and better drainage

Macleaya cordata   Plume poppy (8)
Plant better known for its foliage and structural effect; flowers interesting rather than showy; aggressive

Mirabilis multiflora   Four o'clocks (17)
Sprawling xeriscape plant that struggled in heavy clay and regular watering regime; not floriferous; winter injury

Physalis alkekengi 'Gigantea'   Chinese lantern (5)
Chlorosis and insect damage affect appearance

Rheum australe   Ornamental rhubarb (4)
Foliage appearance poor due to chewing insects; flowers not very showy; appearance poor by end of summer

Sagina subulata   Pearlwort (19)
Yearly winter dessication; revives by mid summer; flowers not showy (very tiny)

Salvia cyanescens   (7)
Sparse plant that lacks vigor and bloom; over run by other perennials nearby

Stipa tenuissima 'Ponytails'   Silky thread grass (8)
Winter injury; slow to emerge and fill out in spring

Stipa tirsa   Thread grass (8)
Winter injury; lacks vigor and bloom

Symphytum officinale   Comfrey (13)
Coarse herb requiring a lot of space; lodging; leaves often cover flowers

Thermopsis carolina   Carolina lupine (5)
Poor appearance by mid summer; dislikes heat

Thermopsis fabacea   (4)
Poor appearance by mid summer; dislikes heat

Tiarella 'Slick Rock'   Foamflower (4)
Lacks bloom and vigor; very little new growth yet rated well in 4th year for flower aesthetics

Veronica repens   Creeping speedwell (12)
Chlorosis; over run by more vigorous perennials

Vinca minor   Periwinkle (18)
Competition with moneywort and bedstraw make it impossible to judge the performance of this plant; other plantings in Fort Collins perform well

Vinca minor 'Golden Bowles'   (4)
Leaf scorch and lacks flower power

Vinca minor 'Variegata'   (13)
Over run by neighboring plants; not floriferous

Viola spp.   Various
All species grown are short-lived with poor vigor due to dry soil and lack of shade

Waldsteinia fragaroides   Barren strawberry (9)
lacks flowers and vigor; shaded and crowded

Zauschneria arizonica   Hardy hummingbird trumpet (8)
Late season bloom often frost damaged; chlorosis, skeletonizing insects affect appearance

APPENDIX 5
TAXA STILL IN EVALUATION

The following species have been grown in the perennial garden for two years or less or have not had at least three years worth of data collected on them. They are still under evaluation and details on their performance will be reported in future editions of this publication.

Achillea teretifolia
Adenophora liliifolia
Agastache foeniculum
Agastache foeniculum 'Blue Fortune'
Agastache barberi 'Tutti Frutti'
Agastache cana
Ageratina altissima 'Chocolate' (*Eupatorium rugosum* 'Chocolate')
Alyssum markgrafii
Anacyclus pyrethrum var. *depressus*
Anchusa azurea 'Loddon Royalist'
Artemisia 'Mori's Form'
Artemisia capalarus
Artemisia lactiflora 'Guizho'
Bolax gummifera
Calamintha nepetoides 'White Cloud'
Chamaemelum nobile 'Flore-Plena' (*Anthemis nobilis* 'Flore-Plena')
Coreopsis 'Tequila Sunrise'
Cotula spp.
Delphinium 'Magic Fountain'
Delphinium 'King Arthur'
Dianthus plumarius 'Sweet Memory'
Dierama robustum
Dierama mossii
Digitalis thapsi SPANISH PEAKS™
Echinops 'Arctic Glow'
Echium russicum
Epilobium canum ssp. *canum* 'Siskyou Dwarf' (*Zauschneria californica* 'Siskyou Dwarf')
Eryngium variifolium 'Silver Gray'
Euryops depressus
Gaillardia aristata 'Fackelschein'
Gaura lindheimeri 'Siskyou Pink'
Gazania linearis COLORADO GOLD™
Helenium 'Coppelia'
Helianthemum 'Dazzler'

Helianthemum 'Wisely Primrose'
Helleborus orientalis 'Royal Heritage Strain'
Hemerocallis 'Pardon Me'
Hemerocallis 'Fairy Tale Pink'
Hosta 'Halcyon'
Iris pallida 'Variegata'
Kalimeris pinnatifida
Kniphofia 'Shining Sceptre'
Lamium maculatum 'White Nancy'
Lavandula 'Blue Cushion'
Lavandula 'Lady'
Leontopodium jacotianum
Lysimachia ciliata purpurea
Lysimachia punctata 'Alexander'
Morina longifolia
Onobrychis spp.
Osteospermum LAVENDER MIST™
Osteospermum barberiae var. *compactum* PURPLE MOUNTAIN™
Pachysandra terminalis 'Green Sheen'
Papaver triniifolium
Patrinia scabiosifolia
Penstemon mensarum
Penstemon hirsutus 'Pink'
Penstemon rydbergii
Persicaria amplexicaulis var. *pendula* 'Taurus'
Phlomis alpina
Phlox hoodii
Potentilla nepalensis 'Ron McBeath'
Potentilla argentea var. *calabra*
Ranunculus gramineus
Ratibida columnifera
Rudbeckia 'Viette's Little Suzy'
Salvia lyrata 'Knockout Purple'
Silene uniflora 'Robin Whitebreast'
Symphyandra hofmannii
Tanacetum niveum
Tanacetum densum amani
Trollius europaeus
Verbascum 'Southern Charm'
Verbascum xantophoenicium
Veronica prostrata
Viguiera multiflora
Wulfenia carinthiaca
Zaluzianskya spp.

APPENDIX 6
COLORADO STATE NOXIOUS WEEDS

The following plants can not be sold as nursery stock or contaminate nursery stock in the State of Colorado as of July 1, 2000. The plants in boldface type are ornamental varieties that may be offered in catalogs or in other states. Their use in Colorado is greatly discouraged.

Scientific Name	Common Name
Abutilon theophrasti	Velvetleaf
Aegilops cylindrica	Jointed goatgrass
Alhagi pseudalhagi	Camelthorn
Anthemis arvensis	**Scentless chamomile**
Anthemis cotula	Mayweed chamomile
Arctium minus	Common burdock
Brassica kaber	Wild mustard
Bromus tectorum	Downy brome
Cardaria draba	Hoary cress
Carduus nutans	Musk thistle
Carduus acanthoides	Plumeless thistle
Carum carvi	Wild caraway
Cenchrus longispinus	Longspine sandbur
Cenchrus pauciflorus	Field sandbur
Centaurea diffusa	Diffuse knapweed
Centaurea maculosa	Spotted knapweed
Centaurea nigra	Black knapweed
Centaurea repens	Russian knapweed
Centaurea solstitialis	Yellow starthistle
Centaurea virgata	Squarrose knapweed
Chondrilla juncea	Rush skeletonweed
Chorispora tenella	Blue mustard
Chrysanthemum leucanthemum	**Oxeye daisy**
Cichorium intybus	Chicory
Cirsium arvense	Canada thistle
Cirsium vulgare	Bull thistle
Clematis orientalis	**Chinese clematis**
Conium maculatum	Poison hemlock
Convolvulus arvensis	Field bindweed
Cynoglossum officinale	Houndstongue
Cyperus esculentus	Yellow nutsedge
Descurainia sophia	Flixweed
Dipsacus fullonum	Teasel
Elytrigia repens	Quackgrass
Erodium cicutarium	Redstem filaree
Euphorbia cyparissias	**Cypress spurge**
Euphorbia esula	Leafy spurge
Halogeton glomeratus	Halogeton
Hesperis matronalis	**Dame's rocket**
Hyoscyamus niger	Black henbane
Hypericum perforatum	**Common St. Johnswort**
Isatis tinctoria	Dyer's woad
Kochia scoparia	Kochia
Lepidium latifolium	Perennial pepperweed
Linaria dalmatica	Dalmation toadflax
Linaria vulgaris	**Yellow toadflax**
Lythrum salicaria	**Purple loosestrife**
Lythrum virgatum	**Loosestrife**
Madia sativa	Coast tarweed
Onopordum acanthium	Scotch thistle
Onopordum tauricum	Bull cottonthistle
Panicum miliaceum	Wild proso millet
Peganum harmala	African rue
Potentilla recta	**Sulfur cinquefoil**
Salsola collina	Russian thistle
Salsola iberica	Russian thistle
Salvia aethiopis	Mediterranean sage
Saponaria officinalis	**Bouncingbet**
Senecio vulgaris	Common groundsel
Setaria glauca	Yellow foxtail
Setaria viridis	Green foxtail
Solanum nigrum	Black nightshade
Solanum sarrachoides	Hairy nightshade
Sorghum halepense	Johnsongrass
Tamarix parviflora	**Saltcedar**
Tamarix ramosissima	**Saltcedar**
Tanacetum vulgare	**Common tansy**
Tribulus terrestris	Puncturevine
Verbascum thapsus	Common mullein

SCIENTIFIC NAME INDEX

Acanthus balcanicus — 13
    hungaricus - see *A. balcanicus*
    longifolius - see *A. balcanicus*
Achillea — 13-14
    eupatorium - see *A. filipendulina*
    filipendulina — 13
        'Parker's Variety' — 13
    x *filipendulina* 'Coronation Gold' — 14
    millefolium — 14
        'Red Beauty' — 14
        'Rosea' — 14
    'Moonshine' — 14
    ptarmica 'The Pearl' — 14
Achnatherum brachytricha- see *Calamagrostis brachytricha*
Agastache — 14-15
    barberi — 15
    rupestris — 15
Ajuga — 15-16
    metallica - see *A. pyramidalis* 'Metallica Crispa'
    pyramidalis 'Metallica Crispa' — 15
    reptans 'Bronze Beauty' — 16
Alcea — 16
    rosea Chater's Double Hybrids — 16
    rugosa — 16
Alchemilla mollis — 17
    'Auslese' — 17
    vulgaris - see *A. mollis*
Althaea rosea - see *Alcea rosea*
    rugosa - see *Alcea rugosa*
Alyssum saxatile - see *Aurinia saxatilis* 'Compacta'
Anaphalis margaritacea — 17
Anchusa myosotidiflora - see *Brunnera macrophylla*
Andropogon gerardii — 84
    scoparius - see *Schizachyrium scoparium*
Anemone — 17-18
    alba - see *A. sylvestris*
    hupehensis var. *japonica* 'Prince Henry' — 18
    pulsatilla - see *Pulsatilla vulgaris*
    serotina - see *Pulsatilla vulgaris*
    sylvestris — 18
    tomentosa — 18
    vitifolia - see *A. tomentosa*
Anthemis biebersteinii - see *A. marschalliana*
    marschalliana — 19
    rudolphiana - see *A. marschalliana*
Aquilegia — 19
Armeria maritima — 19-20
    var. *compacta* — 20
    'Dusseldorf Pride' — 20
    'Victor Reiter' — 20
Asperula odoratum - see *Galium odoratum*
Aster novi-belgii — 20-21

    'Eventide' — 20
    'Finalist' — 20
    'Violet Carpet' — 20
    'White Opal' — 21
    'Winston S. Churchill' — 21
    'White Fairy' — 21
Aurinia saxatilis 'Compaçta' — 21
Avena sempervirens - see *Helictotrichon sempervirens*
Baptisia australis — 21-22
Bergenia — 22
    'Evening Glow' — 22
    'Sunningdale' — 22
Boltonia asteroides 'Snowbank' — 22
Brauneria purpurea - see *Echinacea purpurea*
Brunnera macrophylla — 22-23
Buphthalmum helianthoides - see *Heliopsis helianthoides*
Calamagrostis — 84-85
    x *acutiflora* 'Overdam' — 84-85
    brachytricha — 85
Callirhoe involucrata — 23
Calylophus berlandieri - see *Oenothera speciosa* 'Siskiyou'
Campanula — 23-25
    carpatica — 23-24
        'Blue Clips' — 24
        'Blue Uniform' — 24
        'White Clips' — 24
    cochleariifolia — 24
    glomerata 'Superba' — 24
    grandiflorus - see *Platycodon grandiflorus*
    persiciflora - see *C. persicifolia*
    persicifolia — 24-25
        'Chettle Charm' — 25
        'Telham Beauty' — 25
    polymorpha - see *C. rotundifolia*
    pulsilla - see *C. cochleariifolia*
    rotundifolia — 25
    turbinata - see *C. carpatica*
Centaurea — 25-26
    dealbata 'Rosea' — 25
    macrocephala — 25
    montana — 26
Centranthus ruber — 26
    'Albus' — 26
Cerastium tomentosum 'Silver Carpet' — 26-27
Ceratostigma plumbaginoides — 27
Chamaenerion angustifolium - see *Epilobium angustifolium*
Chamerion angustifolium - see *Epilobium angustifolium*
Chrysanthemum maximum - see *Leucanthemum x superbum* x *morifolium* — 27-28
    'South Pass' — 28
    'Mary Stoker' — 28
    'Sheffield's Hillside Pink' — 28
    serotinum - see *Leucanthemella serotina* 'Herbstern'

x superbum - see *Leucanthemum x superbum*
uliginosum - see *Leucanthemella serotina* 'Herbstern'
Chrysopsis villosa - see *Heterotheca villosa*
Clematis 28-29
davidiana - see *C. heracleifolia*
heracleifolia 28
integrifolia 28
recta 29
Coreopsis verticillata 29
'Moonbeam' 29
rosea 29
Delosperma congestum - see *D. nubigenum*
nubigenum 29-30
Dendranthema x grandiflorum - see *Chrysanthemum x morifolium*
Deschampsia caespitosa 85
Dianthus 30-32
barbatus 30
blandus - see *D. plumarius*
caryophyllus 30-31
caesius - see *D. gratianopolitanus* 'Tiny Rubies'
gratianopolitanus 'Tiny Rubies' 31
hybrids 31
nardiformis 31
plumarius 31-32
'Tiny Rubies' - see *D. gratianopolitanus* 'Tiny Rubies'
winteri - see *D. plumarius*
Dicentra spectabilis 32
'Alba' 32
Dictamnus albus 'Purpureus' 32-33
caucasicus - see *Dictamnus albus* 'Purpureus'
fraxinella - see *Dictamnus albus* 'Purpureus'
Digitalis ambigua - see *D. grandiflora*
grandiflora 33
Dracocephalum virginianum - see *Physostegia virginiana*
Echinacea purpurea 33-34
'Bright Star' 34
'White Swan' 34
Echinops ritro 34
'Taplow Blue' 34
Epilobium angustifolium 34
spicatum - see *E. angustifolium*
Erianthus ravennae - see *Saccharum ravennae*
Eulalia japonica var. *gracillima* - see *Miscanthus sinensis* 'Gracillimus'
Eupatorium maculatum 35
Festuca 85-86
amethystina 'Superba' 86
cinerea 86
glauca - see above
ovina (var. *glauca*) - see *F. cinerea*
Filipendula hexapetala - see *F. vulgaris*
vulgaris 35
Gaillardia 35-36
aristata 36

x grandiflora 'Goblin' 36
'Kobold' - see 'Goblin'
Galeopsis galeobdolon - see *Lamium galeobdolon* 'Herman's Pride'
Galium odoratum 36
Gaura lindheimeri 36-37
Gentiana septemfida 37
Geranium 37-38
himalayense 37-38
macrorrhizum 'Bevan's Variety' 38
x oxonianum 'A.T. Johnson' 38
platypetalum 38
sanguineum 38
var. *prostratum* 38
var. *striatum* - see var. *prostratum*
Geum 39
chiloense 'Mrs. Bradshaw' 39
coccineum - see *G. chiloense* 'Mrs. Bradshaw'
quellyon - see *G. chiloense* 'Mrs. Bradshaw'
triflorum 39
Goniolimon tataricum 39-40
Gypsophila 40
dubia - see *G. repens*
paniculata 'Pink Fairy' 40
prostrata var. *fratensisn* - see *G. repens*
repens 40
Helianthemum chamaecistus - see *H. nummularium*
mutabile - see *H. nummularium*
nummularium 41
'Single Yellow' 41
'Wisley Pink' 41
Helictotrichon sempervirens 86
Heliopsis helianthoides 'Incomparabilis' 41
Hemerocallis 42
'Butter Curls' 42
'Magic Wand' 42
Heterotheca villosa 42-43
Heuchera 43-44
micrantha 'Chocolate Ruffles' 43
'Palace Passion' 43
'Palace Purple' 43
sanguinea 44
Bressingham hybrids 44
Hosta 44-45
'Francee' 44-45
'Ginkgo Craig' 45
tsushimensis 45
Hylotelephium 45-46
spectabile 'Autumn Glory' 45
telephium 46
Hypericum calycinum 46
Iberis grarrexiana - see *I. sempervirens*
sempervirens 'Autumn Snow' 46
'Little Gem' 46
'Snowmantle' 46
Iris 47-48

120

(bearded hybrids)
    'Babbling Brook' 47
    'Before the Storm' 47
    'Stepping Little' 47
    'Summit Angel' 47
    'Summit Queen' 47
    'Termination Dust' 47
    'Time Piece' 48
  lactea 48
    var. *oltriensis* 48
  maritima - see *I. sibirica*
  sibirica 48
Knautia macedonia 48-49
Kniphofia alooides - see *K. uvaria*
  uvaria 49
Laciniaria pychnostachya - see *Liatris pychnostachya*
'Alba'
  spicata - see *Liatris spicata*
Lamiastrum galeobdolon - see *Lamium galeobdolon*
'Herman's Pride'
Lamium 49-50
  galeobdolon 'Herman's Pride' 49
  maculatum 'Pink Pewter' 49
Lavandula angustifolia 50
  officinalis - see *L. angustifolia*
Lavatera olbia - see *L. thuringiaca*
  thuringiaca 50
Leptandra virginica - see *Veronicastrum virginicum*
Leucanthemella serotina 'Herbstern' 50
Leucanthemum x superbum 51
    'Becky' 51
    'Esther Read' 51
Liatris 51-52
  callilepis - see *L. spicata*
  pychnostachya 'Alba' 52
  spicata 52
Lilium 52-53
  longiflorum 53
Limonium 52
  gerberi - see *L. latifolium*
  gmelinii 53
  latifolium 53
  platyphyllum - see *L. latifolium*
  tataricum - see *Goniolimon tataricum*
Linum perenne 53-54
Lobelia cardinalis 54
  fulgens - see *L. cardinalis*
  graminea - see *L. cardinalis*
  splendens - see *L. cardinalis*
Lotus ambiguus - see *L. corniculatus* 'Dwarf'
  balticus - see *L. corniculatus* 'Dwarf'
  corniculatus 'Dwarf' 54
Lupinus 54-55
  perennis 55
  Russell Hybrids 55
Lychnis chalcedonica 55-56

    'Molten Lava' 55
Lysimachia nummularia 56
Malva alcea 'Fastigiata' 56
  bismalva - see *M. alcea* 'Fastigiata'
  fastigiata - see *M. alcea* 'Fastigiata'
Miscanthus sinensis 'Gracillimus' 86-87
Monarda didyma 56-57
Nepeta x faassenii 57
    'Souvenir d'Andre Chaudron' 57-58
  sibirica 'Souvenir d'Andre Chaudron' - see above
Oenothera 57-59
  berlandieri - see *O. speciosa* 'Siskiyou'
  blandina - see *O. glazioviana*
  erythrosepala - see *O. glazioviana*
  glazioviana 58
  macrocarpa 58-59
    'Fremontii' 58
  missouriensis - see *O. macrocarpa*
  speciosa 'Siskiyou' 58
Ophiopogon nigresens - see below
  planiscapus 'Nigrescens' 59
    'Niger' - see above
    'Arabicus' - see 'Nigrescens'
Oxalis crassipes 'Rosea' 59-60
Paeonia 59-61
    'Charlie's White' 60
    'Pink Dawn' 60
    'Doreen' 60
    'Vivid Rose' 60-61
Panicum virgatum 87
Papaver orientale 61
Pennisetum alopecuroides 'Hameln' 87
    'Little Bunny'
  japonicum - see *P. alopecuroides*
Penstemon 61-64
  campanulata - see *P. campanulatus*
  campanulatus 62
  digitalis 62-63
    'Husker Red' 62
'Elfin Pink' 62
  x mexicali PIKES PEAK PURPLE™ 63
  pinifolius 63
    'Mersea Yellow' 63
  pulchellus - see *P. campanulatus*
  strictus 63-64
Perovskia atriplicifolia 63
Persicaria affinis 'Border Jewel' - see *Polygonum affine*
'Border Jewel'
Phlomis russeliana 64
Phlox 64-66
  divaricata ssp. *laphamii* 64
  paniculata 65
    'David' 65
    'Franz Schubert' 65
  subulata 66
    'Emerald Blue' 65

Physostegia virginiana 66
Platycodon glaucus - see below
    grandiflorus 66-67
        'Komachi' 66
Plumbago larpentiae - see Ceratostigma plumbaginoides
Polemonium caeruleum 67
Polygonum affine 'Border Jewel' 67
        'Dimity' 67
Potentilla recta 'Macrantha' 67-68
        'Warrenii' - see P. recta 'Macrantha'
        var. warrensii - see P. recta 'Macrantha'
Prunella grandiflora 68
Pseudolysimachion incanum - see Veronica incana
'Minuet'
    spicatum - see Veronica spicata
Pulmonaria officinalis ' Sissinghurst White' - see P.
saccharata 'Sissinghurst White'
    saccharata 'Mrs. Moon' 68-69
        'Roy Davidson' 69
        'Sissinghurst White' 69
Pulsatilla vulgaris 69-70
        'Rubra' 70
    var. serotina - see P. vulgaris
Rudbeckia fulgida var. sullivantii 'Goldsturm' 69
    purpurea - see Echinacea purpurea
Ruta graveolens 'Blue Mound' 70
Saccharum ravennae 87-88
Salvia 70-71
    argentea 70-71
    nemerosa ' May Night' - see S. x sylvestris 'May
Night'
    pratensis 71
    x superba 'May Night' - see below
    x sylvestris 'May Night' 71
Santolina chamaecyparissus 71
    incana - see above
Scabiosa columbaria 'Butterfly Blue' 72
        'Pink Mist' 72
Schizachyrium scoparium 80
Sedum 72-74
    aizoon 72
    floriferum - see S. kamtschaticum 'Floriferum'
    kamtschaticum 'Floriferum' 72
        'Variegatum' 73
        'Weihenstephaner Gold' - see 'Floriferum'
    maximowiczii - see S. aizoon
    nevii 73
    spectabile 'Autumn Glory' - see Hylotelephium
    spectabile 'Autumn Glory'
    spurium 'Dragon's Blood' 73
        var. album 73
        'Bronze Carpet' 73
        'Red Carpet' 73
    telephium - see Hylotelephium telephium
    woodwardii - see S. aizoon
Sempervivum 74

    arachnoideum 74
    tectorum 'Atropurpureum' 74
Sidalcea 'Party Girl' 74-75
Solidago virgaurea 'Peter Pan' 75
x Solidaster luteus 'Lemore' 75
Stachys byzantina 75-76
    lanata - see S. byzantina
    olympica - see S. byzantina
Statice gmelinii - see Limonium gmelinii
    latifolium - see Limonium latifolium
    maritima - see Armeria maritima
    tatarica - see Goniolimon tataricum
Stipa brachytricha - see Calamagrostis brachytricha
Teucrium 76
    canadense 76
    chamaedrys 76
Thalictrum aquilegiifolium 76-77
Thymus 77-78
    pseudolanuginosus 77
    serpyllum 'Coccineus' 77-78
Tradescantia 77
    x andersoniana - see T. virginiana 'Red Cloud'
    ohiensis
    virginiana 'Red Cloud' 78
Tricyrtis hirta 78-79
    japonica - see T. hirta
Tritoma uvaria - see Kniphofia uvaria
Trollius x cultorum 'Golden Queen' 78
    ledebourii - see T. x cultorum 'Golden Queen'
Ulmaria filipendula - see Filipendula vulgaris
Veronica 79-82
    allioni 79-80
    austriaca ssp. teucrium 'Royal Blue' 79
    incana 'Minuet' 80
    liwanensis 80
    pectinata 80
    peduncularis 'Georgia Blue' 80
        'Oxford Blue' - see V. peduncularis 'Georgia
Blue'
    spicata 81
        'Icicle' 81
        'Red Fox' 81
        'Rosea' 81
    'Sunny Border Blue' 81-82
    teucrium - see V. austriaca ssp. teucrium 'Royal
Blue'
    virginica - see Veronicastrum virginicum 'Album'
Veronicastrum virginicum 'Album' 81
Yucca 82
    filamentosa 82
    glauca 82

COMMON NAME INDEX

Aaron's beard	46
Adam's needle	82
Aizoon stonecrop	72
Alum root	43
American germander	76
Apple blossom grass	36-37
Balloon flower	66
Bearded iris	47-48
Beard-tongue	61-63
Bear's breeches	13
Bedstraw	36
Beebalm	57
Bellflower	23
Bergamot	57
Bethlehem sage	69
Big bluestem	84
Big-head knapweed	25-26
Bigroot geranium	38
Bird's-eye	79
Black mondo grass	59
Black root	81
Black-eyed Susan	69
Blanket flower	35-36
Blazing star	51-52
Bleeding heart	32
Bloodred geranium	38
Bloody cranesbill	38
Blue avena grass	86
Blue bouquet iris	48
Blue bugleweed	16

Blue false indigo	21-22
Blue fescue	86
Blue oat grass	86
Blue wild indigo	21-22
Blue woolly veronica	80
Boltonia	22
Border pink	31-32
Bowman's root	81
Broad-petaled geranium	38
Broom sedge	88
Bugleweed	15
Bulgarian geranium	38
Bush clematis	29
Button snakeroot	52
Cardinal flower	54
Carpathian harebell	23-24
Carpet bugleweed	16
Catmint	57
Charity	67
Checker mallow	75
Cheddar pink	31
Chinese-bellflower	66
Clematis	28-29
Clove pink	30-31
Clustered bellflower	24
Columbine	19
Columbine meadow rue	76
Comb speedwell	80
Common bugleweed	16
Common germander	76

Common rue	70	Globeflower	78
Common thrift	19-20	Golden-tuft alyssum	21
Common yarrow	14	Granny's bonnet	19
Compact Mexican evening primrose	58	Grapeleaf anemone	18
Coral bells	44	Gray fescue	86
Cottage pink	31-32	Great willowherb	34
Cranesbill	37	Greek valerian	67
Creeping baby's breath	40	Ground clematis	29
Creeping Jenny	56	Hairy false golden aster	42-43
Creeping phlox	66	Hairy golden aster	42-43
Creeping St. Johnswort	46	Hairy toad lily	78
Creeping thyme	77	Hardy carnation	30-31
Crested gentian	37	Hardy mum	27-28
Crevice alumroot	43	Hardy pampas grass	87-88
Culver's root	81	Harebell	25
Daylily	42	Heal all	68
Deadnettle	49	Hen and chicks	74
Dropwort	35	Herb of grace	70
Dwarf basket-of-gold	21	Herbaceous peony	59-61
Dwarf bird's foot trefoil	54	High daisy	51
Dwarf fountain grass	87	Himalayan cranesbill	37-38
Elephant's ear	22	Himalayan fleeceflower	67
Eulalia grass	86-87	Hollyhock	16
European goldenrod	75	Hollyhock mallow	56
European pasque flower	69	Hosta	44-45
Evening primrose	57-58	Houseleek	74
Evergreen candytuft	46	Hungarian speedwell	79
Fairies' thimbles	24	Indian pink	54
Fall-blooming reed grass	85	Iris	47-48
False chamomile	22	Jacob's ladder	67
False dragonhead	66	Japanese anemone	18
False mallow	75	Japanese silver grass	86-87
False sunflower	41	Jerusalem cross	55-56
Fernleaf yarrow	13	Joe-pye weed	35
Fescue	85	Jupiter's beard	26
Fireweed	34	Kamschatka stonecrop	72
Flag	47-48	Kansas gay feather	52
Florists' mum	27-28	Knapweed	25
Fraxinella	32-33	Knautia	48
Garden fescue	86	Knotweed	67
Garden lily	52	Korean feather reed grass	85
Garden mum	27-28	Lady's mantle	17
Garden peony	59-61	Lambs'-ears	75-76
Garden phlox	65	Large flowered evening primrose	58
Garden pink	30	Large selfheal	68
Gasplant	32-33	Large yellow foxglove	33
Gay feather	51-52	Lavender	50
Geranium	37	Lavender cotton	71-72
German statice	39-40	Leadwort	27
Germander	76	Lilac cranesbill	37-38
Geum	39	Little bluestem	88
Giant daisy	51	Live-forever	72-73
Giant hummingbird mint	15	Live-forever stonecrop	45-46
Globe centaurea	25-26	Lungwort	69
Globe thistle	34	Lupine	54-55

Maltese cross	55-56	Reed grass	84
Marshall chamomile	19	Rock cranesbill	38
Meadow clary	71	Rock rose	41
Meadow sage	71	Rocky Mountain penstemon	63
Meadowsweet	35	Rosebay willowherb	34
Michaelmas daisy	20	Russian sage	63
Milfoil	14	Sage	70-71
Missouri primrose	58	Scarlet lychnis	55-56
Modern pinks	31	Scotch bluebell	25
Moneywort	56	Sea lavender	53
Moss phlox	66	Sea pink	19
Mother-of-thyme	77	Sea thrift	19-20
Mountain-bluet	26	Shasta daisy	51
Mountain-mint	57	Showy stonecrop	45-46
New York aster	20	Siberian iris	48
Obedient plant	66	Siberian statice	53
Old man's whiskers	39	Siberian-bugloss	22-23
Orange coneflower	69	Silver sage	70
Oriental poppy	61	Silver speedwell	80
Orpine	46	Small flowered alumroot	43
Oswego-tea	57	Small scabious	72
Overdam feather reed grass	84-85	Small soapweed	82
Oxeye	41	Sneezewort	14
Ozark sundrops	58	Snowdrop anemone	18
Peach-bells	24-25	Snow-in-harvest	26-27
Peach-leaved bellflower	24-25	Snow-in-summer	26-27
Pearly everlasting	17	Soapweed	82
Penstemon	61-63	Soapwell	82
Perennial baby's breath	40	Solitary clematis	28-29
Perennial candytuft	46	Spanish bayonet	82
Perennial cornflower	26	Speedwell	79
Perennial flax	53-54	Spider-lily	77
Perennial forget-me-not	22-23	Spiderwort	77
Perennial phlox	65	Spike speedwell	81
Perennial sage	71	Spotted dead nettle	50
Persian cornflower	25	Star thistle	25
Pig squeak	22	Statice	52
Pincushion flower	72	Sticky Jerusalem sage	64
Pineleaf penstemon	63	Stiff beard-tongue	63
Plantain lily	44-45	Stonecrop	72-73
Plumbago	27	Strawberry oxalis	59
Plume grass	87-88	Strawberry wood sorrel	59
Poker plant	49	Sulphur cinquefoil	67
Prairie beard grass	88	Sun rose	41
Prairie blazing star	52	Suncups	57
Prairie mallow	75	Sundial lupine	55
Prairie smoke	39	Sundrops	57-58
Purple avens	39	Sunset hyssop	15
Purple coneflower	33-34	Sweet avens	39
Purple poppy mallow	23	Sweet woodruff	36
Pyramid bugle	15	Sweet-William	30
Ravenna grass	87-88	Swiss mat speedwell	79
Red scabiosa	48-49	Switch grass	87
Red valerian	26	Sword lily	47-48
Red-hot poker	49	Tall speedwell	81

Tatarian statice	39-40
Threadleaf coreopsis	29
Thyme	77
Tickseed	29
Torch lily	49
Tree mallow	50
Trinity flower	77
Tube clematis	28
Tufted hairgrass	85
Turkey foot	84
Turkish veronica	80
Tussock bellflower	23-24
Tussock grass	85
Two-row sedum	73-74
Upright bugleweed	15
Vervain mallow	56
Violet sage	71
Virginia spiderwort	78
Virgin's bower	28
Wall germander	76
Whirling butterflies	36-37
Wild blue phlox	65
Wild germander	76
Wild lupine	55
Wild sweet-William	65
Willow-bell	24-25
Wine cup	23
Woodland phlox	65
Woolly betony	75-76
Woolly speedwell	80
Woolly thyme	77
Yarrow	13
Yellow archangel	49
Yellow hardhead	25-26
Yellow ice plant	29-30

REFERENCES

Bloom, A. 1981. Perennials for your Garden. Floraprint U.S.A., Chicago, IL.

Bloom, Alan and Adrian. 1992. Blooms of Bressingham Garden Plants. Harper Collins Publishers, London.

Botanica: The Illustrated A-Z of over 10,000 Garden Plants and How to Cultivate Them. Second Edition. 1998. Chief Editors: R.J. Turner, Jr. and Ernie Wasson, Mynah/Random House Australia Pty Ltd., Milsons Point, Australia.

Bremness, L. 1988. The Complete Book of Herbs: A Practical Guide to Growing & Using Herbs. Penguin Group, Penguin Books U.S.A., Inc., New York, N.Y.

Brooklyn Botanic Garden Native Perennials. 1996. Guest Editor: Nancy Beaubaire, Brooklyn Botanic Gardens, Inc., Brooklyn, N.Y.

Clausen, R.R., and Ekstrom, N.H. 1989. Perennials for American Gardens. Random House, Inc., New York, N.Y.

Darke, R. 1999. The Color Encyclopedia of Ornamental Grasses, Sedges, Rushes, Restios, Cattails, & Selected Bamboos. Timber Press, Portland, OR.

Denver Water. 1998. Xeriscape Plant Guide. Fulcrum Publishing, Golden, CO.

Elliot, J. 1997. The Smaller Perennials. Timber Press, Inc. Portland, OR.

Greenlee, John 1992. The Encyclopedia of Ornamental Grasses: How to Grow and Use Over 250 Beautiful and Versatile Plants; Michael Friedman Publishing Group, Inc. New York, N.Y.

Grenfell, D. 1996. The Gardener's Guide to Growing Hostas. Timber Press, Inc. Portland, OR.

Grenfell, D. 1998. The Gardener's Guide to Growing Daylilies. Timber Press, Inc. Portland, OR.

Grounds, R. 1998. The Plantfinder's Guide to Ornamental Grasses. Timber Press, Portland, OR

Jefferson-Brown, M. and Howland, H. 1995. The Gardener's Guide to Growing Lilies. Timber Press, Inc. Portland, OR.

Knopf, Jim 1991. The Xeriscape Flower Gardener: A Waterwise Guide for the Rocky Mountain Region. Johnson Publishing Company, Boulder, CO.

Lampe, Kenneth F. and McCann, Mary Ann 1985. AMA Handbook of Poisonous and Injurious Plants. American Medical Association, Chicago, IL.

Lewis, P. and Lynch, M. 1998. Campanulas- A Gardener's Guide. Timber Press, Inc. Portland, OR.

Lowe, D. 1995 Cushion Plants for the Rock Garden. Timber Press, Inc. Portland, OR..

Noland, D. A., and Bolin, K. 2000. Perennials for the Landscape. Interstate Publishers, Inc. Danville, IL. Nold, R. 1999. Penstemons. Timber Press Inc. Portland, OR.

Page, M.1997. The Gardeners's Guide to Growing Peonies. Timber Press, Inc. Portland, OR.

Picton, P. 1999. The Gardener's Guide to Growing Asters. Timber Press, Inc. Portland, OR.

Rice, G. 1995. Hardy Perennials. Timber Press, Inc. Portland, OR.

Rock Garden Plants of North America- An Anthology from the Bulletin of North American Rock Garden Society. 1996. Edited by Jane McGary. Timber Press, Inc. Portland, OR.

Sajeva, M. and Costanzo, M. 1994. Succulents- The Illustrated Dictionary. Timber Press, Inc. Portland, OR.

Stebbings, Geoff. 1997. The Gardener's Guide to Growing Irises. Timber Press, Inc. Portland, OR.

Still, S. 1994. Manual of Herbaceous Ornamental Plants. Fourth Edition. Stipes Publishing Co. Champaign, IL.

Strauch, J.G., and Klett, J.E., 1989. Flowering Herbaceous Perennials for the High Plains, Technical Bulletin LTB89-5. Colorado State University Fort Collins, CO.

Sunset Perennials. 1992. Coordinating editor: Suzanne Normand Matheson. Sunset Publishing Corporation, Menlo Park, CA.

Sunset Western Garden Book. 1995., Editor: Kathleen Norris Brenzel, Sunset Publishing Corporation, Menlo Park, CA.

The American Horticultural Society A-Z Encyclopedia of Garden Plants. 1997. Editors-in-chief: Christopher Brickell and Judith D. Zuk, DK Publishing, Inc. New York, N.Y.

The New Royal Horticultural Society Dictionary of Gardening. 1999. Editor-in-chief: Anthony Huxley, Grove's Dictionaries, Inc. New York, N.Y.

Way, D., and James, P. 1998. The Gardener's Guide to Growing Penstemons, Timber Press Inc. Portland, OR.